D0455812

NEW YORK

ENCOUNTER

GINGER ADAMS OTIS

New York Encounter
1st edition – May 2007

Published by Lonely Planet Publications Pty Ltd
ABN 36 005 607 983

Australia	Head Office, Locked Bag 1, Footscray, Vic 3011 ☎ 03 8379 8000 fax 03 8379 8111 talk2us@lonelyplanet.com.au
USA	150 Linden St, Oakland, CA 94607 ☎ 510 893 8555 toll free 800 275 8555 fax 510 893 8572 info@lonelyplanet.com
UK	72–82 Rosebery Avenue, Clerkenwell, London EC1R 4RW ☎ 020 7841 9000 fax 020 7841 9001 go@lonelyplanet.co.uk

This title was commissioned in Lonely Planet's Oakland office and produced by: **Commissioning Editor** Jay Cooke **Coordinating Editor** Elizabeth Anglin **Coordinating Cartographer** Hunor Csutoros **Layout Designer** Wibowo Rusli **Assisting Editor** Helen Christinis, Laura Gibb **Managing Editor** Melanie Dankel **Managing Cartographer** Alison Lyall **Cover Designer** Nic Lehman **Project Manager** Rachel Imeson **Series Designers** Nic Lehman & Wendy Wright **Thanks to** Eli Arduca, Sally Darmody, Michelle Glynn, Laura Jane, Celia Wood

ISBN 978 1 74059 713 5

Printed through Colorcraft Ltd, Hong Kong. Printed in China

Acknowledgement Manhattan Subway Map © 2007 Metropolitan Transportation Authority. Used with permission

Lonely Planet and the Lonely Planet logo are trademarks of Lonely Planet and are registered in the US Patent and Trademark Office and in other countries.

Lonely Planet does not allow its name or logo to be appropriated by commercial establishments, such as retailers, restaurants or hotels. Please let us know of any misuses: www.lonelyplanet.com/ip.

HOW TO USE THIS BOOK

Color-Coding & Maps

Color-coding is used for symbols on maps and in the text that they relate to (eg all eating venues on the maps and in the text are given a green fork symbol). Each neighborhood also gets its own color, and this is used down the edge of the page and throughout that neighborhood section.

Shaded yellow areas on the maps are to denote 'areas of interest' – be that for historical significance, attractive architecture or a strip that's good for bars or restaurants. We'd encourage you to head to these areas and just start exploring!

Prices

Multiple prices listed with reviews (eg $10/5 or $10/5/20) indicate adult/child, adult/concession or adult/child/family.

> Although the authors and Lonely Planet have taken all reasonable care in preparing this book, we make no warranty about the accuracy or completeness of its content and, to the maximum extent permitted, disclaim all liability arising from its use.

Send us your Feedback We love to hear from readers – your comments help make our books better. We read every word you send us, and we always guarantee that your feedback goes straight to the appropriate authors. The most useful submissions are rewarded with a free book. To send us your updates and find out about Lonely Planet events, newsletters and travel news – visit our award-winning website: *lonelyplanet.com/contact*.

Note: We may edit, reproduce and incorporate your comments in Lonely Planet products such as guidebooks, websites and digital products, so let us know if you don't want your comments reproduced or your name acknowledged. For a copy of our privacy policy visit *lonelyplanet.com/privacy*.

GINGER ADAMS OTIS

Ginger Adams Otis is a radio and print reporter who lives and works in Manhattan. When you're in town you may hear her on local radio stations, or see her byline in newspapers like *The Village Voice*, *Newsday*, *New York Magazine* and many other print publications. You may even bump in to her on the subway. When not busy working for city media, Ginger does Lonely Planet guides and reports for the BBC, NPR and the Associated Press, sometimes covering breaking events in the five boroughs, and other times working on assignments that take her around Latin America, where she has done extensive reporting.

GINGER'S THANKS

Ginger would like to thank Jay Cooke, always an inspiring and understanding editor, Brice Gosnell for his interest and encouragement, and the entire Oz team – Elizabeth, Alison and all the cartographers – for their painstaking efforts.

THE PHOTOGRAPHER

Dan Herrick has been a photographer based in New York city for the past six years after having lived and studied in Latin America and Europe. He enjoys documenting the city's continual change as well as its frenetic way of life. On occasion he is able to pull himself away from it all to travel abroad, or more often to travel to one of the many different world s that exist within the city's boundaries.

Our Readers Many thanks to the travelers who wrote to us with helpful hints, useful advice and interesting anecdotes. Tim Allen, Mikael Beck, Arne Fleissner, Jamie Hunter, Darren Jackson, Samantha Knott, Dallene Ng, Catherine Paul, Clare Pritty, Allison Rogers, Karen Smith, Victoria Spackman.

Photographs p53, p121, p165, p185, p225 by Ginger Adams Otis. All other photographs by Lonely Planet Images, and by Dan Herrick except p4, p16, p20, p35, p36, p136, p159, p249 Angus Oborn; p8, p23, p252 Richard l'Anson; p11, p15, p27, p28, p29, p32, p33, p173, p182, p184, p191 Corey Wise; p12 Michael Taylor; p22 Eoin Clarke; p46 Wade Eakle; p160, p200 Allan Montaine; p161 Bill Bachmann; p167, p193 Ionas Kaltenbach; p190, p250, p258 Kim Grant; p234 Esbin Anderson Photography; p259 Christopher Groenhout. **Cover photograph** Woman walking by taxicabs, James Doberman/Getty Images. All images are copyright of the photographers unless otherwise indicated. Many of the images in this guide are available for licensing from **Lonely Planet Images**: www.lonelyplanetimages.com.

PASSENGER
CARS ONLY

NO STANDING

Pedestrians on a New York street

CONTENTS

THIS IS NEW YORK

When you set foot in New York City you're not simply stepping into a metropolis – you're entering one helluva global village. It's big, brash and sprawling, and yet, when you get right down to it, just a series of interlocking neighborhoods, each as exciting and vibrant as the next. Where else can you take the subway four stops and get from Little Korea to Little Italy?

New York is full of dynamic contrasts. Teeming with wall-to-wall buildings and close to nine million people, each enclave has its own unique flavor and pace. Nowhere is its multiculturalism more apparent than in its people. New Yorkers eat kimchi and Korean BBQ, falafel, gyros and borscht. They dance salsa, merengue, and *bachata* when the mood strikes, head to Little Brazil for some *fútbol,* and generally think of national and international politics as something that's happening in their own backyard. Hey, when you've got the UN and more foreign and domestic embassies, corporations, foundations and cultural institutions headquartered here than anywhere else, you get used to talking politics.

There's always something going on, and New Yorkers have rarely met a cause they weren't ready to rally for. If it seems strange that such a capitalist city retains strong democratic roots, remember that the abolitionist movement that pushed Abraham Lincoln into the Civil War held many of its initial meetings in Lower Manhattan. The suffragist movement that garnered women voting rights was born among the tenements of the East Side, and the 1969 Stonewall Riots that gave rise to the fight for gay rights grew out of the Village's egalitarian heritage.

Take a deep breath and dive right in. First-rate ballet? Museum tours and pub crawls? All-night Lower East Side poetry slams? It's all there, and more. Mix and mingle, meet and greet, and, as the locals do, let it all hang out. How much can happen in a New York minute? Brace yourself – you're about to find out.

Top left Bohemian Hall & Beer Garden **Top right** One of the last authentic meatpacking workers lends a light to the now more fashionable meatpacking visitor **Bottom** Shopping on 125th Street in Harlem

NEW YORK >7

>HIGHLIGHTS

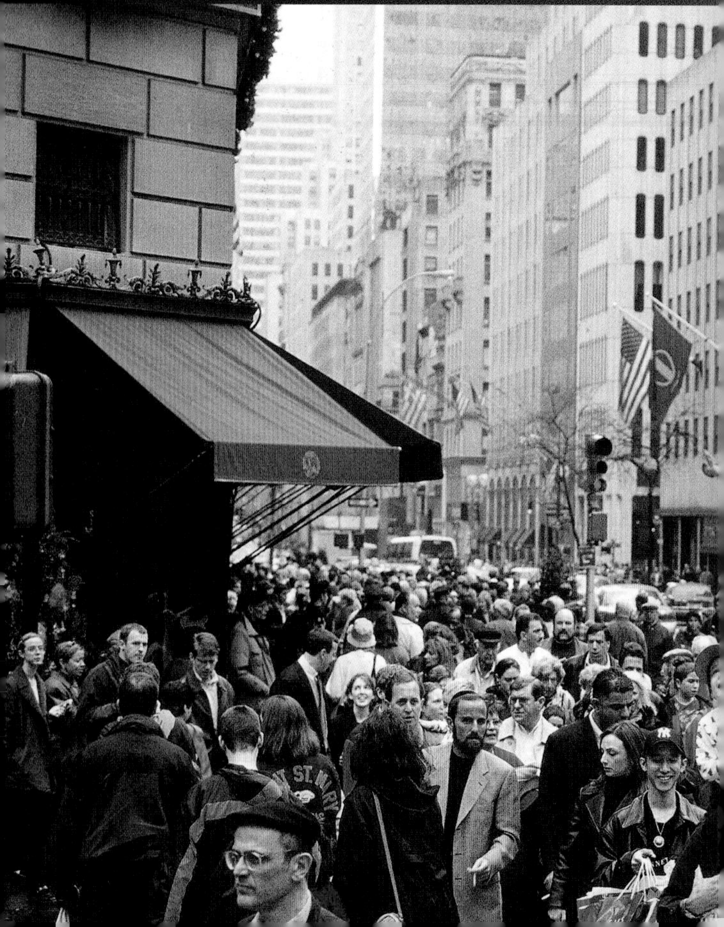

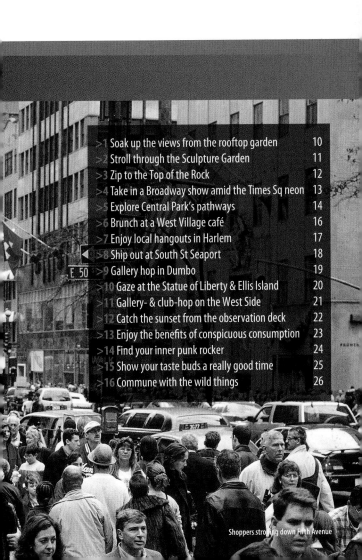

E 50

Shoppers strolling down Fifth Avenue

>1 METROPOLITAN MUSEUM OF ART
SOAK UP THE VIEWS FROM THE ROOFTOP GARDEN

With nearly three million pieces in its collection, five million visitors a year and an annual budget of $120 million, the Met (p190) is New York's biggest, richest and most celebrated cultural institution. It could take a lifetime to appreciate all that is has to offer. Its $155 million renovation, started in 2004 and due for completion in 2007, has added a new Roman Court and brought loads of hidden antiquities (including an Etruscan chariot) out of storage. They've renovated galleries dedicated to Roman and modern art and pumped up the number of Hellenistic works on display to 7500.

You'll want plenty of time to explore this behemoth; the European galleries above the marble staircase at the Fifth Ave entrance could easily consume a day, as could the larger-than-ever Greek and Roman galleries, and the newly-expanded Egyptian gallery, with its perfectly preserved mummies and entire Temple of Dendur, saved from submersion in the waters of the Aswan Dam.

Behind the temple is the American wing, with an incongruous combination of Tiffany glass, baseball cards and the facade of a US Bank. The dark, lovely medieval galleries appear next, filled with iconic artifacts, Byzantine enamels and religious jewelry. Then comes the calm oasis of the Lehman Wing, filled with Renaissance paintings by Rembrandt, Memling and El Greco. There are also Africa, Oceania and the Americas galleries, an Asian art gallery and many special art collections.

>2 MUSEUM OF MODERN ART
STROLL THROUGH THE SCULPTURE GARDEN

The MoMA's 1939 facade got an all-over spiffing up in 2004, courtesy of Japanese architect Yoshio Taniguchi, and is now an uptown gem, gleaming and transcendent.

The best way to explore this multilevel building is to start at the old entrance, with a strange, cantilevered canopy that looks like the top of an old baby-grand piano. It's a few doors down from the new entrance on West 53rd St where tickets are sold. Take the elevator to the 6th floor, home to special exhibits. As you look out the windows, you'll get the best appreciation of how Taniguchi integrated the modern MoMA (p159) into the surrounding older architecture.

If you follow the museum's contours, you'll move downward from floor to floor, and chronologically through the major art movements of the 20th century. Floors five and four are MoMA's intro to modern art – Picassos, Matisses, Dalis, Mondrians, Pollocks, de Koonings and a few Marcel Duchamp originals. The 3rd floor is packed with exhibits tracing the development of architecture and design. The 2nd floor contains prints, illustrated books, and exhibits about film and media that often coincide with film series put on in the new theaters below the lobby. Beyond the second floor atrium is an informal café and espresso bar with homey, communal tables. The 1st floor surrounds the wondrous, inspiring Sculpture Garden – step outside to take in the benches and trees bent into curious shapes.

>3 ROCKEFELLER CENTER
ZIP TO THE TOP OF THE ROCK

With twenty-two ornate, luxurious acres of shops, gardens, banks and art deco sculptures right in the heart of pulsating Manhattan, what could be more magnificent on a cold winter's night than this iconic location with its immense Christmas tree and romantic skating rink? Only the view from 70 stories up. Top of the Rock, the city's most expansive and vertigo-inducing observation deck, shut down for 20 years, is back in business.

Rockefeller Center (p160) was conceived by oil magnate John D. Rockefeller during the Great Depression. Engaging in a mammoth project to house clothing stores and other high-end shops at a time when most Americans barely had two coins to rub together was a risky enterprise. But the decade-long project provided 70,000 workers with jobs and created a celebrated 'city within a city' that now houses several major media corporations, including NBC Studios and the Associated Press.

It also contains more than 100 works of art, including a major mural in each building – all but the one by Mexican artist Diego Rivera. Rivera included Lenin in his work, which didn't please his capitalist boss. It was destroyed, and replaced by Jose Maria Sert's painting of Abraham Lincoln. Other important works include *Prometheus*, overlooking the skating rink, *Atlas* carrying the world on Fifth Ave, and *News*, an installation by Isamu Noguchi at 45 Rockefeller Plaza.

>4 TIMES SQUARE

TAKE IN A BROADWAY SHOW AMID THE TIMES SQ NEON

This maelstrom of human activity and flashing neon lights is definitely the city's most famous intersection. Synonymous in the late 1960s with sex shops, peep shows and colorful offbeat characters, today's Times Sq has a comparatively clean and healthy image (although its 40 miles of neon does turn night into day, and can make you feel a bit like a french fry under a hot lamp). Nonetheless, its trademark, high-energy theater buzz still abounds, especially on weekend nights when the lights are flashing, sidewalks are jumping and everybody is hustling for that 8pm curtain.

Formerly known as Long Acre Sq, this placid horse-trading plaza changed forever in 1904 with the advent of the subway and the addition of the *New York Times* newspaper, which eventually lent its name to the location. The paper threw itself a little party on December 31, which has now become the annual New Year's Eve ball-dropping bacchanalia. Don't worry if you miss it though – the full-on, high wattage effect of Times Sq is a daily occurrence. Known as the Crossroads of the World, it remains the brashest, boldest piece of in-your-face infotainment the world's ever seen. For more on the area, see p168.

>5 CENTRAL PARK

EXPLORE CENTRAL PARK'S PATHWAYS

Welcome to the lungs of New York City, a place where verdant grasses, dappled forests, wild flowers and cool, meandering streams erase the memories of traffic jams and crowded sidewalks. This is the people's park, designed in the 1860s and '70s by Frederick Law Olmsted and Calvert Vaux to provide an open space for everyone.

This oasis of rolling pastures and gardens stretches from midtown to the beautifully restored Harlem Meer. Walkers, joggers, cyclists, in-line skaters, rock-climbers, cross-country skiers and horseback riders share the ample supply of roadways. Couples, friends and sometimes even strangers meet at the center, Betheseda Terrace, recognizable by the famous *Angel of the Waters* statue (p183) in its middle.

So much communing with nature gets done in Central Park that it's hard to believe it's almost entirely artificial – it was the first landscaped park built in US history. To make space for it, several communities and businesses were razed, including Seneca Village (p187), Manhattan's first prominent gathering of free African-American property owners. Olmsted and Vaux also drained a swamp, moved five million cubic yards of soil and built four transverse roads to carry cross-town traffic beneath the park's hills (66th, 79th, 86th and 96th Sts run right underneath).

The park's northern sections were deliberately left untamed, with the exception of the Conservatory Gardens, a sensory overload of tulips and flowering apple trees. Most of the area above 79th St is craggy and wild.

One of the most famous parts of the park is the Great Lawn (p182), between 72nd and 86th Sts, where you can catch the New York Philharmonic Orchestra each summer. Nearby you'll find Delacorte Theater, home to the annual Shakespeare in the Park Festival, panoramic Belvedere Castle, the bird-watching (and gay-male cruising) haven of the Ramble, and Loeb Boathouse, where you can take a romantic row around a glassy pond.

You can also check out the penguins, polar bears, sea lions, pandas and tamarin monkeys at the Central Park Wildlife Center (p182), housing a children's discovery center as well. Sea lions chow down

daily at 11:30am, 2pm and 4pm; you're allowed to join the feeding frenzy by tossing in some fish.

Walkers and joggers will appreciate the Jacqueline Kennedy Onassis Reservoir (p183). Its circular 1.58-mile track is a favorite training ground for the New York City marathon.

On the park's west side, near the 79th St Tranverse, is Strawberry Fields (p183), home to an ever-evolving, changing memorial to John Lennon, who liked to hang out in that ethereal stretch of park and who was shot by a deranged fan while entering his apartment across the street in 1980. The list of must-sees and dos goes on and on in Central Park; for more information, visit the **Dairy Visitor Center** (☎ 212-794-6564; www.centralpark.org).

THE CLOISTERS
Set on 4 acres overlooking the Hudson River, this marvelous extension of the Met, the **Cloisters** (☎ 212-923-3700; www.metmuseum.org), was built in the medieval architectural style and provides a lovely setting for an immense collection of Romanesque sculptures, illuminated manuscripts and paintings. Don't miss the Hunt of the Unicorn tapestries, the *Merode Triptych* or the serene and well-tended gardens.

>6 WEST VILLAGE

BRUNCH AT A WEST VILLAGE CAFÉ

Full of winding streets built on old cow paths, and hidden courtyards behind narrow, tree-lined alleys, the 'Village' was once a hotbed of political activity – a crazy, Bohemian neighborhood where only artists and outcasts dared live. Now it's a privileged enclave for wealthy celebrity residents who, to give them their due, are fighting to preserve its character against an onslaught of modern steel and glass construction.

Much of the Village's storied history has been reduced to a handful of well-known landmarks and celebrations. That's not to say that Greenwich Village (p108) isn't worth visiting – it is, as much for its history as its genteel pace, the shopping and the people-watching.

You'll see century-old clapboard houses and pass many a haunted bar. The Village is rife with spirits – Welsh poet Dylan Thomas drank himself into a coma at the White Horse Tavern. Literary greats who lived and worked here include Edith Wharton, Mark Twain, Willa Cather, James Baldwin, Eugene O'Neill, ee cummings and William Burroughs. While Greenwich Village is no longer the locus of creative life in the city, its energy is distinct enough to merit a look.

>7 HARLEM
ENJOY LOCAL HANGOUTS IN HARLEM
A mecca of urban African American life for over a century, Harlem (p208) has burst out of its 1980s doldrums with a vengeance. Not only have long-standing cultural icons been restored and revitalized, like the Apollo Theater, the Lenox Lounge, the Studio Museum and the Schomburg Center for Black Research (p212), it's put forward a whole new crop of cafés, stores, restaurants and jazz clubs. It's still pockmarked with signs of neglect, but it's reclaiming the artistic vitality that buoyed the community prior to the Great Depression.

City policy makers largely ignored Harlem after the 1930s economic fallout, and decades of neglect came to a head during the 1960s Civil Rights movement as Harlem was beset with riots. The 1980s crack epidemic turned rows of once-prestigious brownstones into abandoned addict havens. But now, thanks mostly to Manhattan's inflated real estate market, Harlem, with its wide boulevards, historic churches, and gorgeous beaux-arts facade buildings, is back on top. Developers, given tax breaks by the city, are pouring in, and community activists are working hard to control the gentrification so that it fosters growth, not displacement, for black residents.

>8 LOWER MANHATTAN
SHIP OUT AT SOUTH ST SEAPORT

An eye-catching combination of old and new, Lower Manhattan contains some of the island's most grandiose skyscrapers, crammed on to tiny colonial streets. This is where the city was born, first as a native Lenape settlement, then as a Dutch colony and later a British stronghold and the (temporary) capital of a new, free nation. Lower Manhattan overflows with both Revolutionary and modern landmarks. George Washington was sworn in at Federal Hall (p46); he worshipped at St Paul's Chapel (p47) and Trinity Church (p48), and buried many of his contemporaries in its cemetery. The New York Stock Exchange (p47) got its start on Wall St, named after the original Dutch fortifying wall, and remains headquartered there.

The World Trade Center towers were the most dramatic element of the NYC skyline and their loss in 2001 left a visible hole. Much has changed of late at Ground Zero (p46). No longer a rough and jagged hole, the viewing platform overlooks a construction site-cum-memorial. The city hopes to start development on new buildings and a contemplation space by 2010. The addition of plaques explaining the timeline of September 11, 2001 have added structure to the area, and a bronze sculpture on the west side of the famous Liberty St firehouse details the Fire Department's personnel loss. Aside from paying tribute to its heroes, though, the city has generally chosen to focus on moving forward rather than on what was irrevocably lost.

>9 DUMBO

GALLERY HOP IN DUMBO

It's only taken about 100 years, but a reversal of fortune is finally at hand for Manhattan's most famous outer borough. It was just over a century ago that Brooklyn's elders made the 'Great Mistake of '98' and linked the formerly independent municipality to greater New York City. The result, of course, was a great fiscal boom for Manhattan and a terrible economic wane for Brooklyn. Now, thanks to a convergence of factors (mostly to sky-high Manhattan housing costs), Brooklyn's more than caught up with – and some say surpassed – Manhattan in terms of nightlife, cultural offerings and great eats.

From the artists' enclave known as Down Under the Manhattan Bridge Overpass (Dumbo, p219), to the respected performances at Brooklyn Academy of Music, trendy, hipster Williamsburg, funky, far-out Coney Island, gritty and innovative Red Hook, and eclectic, welcoming Park Slope, Brooklyn is full of exciting things to explore and experience.

Even if you don't care that restaurants, bars and clubs are cheaper once you cross the East River, and that most of NYC's singles and under 35s live on that side of the bridge, you'll be ignoring the biggest expression of artistic energy seen in this state since Basquiat lit up the East Village in the 1980s with his spray-painted stick figures. If you're in the city and don't cross that slender span of steel, the Brooklyn Bridge, you're missing out.

HIGHLIGHTS

>10 NEW YORK HARBOR

GAZE AT THE STATUE OF LIBERTY & ELLIS ISLAND

She's guarded the entrance to lower Manhattan since 1886, hoisting her torch high overhead in a salute to personal independence, and casting a censorious gaze east toward Europe, an 'unenlightened' entity to the original builders when it came to individual freedoms. The Statue of Liberty (p48), the gorgeous green woman, a gift from France, has welcomed millions of immigrants and inspires awe in all who see her. Sculptor Frederic Auguste Bartholdi built the 305-ft-tall, 225-ton statue, but Gustave Eiffel contributed the skeleton.

Just next to Lady Liberty is Ellis Island (p48), formerly the holding tank, so to speak, for third-class passengers coming off immigrant ships from Europe. Ellis Island's exhibits include leftover trunks and bags from immigrants, pictures of gaunt, hollow-eyed arrivals (who might have left home in decent health but didn't always arrive that way after weeks crammed on a ship), and an interactive display that lets you search among a database of émigrés for your own relatives. It's well worth waiting in line for the ferry that takes you there.

A less-trammeled New York Harbor experience is Governor's Island – formerly a US Naval and Coast Guard administration base. It's being run by the National Parks Service and afternoon tours make a great change of pace.

> 11 CHELSEA'S WEST SIDE

GALLERY- & CLUB-HOP ON THE WEST SIDE

Shopping, drinking, dancing – there's a lot of all of it going on in the abattoir-turned-hipster-hangout known as the Meatpacking District (p122). Back when it was a working butchery and they slaughtered and stored their own product, nobody wanted to live among the fetid, fecund smells. Fast-forward to now and people can't seem to stay away from the place, or from neighboring Chelsea (p132), the trendy, gay-friendly art enclave reinventing Manhattan's far west side.

The area has stellar restaurants, such as the original Pastis that first pioneered the Meatpacking trend, sedate and lovely Paradou, fetching Son Cubano, and laid-back Spotted Pig (p129). Chelsea is surrounded by discount stores, like Filene's on Sixth Ave and the Chelsea Market (p139) on Eighth Ave. It's most famous for the galleries that run from 22nd St to 28th St between Twelfth, Eleventh and Tenth Aves. It's art galore – from powerhouse players like Gagosian, Matthew Marks and Mary Boone, to innovative new projects like gallery group, which put 12 up-and-comers into a former clubhouse on the nabe's far west side.

Chelsea has seven old-fashioned brownstones at Nos 406-418 on West 20th St. Called Cushman Row, it's a lovely example of Greek Revival style in the city. West 20th St also features Italianate style houses at 446-450. Just goes to show that it's a neighborhood with a little bit of everything – and that includes a lot of nightlife!

HIGHLIGHTS

>12 EMPIRE STATE BUILDING

CATCH THE SUNSET FROM THE OBSERVATION DECK

It's facing stiff competition from the newly refurbished Top of the Rock at Rockefeller Center, but the Empire State Building (p158) is still the pinnacle of glorious heights in New York City. From the 86th floor, Manhattan stretches forth in all its glorious immensity – and it only takes 45 seconds in an elevator to get there!

This art deco classic is topped by a vivid spire bathed in a different color combination every night, usually coinciding with current events (green for St Patrick's Day, for example).

Conceived during the prosperous 1920s, the Empire State Building didn't actually go up until after the stock market crash of 1929. Thrown together in 410 days for $41 million, the 102-story landmark opened in 1931 and immediately became the most exclusive business address in the city. Of course, very few could afford the equally exclusive rent: the building sat empty for years, earning it the nickname 'Empty State Building.' The top level was meant to serve as a zeppelin mooring mast, but the Hindenburg disaster in 1937 put a stop to that. The top floor is still closed, but the views from the 86th floor are nothing to sneeze at – it's still the most popular place to propose in New York. To beat the crowds, come very early or late, or buy a combination ticket to the New York Skyride; that line is usually shorter.

>13 FIFTH AVENUE

ENJOY THE BENEFITS OF CONSPICUOUS CONSUMPTION

All the glories of NYC shopping are paraded along Fifth Avenue, where strings of tempting, tantalizing stores will turn your head left and right. Once the home of prominent families living in gracious, stately mansions, it was taken over by the retail industry in the early 1900s. It's now forever associated with fine shopping.

Luxury stores abound, but a few discount chains have moved in and sit cheek by jowl with classics like Brooks Brothers, Bergdorf Goodman (p161) and Cartier. Nowadays the most over-the-top fixture on Fifth Ave is Trump Tower, a gleaming complex of exclusive condominiums and a lobby replete with cascading waterfalls and ritzy boutiques. Just up the street is Grand Army Plaza, presided over by the famed Plaza Hotel, now filled with private condos. This romantic square abuts Central Park, and there are plenty of hansom cabs waiting to whisk you away. If you get tired of trawling through stores like Burberry, Chanel, Christian Dior and Yves St Laurent, St Patrick's Cathedral (p161) is around the corner and the New York Public Library (p159) just down the street.

> 14 HISTORIC LOWER EAST SIDE

FIND YOUR INNER PUNK ROCKER

At once glittery and grungy, the ersatz earthiness of the East Village (p94) spawned a revolution in eating, drinking and socializing that's made it one of New York's most exciting neighborhoods. This former rocker-filled enclave housed a young Madonna, jazz great Charlie Parker, guitarist extraordinaire Jimi Hendrix and social raconteur Margaret Sanger, arrested for distributing pamphlets about birth control.

Remnants of those wild times still infuse the neighborhood with a singular, electric energy, even as waves of gentrification knock down squatter tenements and turn community-run cooperatives into luxury condos. It's safer and cleaner than it once was, but it's still the East Village: the best place for a poetry slam (Nuyorican Café, p106), cutting-edge performance art or avant-garde gallery showing (La MaMa, p106), or an all-night pub crawl along Second Ave (and increasingly Avenues A and B).

Across Houston St, just one block to the south, the long-forgotten Lower East Side has been rediscovered. Fueled by a daring group of restaurateurs, the Lower East Side is experiencing a culinary renaissance setting off a chain reaction all the way down to Chinatown. These neighborhoods are an exciting blend of old and new that manage to coalesce into an entrancing now.

>15 NYC DINING
SHOW YOUR TASTE BUDS A REALLY GOOD TIME

Dining in New York City is more than a pleasurable pastime, bigger than a ritual celebration, and rarely just about slaking bodily hunger. For foodies, eating is an art, a philosophy, a transformation of yet another mundane act into a larger-than-life event, all the better to fit into the supercharged and turbo-energized pace of the city.

New and innovative cuisines are part of what makes NYC such a gustatory delight. Ingredients from the furthest corners of the globe show up in the tamales on street corners and the homemade chilis and pasties at local markets.

Fads and flavors come and go in the time it takes you to cab in from the airport, but one trend that's sticking around is an obsession for appetizers. Time-crunched Manhattanites order a bunch of these small plates and nosh like crazy. They've also discovered 'lounge food,' a replacement for hard-to-get reservations at in-demand restaurants. If Del Posto is booked when you're in town, eat at the 'lounge' (the bar in a less posh establishment): it's the same food and often half the sit-down price.

Certain locations are hot, hot, hot for restaurant openings – namely, the East Village (p94), Lower Manhattan (p44), the Meat-packing District (p122) and the Lower East Side (p66). The Upper West Side is probably the most culinary-deprived neighborhood, but even it has a couple of solid standbys. You'll never go hungry in NYC, unless, of course, you can't decide where to eat.

>16 THE BRONX ZOO
COMMUNE WITH THE WILD THINGS

Giving new meaning to the term 'urban jungle,' the 265-acre Bronx Zoo works hard to entertain and educate½ visitors while preserving the natural needs and rhythms of the animals it houses. More than 4500 creatures totaling more than 600 species roam through the mostly unfenced outdoor settings, often separated from the public by nothing more than a moat or other natural barrier. Opened in 1899, the Bronx Zoo has survived by changing with the times. Check out the high-tech Congo Gorilla Forest for example. It's a 6 ½ acre re-creation of an African rain forest, with treetop lookouts, natural pathways, overflowing greenery and about 300 animals, including two troops of lowland gorillas and some red river hogs.

Admission fees go toward caring for the zoo animals, and to the Wildlife Conservation Society's projects around the world. The Bronx Zoo often takes in wounded, sick or endangered animals that WCS partner programs discover in the wild. Three different rides, a monorail, an aerial tram and a shuttle offer you alternative perspectives of the park. Kids go wild for the mini-zoo built to their scale, and the monarch butterfly exhibit is positively otherworldly.

>A YEAR IN NEW YORK

From salsa and swing at Lincoln Center to blues in Battery Park, there's always a festival or party somewhere in the city. The biggest cultural, traditional and artistic events include New Year, Chinese New Year, the Puerto Rican Day Parade, Gay Pride Month, Fourth of July, the West Indian Day Parade, Halloween and the Thanksgiving Day Parade. In December, when Hanukkah, Christmas and Kwanza usually collide, the city is truly a moveable feast.

Dressed as a computer virus, celebrating Halloween in Greenwich Village

JANUARY

Three Kings Parade
www.eastharlempreservation.org
On January 5, Spanish Harlem, up Fifth Ave
to 116th St, is full of parading schoolchildren,
donkeys and sheep.

Winter Restaurant Week
www.nycvisit.com
High-profile restaurants offer three-course
lunches or dinners from between $20 and $30.

Martin Luther King Jr Parade
Civil rights leader Martin Luther King is com-
memorated annually with a birthday gala
parade down Fifth Ave from 86th to 61st Sts.

FEBRUARY

Olympus Fashion Week
www.olympusfashionweek.com
The couture world descends upon Manhattan the second week of February to flounce,
and gawk at the new looks. A second
fashion week is held the second week of
September.

Westminster Kennel Show
www.westminsterkennelclub.org
Catch the much-mocked parade of show
dogs at this dead-serious annual showcase
for purebreds.

MARCH

St Patrick's Day Parade
www.saintpatricksdayparade.com/NYC
/newyorkcity.htm
Everything goes green along Fifth Avenue,
from 44th to 86th Sts, on March 17 when the
world-famous parade (pictured left) starts
at 11am.

APRIL

Easter Parade

www.ny.com

From 10am to 4pm on Easter Sunday, cars are blocked off of Fifth Ave from 57th to 49th Sts. People show off their Easter costumes and fine, fluffy Easter hats.

Orchid Show

www.rockefellercenter.com

This massive display of the rare flowers, well into its second decade, includes competitions in both the orchid-art and fragrance categories.

MAY

Bike New York

www.bikemonthnyc.org

May is Bike Month (pictured above), with weekly bike-oriented tours, parties and other events for pedal-pushing New Yorkers.

Fleet Week

www.intrepidmuseum.com

Ships arrive from around the world for this annual end-of-the-month celebration.

JUNE

Puerto Rican Day Parade
www.nationalpuertoricandayparade.org
Thousands of revelers show up the second week of June for this massive march along Fifth Ave from 44th to 86th Sts.

Lesbian, Gay, Bisexual & Transgender Pride
www.heritageofpride.org
Gay Pride Month lasts throughout June and culminates in a major march (pictured above) down Fifth Ave on the last Sunday of the month.

Restaurant Week
www.nycvisit.com
Big-time discounts at top-notch eateries during the last week of June; three-course lunches and dinners for $20 to $35.

Mermaid Parade
www.coneyisland.com
Elaborately costumed folk display their mermaid finery along the Coney Island boardwalk on the last Saturday of the month.

JULY

July Fourth Fireworks

www1.macys.com

Independence Day fireworks start at 9pm. For good viewing spots, try the LES waterfront park, Williamsburg, Brooklyn or high rooftops.

Nathan's Hot Dog Eating Contest

www.nathansfamous.com

A celebration of gluttony (below) brings food inhalers to Coney Island each Fourth of July.

Philharmonic in the Park

www.newyorkphilharmonic.org

Enjoy free concerts in Central Park, Prospect Park, Queens, the Bronx or Staten Island.

AUGUST

Fringe Festival

www.fringenyc.org

This annual festival features the edgiest, most creative stage talent in New York.

Howl! Festival

www.howlfestival.com

A week-long celebration of arts in the East Village, including the Charlie Parker Jazz Festival and other readings and performances.

US Open Tennis Tournament

www.usopen.org

One of the four Grand Slam tournaments for professional tennis players, held in Queens.

A YEAR IN NEW YORK CITY

SEPTEMBER

West Indian American Day Carnival
www.wiadca.com
Two million Caribbean Americans head to Eastern Parkway in Brooklyn for the annual Carnival Parade (pictured above).

Olympus Fashion Week
www.olympusfashionweek.com
Round two for designers and fashionistas strutting their stuff on the catwalk.

OCTOBER

D.U.M.B.O. Art under the Bridge Festival
www.dumboartscenter.org
Celebrating local artists, you can enjoy open studios, performances and street displays.

Open House New York
www.ohny.org
For one weekend a year, the doors to New York's secret places are thrown open.

Halloween Parade
www.halloween-nyc.com
Freaks and geeks gather in the streets for a wild night of prancing about in costume.

NOVEMBER

New York City Marathon

www.ingnycmarathon.org

This annual 26-mile run (pictured below) through the five boroughs draws thousands of athletes from around the world.

Thanksgiving Day Parade

www.macys.com

Famous floats waft down Broadway, from 72nd St to Herald Sq. Balloons are inflated at the southwest corner of Central Park the night before.

DECEMBER

Rockefeller Center Christmas Tree Lighting

Join the hundreds encircling Rockefeller Center in Midtown and watch the world's tallest Christmas tree lit up to a chorus of 'ooohs' and 'aaahs.'

New Year's Eve

www.nycvisit.com

In addition to the world-famous countdown to midnight in Times Sq, the city has plenty of other celebratory events, namely the **Midnight Run in Central Park** (☎ 212-860-4455), and midnight fireworks in Central Park, Prospect Park and the South St Seaport.

ANNUAL FESTIVALS

Chinese Lunar New Year Festival (www.explorechinatown.com) An awesome display of fireworks and dancing dragon parades, sometimes in late January but usually early February following the Chinese calendar.

Cherry Blossom Festival (www.bbg.org) Held the first weekend in May, the annual Japanese tradition of Sakura Matsuri celebrates the flowering of cherry trees in Brooklyn's Botanic Gardens.

Tribeca Film Festival (www.tribecafilmfestival.com) This film fest invigorates Lower Manhattan the first week of May, filling it full of celebrities anxious to show their indie credibility.

JVC Jazz Festival (www.festivalproductions.net/jvcjazz.htm) More than 40 jazz shows go on in clubs around the city for this mid-June fest, with big names such as Abbey Lincoln, João Gilberto and Ornette Coleman.

River to River Festival (www.rivertorivernyc.org) Lasting through the summer but most popular in June, hundreds of creators and performers bring theatre, music, dance and film to downtown parks.

San Gennaro Festival (www.sangennaro.org) Rowdy, loyal crowds descend on Little Italy for carnival games, sausage-and-pepper sandwiches, deep-fried calamari and more Italian treats than you can imagine. For more than 75 years, it's been a sight to behold.

>ITINERARIES

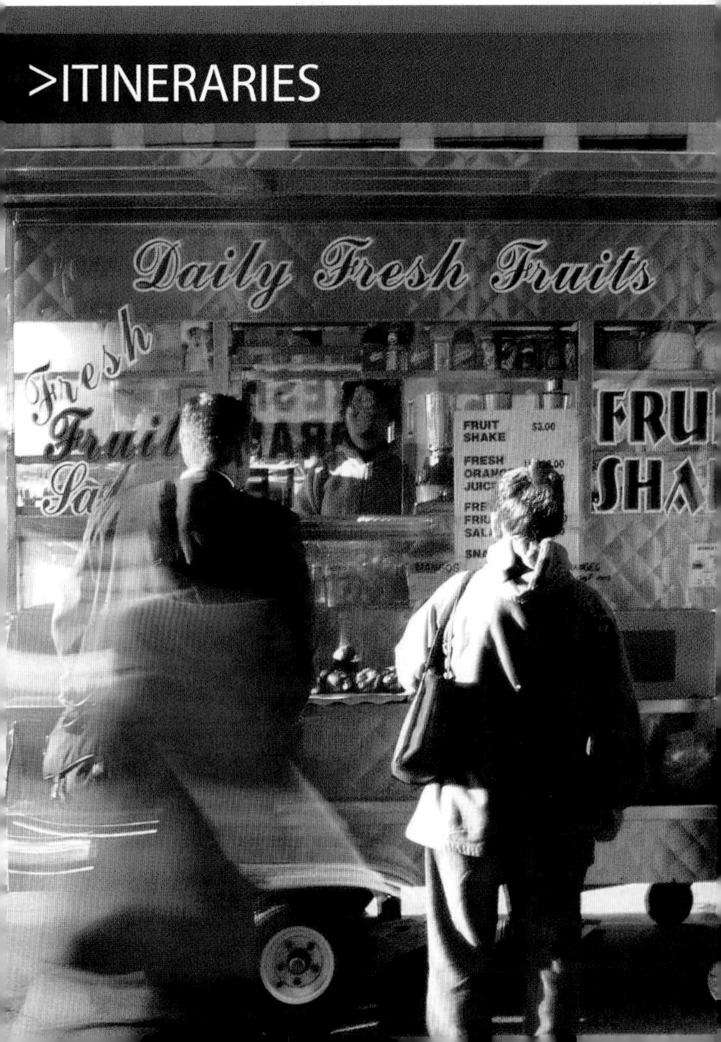

ITINERARIES

If you're willing to overlook the occasional odd smell and delayed start, public transportation can be your best friend in New York City. The century-old subway system zips up and down Manhattan with fairly dependable regularity. For the scenic route, take the aboveground buses that trundle along Manhattan's famous avenues – they're slower, but a great way to sightsee.

Pick up a MetroCard (p269) from any newsstand or subway station and start planning; taking a bus or subway to an area you want to explore and then sauntering from sight to sight is an efficient way to visit attractions. Mind those cross-town blocks though – they're deceptively long. Taxis are a good option if you're trekking to the far edges of the city that aren't equipped with subway services, but during rush hour in particular (anywhere from 7am to 9am and 4pm to 7pm), traffic can be brutal.

ONE DAY

Greet the morning on the West Side and stroll through Central Park (p180), exiting at 79th or 85th St at Fifth Avenue. Check out the fabled Metropolitan Museum of Art (p190) on 82nd St, and then hop onto the M1 bus (labeled South Ferry) heading downtown to Houston St along Fifth Avenue. Work your way south through Nolita to Barbossa (p88) for lunch, and then window-shop around Tribeca and Soho (p84). Catch the splendid night view from the top of the Empire State Building (p158), and dine amid the neon of Times Sq.

TWO DAYS

Start by exploring the shops and cafés of the Meatpacking District, including delicious Chelsea Market (p139). Meander south into Greenwich Village, noting the literary and artistic history at places like White Horse Tavern and Chumleys (p118). Walk down Bleecker St and into Washington Sq Park, then north into Union Sq and Gramercy Park. After a break at Pete's Tavern (p153), a short bus or subway ride transports you to the Lower East Side (p66), where you can gallery- and boutique-hop your way into the East Village (p94), checking out Tompkins Sq Park (p98) and St Marks Pl. Pub-crawl or enjoy a laid-back dinner on Second Avenue.

Top left Shoppers at B & H Photo **Top right** Playing chess in Washington Sq Park **Bottom** First screen test: learning through play at the Children's Museum of Manhattan **Previous Page** Sidewalk food vendors

THREE DAYS

Start by taking a peek at the American Museum of Natural History (p200) on Manhattan's Upper West Side, then move to Riverside Park (p201) at 100th St and stroll around, noting the sculpture dedicated to city firefighters, eventually ending up at St John the Divine. The Schomburg Center, Studio Museum (p212) and Striver's Row are all just around the corner in Harlem, and Amy Ruth's soul food (p214) at Lenox Ave and 116th St is a perfect stop for lunch. After a comforting lunch, walk to Central Park's Harlem Meer and enjoy the Conservatory Gardens, or follow the Museum Mile on Fifth Avenue, starting with the Museum of the City of New York (p211) and El Museo del Barrio (p211) near 105th St.

RAINY DAY

The MoMA (p159) is perfect for any inclement weather because the out-of-this-world atmosphere creates its own little reality bubble anyway. Spend the morning enjoying the museum from the sixth floor down to the basement, and then make a pit stop at The Modern, the museum's plush café and restaurant. Head down to Union Sq, to Bowlmor Lanes (p154), and expend some energy knocking down a few frames. From there it's an easy trip to the Film Forum to catch some classic new wave French cinema. Top the night off with a romantic Greenwich Village dinner at Surya or Blue Hill (p116).

NYC ON A SHOESTRING

Believe it or not, there are plenty of things to do on expensive Madison Ave for under $10. Start off with a visit to Madison Sq Park (p148) and

FORWARD PLANNING

Three weeks before you go Pick a Broadway show you want to see and book tickets. Pick a back up as well in case you need to try your luck at the TKTS (Theater Development Fund, www.tdf.org/tkts) booth when you're there.
Two weeks before you go Make a reservation at Thalassa (p51) or another restaurant you'd like to try through www.opentable.com.
Three days before you go Sign up for the Manhattan User's Guide (www.manhattan usersguide.com) and Daily Candy (www.dailycandy.com).
The day before you go Check out the art, club and literary event websites (www.club freetime.com/new_york.asp; www.freenyc.net) to find out what's on for your first night in town.

take a good look at the Flatiron Building (p148). You can walk to the Municipal Art Society, and then head to St Patrick's Cathedral (p161). You'll also pass La Maison du Chocolat, a good place for a snack to fortify you for the Whitney Museum of American Art (p192). Finish off the day with a walk up Museum Mile on Central Park's east side, trying to catch the sunset at the Harlem Meer. A little further north you can seek refuge in St Nick's Pub (p217) and hear some jazz.

OPEN ALL DAY

Many museums are closed on Monday, making that the perfect day to really explore Central Park (p180). Start at the northern tip and head south, through the Ramble, the Mall, taking a peek at the Central Park Wildlife Center, the Dairy, the Carousel, and Strawberry Fields. If you emerge on the park's west side, take the subway to Chelsea. Not all the galleries will be open – but the stores will be. Do a little window-shopping and inhale the fresh cookie smell of the Chelsea Market (p139). After some gourmet bar snacks at the Spotted Pig, continue on to Lower Manhattan (p44). Ground Zero (p46), St Paul's Chapel (p47) and Trinity Church (p48) are all open daily, and then it's an easy stroll east on Wall St to South St Seaport (p47), which has free concerts in the summer and a convivial, late-night atmosphere.

>NEIGHBORHOODS

Bookshop in Dumbo, Brooklyn

NEIGHBORHOODS

It's easy to float through Manhattan on a wave of sensory delight, savoring sights and smells among the varying pockets of neighborhood culture and color. It's only when you want to pinpoint an actual street that problems might occur; the barrage of names can be utterly confusing. Here's the insider's guide to Manhattan nomenclature, starting at the southern tip and heading north.

Wall St and Battery Park (aka Lower Manhattan, the 'concrete canyon') are filled with huge, hulking skyscrapers crammed into an area built on a colonial scale, making for some fascinating architecture and cityscapes.

North of the Brooklyn Bridge, vibrant Chinatown explodes along Canal St and into what used to be known as Little Italy, now largely confined to Mulberry St, where remaining Italian American families work hard to keep 'old country' traditions alive. North of Broome St, but still below Houston St, is Nolita (North of Little Italy), formerly a gritty area but now a bright and bubbly upscale quadrant of pretty city blocks.

To the west of Lafayette St, galleries, boutiques and cobblestone roads give both Soho and Tribeca a gentle fin-de-siècle feel. Nineteenth-century factories filled this area until artists turned the derelict cast-iron buildings into soaring loft spaces in the sixties.

North of Houston St is Greenwich Village, or more familiarly, 'the Village.' On the east side, from Sixth Ave and 14th St, and the southeastern edge of Chinatown below Houston St, the East Village flows into the Lower East Side. Above 14th St, Union Sq is a popular gathering spot at the nexus of major subway and bus lines. West along 14th St to Ninth Ave takes you to the Meatpacking District and Chelsea, while teeming Midtown has many of the city's popular attractions. The Upper East Side kicks in above 59th St, and the Upper West Side, with tree-lined boulevards parallel to Central Park, leads into Harlem, home to gospel, jazz, good food and some of the most beautiful brownstones in Manhattan.

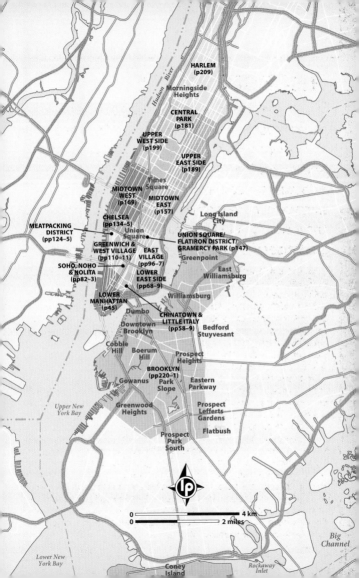

HARLEM
(p209)

Morningside
Heights

CENTRAL
PARK
(p181)

UPPER
WEST SIDE
(p199)

UPPER
EAST SIDE
(p189)

Times
Square

MIDTOWN
WEST
(p169)

MIDTOWN
EAST
(p157)

Long Island
City

CHELSEA
(pp134–5)

Union
Square

MEATPACKING
DISTRICT
(pp124–5)

UNION SQUARE/
FLATIRON DISTRICT/
GRAMERCY PARK (p147)

GREENWICH &
WEST VILLAGE
(pp110–11)

Greenpoint

EAST
VILLAGE
(pp96–7)

East
Williamsburg

SOHO, NOHO
& NOLITA
(pp82–3)

LOWER
EAST SIDE
(pp68–9)

LOWER
MANHATTAN
(p45)

Williamsburg

Dumbo

CHINATOWN &
LITTLE ITALY
(pp58–9)

Downtown
Brooklyn

Bedford
Stuyvesant

Cobble
Hill

Boerum
Hill

Prospect
Heights

Gowanus

BROOKLYN
(pp220–1)

Park
Slope

Eastern
Parkway

Greenwood
Heights

Prospect
Lefferts
Gardens

Prospect
Park
South

Flatbush

Hudson River

Upper New
York Bay

Lower New
York Bay

Coney
Island

Rockaway
Inlet

Big
Channel

0 —————————— 4 km
0 —————————— 2 miles

>LOWER MANHATTAN

Defined by world-famous Wall St, named after the barrier put in place by the Dutch over 200 years ago, Lower Manhattan has enjoyed a slow rebirth from the painful travails of September 11, 2001.

The gaping hole left by the destruction of the World Trade Center hasn't disappeared, but with characteristic fortitude, New Yorkers have simply accepted it. Lower Manhattan is the latest neighborhood to enjoy an influx of fine wining and dining options, as trendy cafés and five-star restaurants open along its small, colonial byways. It's still a little challenged in the nightlife department, but it does have the South St Seaport, overlooking the East River. With the Fulton Street Fish Market gone, the area has suddenly became a hot spot for drinking and dancing, especially during the summer. The old docks house a mini-mall hawking typical tourist wares, but the historic and briny atmosphere from when this was an actual working port imparts a sense of authenticity.

LOWER MANHATTAN

◎ SEE
Battery Park 1   B6
Bowling Green 2   B5
Federal Hall 3   C4
Ferry to Statue of
Liberty/Ellis Island .. 4   B6
Ground Zero 5   B3
National Museum of
the American Indian .. 6   B5
New York City Police
Museum 7   C5
New York Stock
Exchange 8   B4
South St Seaport 9   D4
St Paul's Chapel 10   B3
Trinity Church 11   B4

⌂ SHOP
Century 21 12   B4
Issey Miyake 13   A1
J&R 14   B3

▒ EAT
Blaue Gans 15   B2
Bouley 16   B2
Bridge Café 17   D3
Bubby's Pie Company. 18   A1
Financier Patisserie 19   C5
Franklin Station Café . 20   B1
Fraunces Tavern 21   C5
Les Halles 22   B4
Soda Shop 23   A1
Thalassa 24   B2
Zaitzeff 25   C4

▼ DRINK
Another Room 26   B1
Blue Bar at Bayard's ... 27   C5
Jeremy's Ale House ... 28   D3
Rise 29   B5
Ulysses 30   C5

★ PLAY
Staten Island Ferry
Terminal 31   C6
Tribeca Film Center ... 32   A1
Tribeca Performing
Arts Center 33   A2
Washington Market
Park 34   A2

◉ SEE

◎ BATTERY PARK
☎ 311; www.nycgovparks.org;
Broadway at Battery Pl; ⏲ sunrise-1am;
◎ 4, 5 to Bowling Green, 1 to South
Ferry; ♿
Embracing the tip of lower Manhattan, Battery Park's a breezy, delightful swath of color with 13 works of public art, 35 acres of greenery, the Holocaust Memorial, the NYC Police Memorial, the Irish Hunger Memorial, the rose-filled Hope Garden and sweeping views of Lady Liberty.

◎ BOWLING GREEN
Cnr of Broadway & State St; ◎ 4, 5 to
Bowling Green
A handkerchief-sized piece of grass, Bowling Green has nonetheless played an important role in the city's history. It's believed to be the spot where Dutch settler Peter Minuit paid $24 to the Lenape for the island of Manhattan. Now it's home to *Charging Bull*, Arturo di Modica's famous bronze statue symbolizing America's economic vitality.

◎ FEDERAL HALL
☎ 212-825-6888; www.nps.gov/feha;
26 Wall St; admission free; ⏲ 10am-4pm
Mon-Fri; ◎ 2, 3, 4, 5 to Wall St
The museum inside, dedicated to postcolonial New York and its struggle to define freedom of the press, is well worth a visit. Now a part of the National Parks Service, its classic Greek Revival style reflects the founding fathers' appreciation for democracy. George Washington was inaugurated here, and still stands at the entrance today in the form of a big bronze statue.

◎ GROUND ZERO
Church St btwn Vesey & Liberty; ◎ 2, 3,
E to World Trade Center, N, R to Rector St
The foundation of the former World Trade Center, with its raw, rusty rivets sticking out, is still

plainly visible from all sides of the Ground Zero visitor platform. Parts of it will remain even as development of the site moves forward. For another permanent memorial, check out the bronze, three-panel plaque that tells the story of September 11 on the side of the firehouse at Liberty and Greenwich Sts.

⬡ NATIONAL MUSEUM OF THE AMERICAN INDIAN

☎ 212-514-3700; www.nmai.si.edu; 1 Bowling Green; admission free; ◷ 10am-5pm Fri-Wed, 10am-8pm Thu; ⊖ 4, 5 to Bowling Green

Run by the Smithsonian Institute, this museum is housed in the former US Customs House where Herman Melville wrote parts of *Moby Dick*. The collection of crafts, art and everyday objects from American Indian tribes is augmented by interactive displays offering insights into Indian beliefs and culture.

⬡ NEW YORK STOCK EXCHANGE

☎ 212-656-5168; www.nyse.com; 8 Broad St; ⊖ 1, 2, 4, 5 to Wall St, J, M, Z to Broad St

Strictly enforced security meas-ures keep visitors out of the NYSE these days, but you can still take in its gorgeous Romanesque facade and the hordes of blue-jacketed

traders milling about. During the holiday season Exchange Place gets seriously decked out – it even rivals Rockefeller Center with the size of its tree.

⬡ SOUTH ST SEAPORT

☎ 212-732-7678; www.southstseaport .org; Pier 17 btwn Fulton & South Sts; ◷ 10am-9pm Mon-Sat, 11am-8pm Sun; ⊖ 3, 4, 5, J, Z to Fulton St; ♿

New Yorkers tend to eschew the mini-mall at Pier 17, home to chain restaurants and kitschy T-shirts, but they do like to party at South St Seaport, especially during the summer when there's live music. You can tour old boats, look at naval memorabilia, and tramp about the cobblestones in perfect tranquillity at this pedestrian-only location.

⬡ ST PAUL'S CHAPEL

☎ 212-233-4164; www.stpaulschapel .org; Broadway at Vesey St; ⊖ 2, 3 to Park Pl

Part of the Trinity Church parish, St Paul's Chapel was built as a companion to its larger, more elaborate sister house of worship. Its homey style wasn't too humble for George Washington, who had a pew inside. St Paul's was the center of rescue and recovery op-erations post–September 11 and has a permanent exhibit about that effort.

STATUE OF LIBERTY & ELLIS ISLAND

☎ 212-363-3200 (ferry info), 212-269-5755 (Time Passes), 866-782-8834 (toll-free reservation number); www.nps.gov/stli, www.statuereservations.com; Circle Line ferry adult/child $10/4, departs Battery Park every 20-30 min from 8:30am to late afternoon, stopping at Liberty Island first, then continuing to Ellis Island; ☼ park hrs 9am-5pm (6:30pm Jun-Aug); ♿

Lady Liberty's upper section is closed up tight for security reasons, but a visit is definitely in order if you haven't been before. The sheer size of her, seen up close, is mesmerizing. If you want to enter the monument base, make a reservation for a Time Pass, otherwise you can't get inside. Nearby Ellis Island is even more fascinating. Its carefully assembled exhibits and detailed accounts of immigrant life are moving and informative.

☺ TRINITY CHURCH

☎ 212-602-0800; Broadway at Wall St; ☼ 8am-6pm Mon-Fri, 8am-4pm Sat, 7am-4pm Sun; ◉ 2, 3, 4, 5 to Broadway, N, R to Rector St

A hugely influential church in the annals of New York history, Trinity was built in 1697 by King William III. Its clergy were required to be Loyalists, even though many of its members were dedicated to American independence by the mid-1700s. Its serene and tiny cemetery has headstones bearing some last names that would be very familiar to any student of the American Revolution.

🛍 SHOP

Lower Manhattan is not a shopping mecca, although it does have one notable exception: discount giant Century 21. It's got a pedestrian mall around Fulton and Nassau Streets, and does what it can to encourage consumption, but the offerings are assembly-made key chains and T-shirts, not one-of-a-kind gifts. Tribeca's known for glossy furniture, super-cute kids shops and a few designer outposts.

☐ CENTURY 21

☎ 212-227-9092; www.c21stores.com; 22 Cortland St at Church St; ☼ 7:45am-8pm Mon-Wed & Fri, to 8:30pm Thu, 10am-8pm Sat, 11am-7pm Sun; ◉ A, C, 4, 5 to Fulton St-Broadway-Nassau St

Welcome to New York's worst-kept secret. Deep discounts on really high-end couture line the racks of this square-shaped downtown department store. Most of the time it's a mob scene, but you can walk out with some gorgeous designer duds.

NEIGHBORHOODS

LOWER MANHATTAN

ISSEY MIYAKE
☎ 212-226-0100; 119 Hudson St;
⏰ 11am-7pm Mon-Sat, noon-6pm Sun;
🚇 1 to Franklin St

Gorgeous skirts, pretty pleats and tons of snazzy, silky shirts line the racks at Issey Miyake's downtown store. The merchandise fits in perfectly with the neighborhood, but the prices are more uptown than downtown.

J & R
☎ 800-221-8180; www.jr.com; 15 Park Row; ⏰ 9am-7:30pm Mon-Sat, 10:30am-6:30pm Sun; 🚇 4, 5, 6 to Brooklyn Bridge

Anything and everything related to technology, video games, sound systems and music can be found in J&R's three multistory stores between Ann and Beekman Streets.

EAT
BLAUE GANS
Austrian Comfort Food $-$$
☎ 212-571-8880; 139 Duane St;
⏰ lunch & dinner; 🚇 1, 2, 3 to Chambers St; ♿

Critics called this latest effort from Austro-American whiz kid Kurt Gutenbrunner 'slapdash,' but everybody else loves the red cabbage salad, big sausages and chicken fried à la Viennese, with venison goulash and potato salad.

Austrian wines and desserts add to the fun; it's a no reservations, children welcome, sit back and unbuckle your belt kind of place.

🍴 BOULEY *French* $$$
☎ 212-694-2525; www.davidbouley .com; 120 West Broadway; ☽ lunch & dinner; ◉ 2, 3, A to Chambers St; ♿
The darling of New York's foodie scene has fallen from his pedestal at times, but he's always bounced back deliciously. David Bouley's flagship restaurant is filled nightly with people dying for a bite of his seasonal dishes, from baby lamb and eggplant moussaka to razor clams and asparagus. Get a reservation or resign yourself to eating at Bouley Bakery, Café & Market next door, or at **Danube** ($$$; ☎ 212-791-3771; 30 Hudson St; ☽ dinner), Bouley's Austrian-inspired creation.

🍴 BRIDGE CAFÉ
American Nouveau $$-$$$
☎ 212-227-3344; bridgecafechef@aol .com; 279 Water St; ☽ lunch 11:45am-4pm Mon-Fri, dinner 4pm-10pm Sun & Mon, 4-11pm Tue-Thu, 4pm-midnight Fri, 5pm-midnight Sat, brunch 11:45pm-4pm Sun; ◉ 2, 3, 4, 5, A, C, J, M, Z to Fulton St-Broadway-Nassau St; ♿ ⚬
It's been around for more than two centuries and is still one of New York's best insider eateries. If you don't mind a possible ghost sighting, Bridge Café's slow,

ambling brunches and happy, hearty dinners are perfect for you. The dishes are far more modern than the decor – fresh ingredients and locally produced cuts of beefsteak, fish and poultry.

🍴 BUBBY'S PIE COMPANY
American & Southern Soul $$
☎ 212-219-0666; www.bubbys.com; 120 Hudson St; ☽ breakfast, lunch & dinner; ◉ 1 to Franklin St; ♿ ⚬
Kids will swoon at the creamy mashed 'taters, juicy dawgs, burgers and fries, and the delectable, homemade, deep-dish pies. For adults, there are pear and arugula and roasted beet salads, as well as hearty soups and sandwiches.

🍴 FINANCIER PATISSERIE
Bakery, Sandwiches & Desserts $-$$
☎ 212-334-5600; 62 Stone St at Mill Ln; ☽ 7am-8:30pm Mon-Fri, 7am-7pm Sat; ◉ 2, 3, 4, 5 to Wall St, J, M, Z to Broad St; ♿ ⚬
A little Left Bank in the Financial District! Early-morning patrons flock here for the fresh-from-the-oven croissants, almond and apricot tarts and deep, dark coffee. The same crowd is back to sample creamy quiche tartlets for lunch, served with a side of pungent salad, and hearty lentil soup and sandwiches.

🍴 FRANKLIN STATION CAFÉ

French Malaysian $-$$

☎ 212-274-8525; 222 W Broadway at Franklin St; ⏲ breakfast, lunch & dinner daily, brunch Sat & Sun; ⊖ 1 to Franklin St, A, C, E to Canal St; ♿

Endearingly small Franklin Station marries curry with other delicate Asian flavors and flair to produce a unique culinary treat. It's a local favorite in a neighborhood over-run with 'it' restaurants that come and go. On top of creamy coconut curried chicken dishes and thick mango smoothies, there's also a regular slideshow on the wall near the door.

🍴 FRAUNCES TAVERN

American Traditional $$-$$$

☎ 212-968-1776; www.frauncestavern .com; 54 Pearl St; ⏲ 11:30am-9:30pm Mon-Fri, 11am-9:30pm Sat (reservations suggested); ♿

How can you really pass on the chance to eat where George Washington (it's been document-ed) supped in 1762? Expect heap-ing portions of tavern stew, clam chowder and beef Wellington, and for dessert, pick from your choice of fruit cobbler, butterscotch bread pudding, spiked fig and apple tart or strawberry shortcake. The bar, filled with friendly locals, is great for a snack and a drink.

🍴 LES HALLES

French Bistro $$-$$$

☎ 212-285-8585; www.leshalles.net; 15 John St btwn Broadway & Nassau; ⏲ lunch & dinner; ⊖ A, C to Broadway-Nassau St

It's hard not to kick up your heels in a cancan dance at Les Halles, a red-roomed wonder of a bistro that serves up classic French fare: *filet de beuf bèarnaise*, *cassoulet toulousain*, *choucroute garnie*, *moules frites*, steak *au poivre*, and plenty of *amuse-gueules* to start.

🍴 THE SODA SHOP

American Comfort $-$$

☎ 212-571-1100; 125 Chambers St; ⏲ 8am-9pm; ⊖ A, C, 2, 3 to Chambers St; ♿ 🐕 V

Lunch and dinner are great – full of American classics like hearty mac 'n' cheese, and spaghetti with rich, flavorful meatballs – but locals love the breakfasts. Soda Shop's homey interior is the perfect place to grab a short stack or fluffy omelette on the way to work.

🍴 THALASSA *Greek* $$$

☎ 212-941-7661; www.thalassanyc .com; 179 Franklin St; ⏲ lunch & dinner; ⊖ 1 to Franklin St; ♿

Greek owned and operated, Tha-lassa was once a cheese and wine storage facility; now it's a sleek, stylish restaurant selling fresh fish by the pound. Pick from *spetsiota*,

V

SEASIDE SNACKS
There's been an explosion of eateries around the suddenly hot South St Seaport area — maybe the removal of the colorful (but odiferous) Fulton Fish Market heralded the change. Keep an eye out for **Meade's** (22 Peck Slip; pub food); **SUteiSHI** (236 Front St; sushi); **Bin No. 220** (220 Front St; wine bar); **Jack's Stir Brew** (222 Front St; vegan scones & coffee); **Il Brigante** (214 Front St; Italian); **Stella Maris** (213-217 Front St; European pub fare); and **Salud!** (142 Beekman St; tapas).

risotto with seafood in olive oil, lobster braised with brandy, cheese, garlic and thyme, braised lamb, silky-sweet wild boar, North African shrimp, and plenty of gorgeous sparkling Greek wines.

ZAITZEFF
Organic Diner $-$$
☎ 212-571-7272; www.zaitzeffnyc.com; 72 Nassau St; 8am-10pm Mon-Fri, 10am-6pm Sat & Sun; 2, 3, 4, 5, A, C, J, M, Z to Fulton St-Broadway-Nassau St;

Finally, healthy and quick organic eats in downtown Manhattan. A former Wall St trader opened this zippy spot and now sells all-natural beef burgers (turkey, too) on whole-grain Portuguese buns for former colleagues. Plenty of organic muffins, salads, sweet-

potato fries and vegetarian options available too (also for takeout or delivery).

DRINK
ANOTHER ROOM
☎ 212-226-1418; 249 West Broadway; 1, 2 to Franklin St
Mellow and artsy and filled with long-time Tribeca residents, Another Room manages to be welcoming despite its narrow space and industrial decor. Wine and beer only; no mixed drinks.

BLUE BAR AT BAYARD'S
☎ 212-514-9454; www.bayards.com; 1 Hanover Sq btwn Pearl & Stone Sts 4:30pm-11pm Mon-Sat; 2, 3 to Wall St, 4, 5 to Bowling Green, J, M, Z to Broad St, R, W to Whitehall St
A dark-hued bar with a maritime theme, Blue Bar is tucked inside the opulent brownstone that houses Bayard, a highly-acclaimed restaurant. Blue Bar's sedate atmosphere lightens a bit on Wednesday nights, thanks to the live piano, but it's always a great place for a quiet, romantic drink.

JEREMY'S ALE HOUSE
☎ 212-964-3537; 228 Front St; 8am-midnight Mon-Fri, 10am-midnight Sat, noon-11pm Sun; 2, 3, 4, 5, A, C, J, M, Z to Fulton St-Broadway-Nassau St

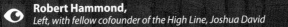

Robert Hammond,
Left, with fellow cofounder of the High Line, Joshua David

What's your favorite season in the city? Summer weekends – I'm one of the few people who love being in the city on warm, summer weekends. **What will your neighborhood look like in 5 years?** I'm looking forward to having more art in the neighborhood with the Whitney Museum extension. I think that corner of Washington and Gansevoort Sts will be one of the most exciting corners in the world – entrance to the High Line, the Whitney, the energy of the West Village and the Meatpacking District. It's a great anchor to the High Line – you can see the world's most interesting contemporary art in Chelsea and then see Hoppers and Warhols in the Whitney permanent collection. **Do you have any 'only in New York ' moments to share?** Swimming around Manhattan in a relay race organized by www.swimnyc.org.

NEIGHBORHOODS

LOWER MANHATTAN

It's a ramshackle kind of place, but Jeremy's Ale House has always had a loyal following – it's a great bunch of mainly blue-collar construction workers who come in for the fried clams, cold beer and cheery bonhomie.

⌾ RISE
☎ 917-790-2626; www.ritzcarlton .com; Ritz Carlton at 2 West St at Battery Pl; ⊕ N, R, W to Rector St, 4, 5 to Bowling Green
What better place to sip a drink than 14 stories over the Hudson River? Rise is a sleek, sexy, comfortable bar that's great anytime of year, but absolutely phenomenal in the summer months when it opens up the outdoor patio. The dress code calls for 'casual chic,' meaning smart but not fussy.

⌾ ULYSSES
☎ 212-482-0400; 95 Pearl St; ⊕ 2, 3 to Wall St
An Irish bar with big easy chairs and comfy couches, Ulysses is part laid-back lounge and part neighborhood watering hole. The crowd's diverse and fun, the choice of drinks immense, and the owners run a shuttle between this and their two other bars, Puck Fair and Swift.

★ PLAY

★ RIVER TO RIVER FESTIVAL
www.rivertorivernyc.com; South St Seaport, Battery Park & Lower Manhattan; admission free; ⊕ any train to Lower Manhattan; ♿
All summer long this nonprofit organization puts on film screenings, live music performances, dance nights, children's events and many other culturally enriching activities all across Lower Manhattan. Each summer's schedule is posted on the website. Favorite local choices include Latin nights at South St Seaport.

★ STATEN ISLAND FERRY
☎ 718-815-BOAT; www.nyc.gov/html /dot/html/masstran/ferries/statfery

---

RICHMOND GALLERIES
The best place for antiques, one-of-a-kind furniture, first-edition books and more is a century-old family-run **auction house** (☎ 718-273-1120; www.richmondgalleries .com) in Staten Island . It's the best-kept secret in New York, although queues on auction day are growing longer, as details of great finds leak out. The Brown family began hoarding furniture 100 years ago as part of a moving business; when a client couldn't pay, the family kept the goods. Call for details on preview days and upcoming auctions.

.html; Whitehall Terminal at Whitehall & South Sts; admission free; ⏰ 24hr; ♿
This is the life – a nice breeze, plenty of room, and a good long look at Lower Manhattan, the Statue of Liberty and Ellis Island – and it costs nothing. The Staten Island Ferry has got to be the best deal in town.

⭐ TRIBECA FILM CENTER
☎ 212-941-2000; www.tribecafilm.com; 375 Greenwich St btwn N Moore & Franklin Sts; ⊕ 1 to Franklin St
It's not a working movie theater, but this labor of love from movie legend Robert DeNiro encourages the public to attend special screenings held throughout the year. It's also the de facto headquarters of the Tribeca Film Festival, another DeNiro production.

⭐ TRIBECA PERFORMING ARTS CENTER
☎ 212-220-1460; www.tribecapac.org; 199 Chambers St; ⊕ A, C, 1, 2, 3 to Chambers St
A grassroots artists' collective, TribecaPAC likes to put on performances from local residents on diverse topics related to city life. Works are multidisciplinary and unexpected, like *Lost Jazz Shrines*, celebrating New York jazz clubs no longer in existence.

⭐ WASHINGTON MARKET PARK
☎ 212-964-1133; www.washingtonmarketpark.org; Greenwich St & Chambers; ⏰ 6am-dusk; ⊕ 1, 2, 3 to Chambers St
In 1858 locals came to this 3-acre site to buy food; now it's a popular neighborhood playground and hangout.

>CHINATOWN & LITTLE ITALY

A living example of how immigrant communities arrive, thrive and move on in New York, what was once Little Italy is now almost entirely China-town, save for one or two small blocks right above Canal St. Regardless of which ethnicity calls this neighborhood home (although, with 150,000 Chinese-speaking residents living there, it's pretty clear who's in charge), it's a vibrant and exotic location.

With a growing Vietnamese presence and waves of Chinese immigrants from Fuzhou, Guangdong and Toisan, there's a constant overlapping of festivals, holidays and traditions – and a whopping 200-plus restaurants and bars.

The city's layered immigrant history is evident everywhere. To get oriented, stop by the official **Explore Chinatown information kiosk** (☎ 212-484-1216; www.explorechinatown.com; Canal St btwn Baxter and Walker Sts; ☽ 10am-6pm Mon-Fri & Sun, 10am-7pm Sat) where helpful, multilingual folk can guide you to specific eateries, shops, sights and events.

Explore on your own as well because there's nothing as exciting as these fragrant, packed, jaw-droppingly busy streets. Or, to switch cultures, head to Mott and Mulberry Sts, where alfresco dining is the norm in warmer months.

CHINATOWN & LITTLE ITALY

🅒 SEE
Columbus Park 1 C6
Eastern States
Buddhist Temple 2 D5
Mahayana Buddhist
Temple.......................3 E4
Mulberrry St...............4 C3
Museum of Chinese
in the Americas 5 C5

🅗 SHOP
Canal St 6 G4
Pearl Paint Company..7 A4
Pearl River Mart 8 A3
Wing Fat Shopping 9 D6

🍴 EAT
Bo Ky Restaurant......10 C5
Canoodle 11 C5
Canton......................12 E5
Da Nico 13 C3
Doyers Vietnamese
Restaurant 14 D6
Jaya 15 C5
La Esquina 16 B2
Mei Lai Wah Coffee
House 17 D5
Original Chinatown
Ice Cream Factory...18 D5
Peking Duck House 19 D6

🅨 DRINK
Double Happiness 20 C2
Happy Ending............21 E2
Mare Chiaro...............22 C2
Winnie's 23 C5

⭐ PLAY
Explore Chinatown
Information Kiosk 24 C5

Please see over for map

SEE

BUDDHIST TEMPLES
There are Buddhist temples are all over Chinatown, but the **Eastern States Buddhist Temple** (64 Mott St btwn Bayard & Canal Sts) holds hundreds of the roly-poly statues in all different sizes. It's a landmarked site, as is the **Mahayana Buddhist Temple** (133 Canal St & Manhattan Bridge Plaza), which holds one large, 16-ft Buddha. You'll know you've arrived when you see two golden lions guarding a door.

COLUMBUS PARK
☎ Mulberry & Park Sts
You'd never guess from the gentle sounds of neighborhood residents playing mah-jongg and dominoes, but this park was once part of the notorious Five Points neighborhood that was the inspiration for Martin Scorsese's *Gangs of New York*. Although the tiny triangle is now a peaceful playground, the surrounding tenements are the same ones that were built in 1890.

MULBERRY ST
Ⓜ C, E to Spring St
Even though the original Italian essence is long gone, Mulberry St still bursts with true ethnic pride. Mobster Joey Gallo was shot to death in **Umberto's Clam House**

(☎ 212-431-7545; 386 Broome St at Mulberry St) in the '70s, the old-time bar **Mare Chiaro** (p64) was one of the favorite haunts of the late Frank Sinatra, and the **Ravenite Social Club** (247 Mulberry St), now a gift shop, used to be the Alto Knights Social Club, where mobsters like Lucky Luciano spent some time. The Ravenite was also a favorite hangout of John Gotti (and the FBI) before he was arrested and sentenced to life imprisonment in 1992.

MUSEUM OF CHINESE IN THE AMERICAS
☎ 212-619-4785; www.moca-nyc.org; 70 Mulberry St at Bayard St; ⊗ noon-5pm Tue-Sun; Ⓜ J, M, N, Q, R, W, Z, 6 to Canal St
At press time, this museum was getting ready to move into a new 12,350-sq-foot space on Lafayette between Grand and Howard Sts with a luxurious visitors lounge and opulent settings for its aged exhibits. MOCA details the history of Chinatown through artifacts, stories and photographs.

 # SHOP

CANAL ST
Ⓜ M, N, Q, R, W, Z, 6 to Canal St
A bustling, busy and perpetually congested avenue, Canal Street is packed with everything from treasure to junk; sifting through

Browsing the curio stores along Canal St

takes a keen eye and loads of patience. Or, you can simply walk around, taking in the strange creatures flopping in the food markets, the homeopathic drugstores with Chinese remedies, and the sound of a thousand tongues speaking at once.

🏠 PEARL PAINT COMPANY
☎ 212-431-7932; 308 Canal St; 🕐 10am-7pm Mon-Fri, 10am-6:30pm Sat, to 6pm Sun; 🚇 J, M, N, Q, R, W, Z, 6 to Canal St
An institution in art circles, Pearl Paint sticks out a mile on Canal St. Taking up four floors of a sprawling warehouse, it's got an obscene amount of space and it's all filled

with anything and everything to do with painting, drawing, arts and crafts, gold leaf, glitter, glue – the list is endless.

🏠 PEARL RIVER MART
☎ 212-431-4770; 477 Broadway; 🕐 10am-7pm; 🚇 J, M, N, Q, R, W, Z, 6 to Canal St
An Asian emporium that stocks all sorts of knick-knacks, Pearl River Mart has moved a few blocks north of Canal St into swanky Soho surroundings, all the better to show off its bright kimonos, bejeweled slippers, Japanese teapots, paper lanterns and jars of mysterious spices, herbs, teas and more.

VENDY AWARDS
Hardworking New Yorkers like to recognize anyone who does his or her job exceptionally well, and that includes the thousands of nimble-fingered food cart vendors who populate the streets from sunrise to sunset selling delicious treats, often specialties from the owner's native land. Every year the nonprofit Street Vendors Project organizes a cook-off among top nominated food sellers. A perpetual third-place finisher for the 'Vendy Prize' is Thiru 'Dosa Man' Kumar (at Washington Sq Park South and Sullivan St); his vegan *dhosas* are legendary, but he can't wrest first place from Sammy's Halal at 73rd St and Broadway in Queens. For a list of current winners, or to nominate a vendor, go to www.streetvendor.org.

WING FAT SHOPPING
8-9 Bowery btwn Pell & Doyers St;
J, M, N, Q, R, W, Z, 6 to Canal St
One of the most unique malls you'll ever see, it lies underground and has businesses offering reflexology, collectible stamps and feng shui services. The most fascinating aspect is its history, as the tunnel is said to have served as a stop on the Underground Railroad, as well as an escape route in the early 20th century for members of rival Tong gangs. They'd wage battle up on the street and then disappear down into the darkness before police could even begin to search.

EAT
BO KY RESTAURANT
Pan Asian $
212-406-2292; 80 Bayard St btwn Mott & Mulberry Sts; breakfast, lunch & dinner; J, M, N, Q, R, W, Z, 6 to Canal St; V

Cheap, quick and delicious, Bo Ky's meat-studded soups, fish-infused flat noodles and curried rice dishes keep customers rotating in and out the door, usually in clumps of twos and threes. Join the crowds and dig in.

CANOODLE *Chinese* $
212-349-1495; 79 Mulberry St; breakfast, lunch & dinner (to 9pm); J, M, N, W, Z, 6 to Canal St;
An old-school favorite, Canoodle's famous for its sausage fried rice, minced quail with lettuce, baby silverfish and Peking Duck. It opens early and closes early (for Chinatown), and despite a few design quirks, is packed all the time.

CANTON *Cantonese* $$$
212-226-4441; 45 Division St btwn Bowery & Market St; lunch & dinner; F to East Broadway;
It's been around for 50 years, so Canton must be doing something

right – no, make that everything right. Underneath the Manhattan Bridge, it churns out delectable dishes like ginger scallion noodles, sautéed tofu (with pork), mixed vegetables and garlicky chicken.

DA NICO *Italian* $$-$$$
☎ 212-343-1212; 164 Mulberry St; ☻ lunch & dinner; ◉ J, M, N, Q, R, W, Z, 6 to Canal St; ⓰

This is one of the few places in Little Italy where you can step back from the street and enjoy a shred of Old World ambience. Da Nico's enormous outdoor patio is as much an attraction as its giant scampi, *pollo scarpariello* and pizza napoletana. Although there isn't much in touristy Little Italy that stands out anymore, this family-run establishment is still a winner.

DOYERS VIETNAMESE RESTAURANT *Vietnamese* $
☎ 212-513-1521; 11 Doyers St btwn Bowery & Pell St; ☻ lunch & dinner; ⓰ Ⓥ

A huge part of the appeal at Doyers is the fascinating street it's on – it used to be known as the 'Bloody Triangle' during the area's gang days. The menu's as long as your arm and has veggie and meat dishes, served in the below-ground dining room.

JAYA *Malaysian* $$
☎ 212-219-3331; 90 Baxter St btwn Walker & White Sts; ☻ lunch & dinner; ◉ J, M, N, Q, R, W, Z, 6 to Canal St; ⓰ Ⓥ

Thirty types of noodles, topped with tofu, vegetables, shrimp, spicy chilies, pork, beef and chicken are the main staple at Jaya, although it's also got house specials like coconut fried rice, basil stir-fried beef and fish soup.

LA ESQUINA *Mexican* $-$$
☎ 646-613-1333; 106 Kenmare St; ☻ 24 hrs; ◉ 6 to Spring

If you glimpse this place out of the corner of your eye as your cab

speeds by, it looks like a frat boy's late-night drunken diner. It is, in the wee hours, but it serves great Mexican fare, perfect for settling the stomach. Make a reservation and you can get into the inner sanctum: a cool sit-down lounge and eatery in La Esquina's lower level.

☎ MEI LAW WAH COFFEE HOUSE *Bakery* $

☎ 212-925-5438; 64 Bayard St at Elizabeth St; ☽ breakfast, lunch & dinner; ⊕ J, M, N, Q, R, W, Z, 6 to Canal St; ⚭ V

Authentic steamed pork buns and rich, thick coffee are a great way to greet the morning. Join the throngs of early morning workers who grab a snack on their way past this Chinatown institution.

☎ ORIGINAL CHINATOWN ICE CREAM FACTORY *Ice Cream* $

☎ 212-608-4170; www.chinatown icecreamfactory.com; 65 Bayard St; ☽ 11am-10pm; ⊕ J, M, N, Q, R, W, Z, 6 to Canal St; ⚭ V

Ask the servers here and they'll tell you ice cream was invented in China during the Tang dynasty – based on the flavors the Factory can produce, you might just believe them. Sorbets and more in flavors like avocado, durian, sesame and peppermint, plus the standards like vanilla and chocolate.

☎ PEKING DUCK HOUSE
Chinese $-$$

☎ 212-227-1810; 28 Mott St; ☽ lunch & dinner; ⊕ J, M, N, Q, R, W, Z, 6 to Canal St; ⚭ ☖ V

You already know what the specialty of the house is – big, brown, crispy glazed duck, served with sides of pancakes and *hoisin* sauce for tearing, rolling and dipping. There are plenty of other dishes to choose from, all bearing imprints of Peking, Shanghai and Szechuan flavors, mixed expertly together. Peking Duck's slightly fancier than other Chinatown spots, but not at all stuffy; it's a popular choice for local families celebrating a big event.

⅄ DRINK
⅄ DOUBLE HAPPINESS

☎ 212-941-1282; 173 Mott St btwn Broome & Grand Sts; ⊕ J, M, Z to Bowery, 6 to Spring St

Enter down a flight of stone steps that lead into a dark basement with no sign – it's all part of the fun though, and the well-mannered crowd inside enjoys the joke enough to come back again and again. The narrow room is filled with flickering candles, lending it a sexy and sinister air.

⅄ HAPPY ENDING

☎ 212-334-9676; www.happyending lounge.com; 302 Broome St;

⊙ 10pm-4am Tue; 7pm-4am Wed-Sat; ⊕ B, D to Grand St; J, M, Z to Bowery

Ignore the hideous pink, purple and spangled decor at Happy Ending – it used to be a 'massage parlor,' and the new owners clearly didn't feel the need to refurbish. Focus instead on the groove, hip-hop, funk and electronica. Tuesday nights are 'We Bite' and 'Shit Hammered' events; Wednesday nights feature literary readings (before the dancing starts); there are gay, goth and punk nights, and the 'Human Jukebox' DJ on Saturdays. Note that the entrance awning says 'Xie He Health Club' – the owners apparently didn't feel the need to change that, either.

▼ MARE CHIARO
☎ 212-226-9345; 176½ Mulberry St btwn Broome & Grand Sts; ⊕ B, D to Grand St

Take a moment and pay your respects to Ol' Blue Eyes – Frank Sinatra used to belly up to this very same bar and charm the gruff waiters into giving him a double.

▼ WINNIE'S
☎ 212-732-2384; 104 Bayard St btwn Baxter & Mulberry Sts; ⊕ J, M, N, Q, R, W, Z, 6 to Canal St

One of many divey karaoke bars hidden in Chinatown alleys, Winnie's is popular for its potent cocktails and wide selection of '80s pop songs; it's always full of karaoke

Local vegetable market in Chinatown

lovers, some of them good, some of them just bad enough to make you think you could do better.

 PLAY

☆ **EXPERIENCE CHINATOWN**
☎ 212-619-4785; www.moca-nyc.org
To truly penetrate the layers that make up the bustling, insiders' world of Chinatown, you'll need a guide. And trusting one from the Chinatown-based Museum of Chinese in the Americas (p57) is definitely a good move. The tours, given weekly from May through

> **POETRY IN TRIBECA**
> The **Poets House** (☎ 212-431-7920; www.poetshouse.org), a nonprofit collective that celebrates poetry and poets, is located in Soho, but often holds events and readings at the Tribeca Performing Arts Center. Whether you're a bard or simply an aficionado, the talks are inspiring and enlightening.

December, are led by museum docents with family roots in the community and give you a sense of Chinatown's past and present.

>LOWER EAST SIDE

This eclectic neighborhood has been a seedy slum far longer than it's been a hip high-rent district, and yet the changes that are altering the historic face of the Lower East Side are taking root almost overnight. This area was a terrible ghetto not too long ago, even though millions of immigrant and working-class arrivals tried hard to improve their lot here. They built the Eldridge St Synagogue and Ukrainian Church that still inhabit the east side of town today, and fought long and hard to get basic improvements in their tenements. The Lower East Side was Skid Row, the last place you wanted to be because you couldn't go any lower.

Now a revolution is taking place amid a growing desire to preserve what's left, while creating opportunity for what's new. The Lower East Side is alive with possibility for the first time in 100 years; it's great to see the nabe shake itself up.

LOWER EAST SIDE

🅲 SEE
East River Park	1	H2
Eldridge St Synagogue	2	C6
Essex St Market	3	D3
Gallery Onetwentyeight	4	D3
Lower East Side Tenement Museum	5	C4
Participant Inc.	6	C3

🅂 SHOP
48 Hester	7	D5
360 Toy Group	8	B3
Bluestockings	9	C3
Breakbeat Science	10	C2
Economy Candy	11	D3
Elizabeth & Vine	12	A3
Foley + Corinna	13	C3
Jutta Neumann	14	C3
Mary Adams The Dress	15	C3

Orchard Street Bargain District	16	C3

🍴 EAT
'Inoteca	17	C3
Alias	18	E3
Freemans	19	B3
Katz's Deli	20	C2
Little Giant	21	C5
Orchard	22	C3
Schiller's Liquor Bar	23	D3
Tenement	24	C3
Yonah Shimmel Knishery	25	B2
Zucco: Le French Diner	26	C3

🅈 DRINK
Delancey	27	E4
Fontana's	28	C5

Good World Bar & Grill	29	C6
Magician	30	D3
Sapphire Lounge	31	B2
Subtonic Lounge	32	D4
Whiskey Ward	33	D3

⭐ PLAY
Abrons Art Center	34	F4
Arlene's Grocery	35	C3
Bowery Ballroom	36	B4
Landmark Sunshine Cinema	37	B2
Living Room	38	C3
Mercury Lounge	39	C2
Pianos	40	D4
Sarah D Roosevelt Park	41	B5

Please see over for map

🔵 SEE

🔵 EAST RIVER PARK

A $ 4 million facelift can do wonders for a park, even one that sits next to the traffic-clogged FDR highway. This long, narrow bit of playground runs down Manhattan's east side and has ballparks, tennis courts, recently renovated bathrooms, great bike paths and stellar views of the Dumbo waterfront.

🔵 ELDRIDGE ST SYNAGOGUE

☎ 212-219-0888; www.eldridgestreet .org; 12 Eldridge St btwn Canal & Division Sts; 🕑 tours 11am-4pm Sun, Tue, Thu or by appt; 🔵 F to East Broadway

Built in 1887, this landmarked house of worship was once the center of LES Jewish life, attracting thousands to its services. It fell into disrepair in the 1920s and closed in the 1950s. In the 1980s the community started the Eldridge St Project to restore it and it's now almost complete. It hosts concerts, art exhibits, educational lectures and readings, too.

🔵 ESSEX ST MARKET

☎ 212-312-3603; www.essexstreet market.com; 120 Essex St btwn Delancey & Rivington Sts; 🕑 8am-6pm Mon-Sat; 🔵 F, V to Delancey St, J, M, Z to Delancey -Essex St

A mix of Jewish and Latino (just like the neighborhood), this 80-year-old market is a noisy pleasure. Stop by the Essex St Cheese Co if you like milky Comté – it specializes in the French *fromage*. Schapiro Wines, the city's oldest winery, founded in 1899, is the spot for kosher vino. Just follow your nose through stalls selling pickles, meats, olives and homemade bread.

🔵 GALLERY ONETWENTYEIGHT

☎ 212-674-0244; www.onetwenty eight.com; 128 Rivington; 🕑 call for appt; 🔵 F to Second Ave

A small gallery with emphasis on contemporary drawing and painting. Onetwentyeight also likes to turn its space over to local dabblers for impromptu, one-night only shows that are promoted only through word of mouth. If you stumble onto one, consider yourself lucky.

🔵 LOWER EAST SIDE TENEMENT MUSEUM

☎ 212-431-0233; www.tenement .org; 90 Orchard St at Broome St; adults/seniors & students/children under 5 $15/11/free, discounts available for combo-tour tickets; 🕑 visitor center 11am-5:30pm, museum tours every 40min 1pm & 1:20pm until 4:30pm & 4:45pm Tue-Fri (reservations suggested);

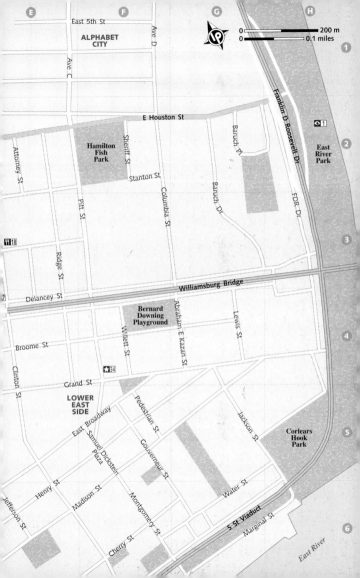

A restored apartment in Lower East Side Tenement Museum

🚇 B, D to Grand St, F to Delancey St, J, M, Z to Essex St; ♿

Get a firsthand look at the crowded conditions endured by Jewish and Eastern European immigrants at the turn of the century. The tours through restored and refurbished apartments raise poignant feelings about early settlers' enthusiasm for a future in America.

🔘 ORCHARD STREET BARGAIN DISTRICT

Orchard, Ludlow & Essex Sts btwn Houston & Delancey Sts; ⏰ Sun-Fri; 🚇 F to Delancey St, J, M, Z to Essex St

Back in the day, this large intersection was a free-for-all as Eastern European and Jewish merchants sold anything that could command a buck from their pushcarts. The 300-plus shops you see now aren't as picturesque, but it's a good place to pick up some cheap shirts, tees and jeans. If you like to haggle, take a shot at bargaining over the price.

🔘 PARTICIPANT INC

☎ 212-254-4334; 95 Rivington St btwn Ludlow & Orchard Sts; ⏰ Wed-Sun noon-7pm; 🚇 F to Second Ave

Part gallery, part performance art space, Participant Inc uses its second floor for all sorts of innovative fun. Opened in 2002 by founder Lia Gangitano, it's stayed

TENEMENT MUSEUM TOURS

When you visit, you'll find three recreations of turn-of-the-20th-century tenements, including the late-19th-century home and garment shop of the Levine family from Poland, and two immigrant dwellings from the Great Depressions of 1873 and 1929. On weekends the museum has an interactive tour where kids can dress up in period clothes and touch anything in the restored apartment (from around 1916) of a Sephardic Jewish family. Walking tours of the neighborhood are held from April to December, and usually include stops at the **Streit's Matzo Company** (148-154 Rivington St), which opened in the 1890s, and the **First Shearith Israel Graveyard** (55-57 St James Pl btwn James & Oliver Sts), which was the burial ground of the country's first Jewish community. Gravestones date from the late 1600s and include those who escaped the Spanish Inquisition.

afloat even as many other galleries disappear. It has a rotating roster of international artists, but also makes a point of showcasing LES-based work.

SHOP

▣ 48 HESTER
☎ 212-473-3496; 48 Hester St at Ludlow St; ◷ noon-7pm Tue-Fri, 11am-6pm Sat & Sun; ◉ F, V to Lower East Side-Second Ave

Owner Denise Williamson stocks this boutique with her favorite designers – Ulla Johnson, Kristen Lee, sass & bide, Rag & Bone and Franck and features cotton separates made by Ms Williamson herself.

▣ 360 TOY GROUP
☎ 646-602-0138; 239 Eldridge St btwn Houston & Stanton Sts; ◷ 11am-7pm Sun, noon-6pm Mon; ◉ F, J, M, Z to Delancey St-Essex St

Ranging from mildly quirky to never-before-heard-of, these toys are imported from all over Asia (particularly Hong Kong and Japan) by owner Jakuan. Figurine collectors will be happy to find the oddball character Michael Lau, rain-hat-wearing Bathing Apes, robotic Bounty Hunters, and abstract creations from Jakuan's Rock Hard clothing line.

▣ BLUESTOCKINGS
☎ 212-777-6028; www.bluestockings.com; 172 Allen St; ◷ 1-10pm daily; ◉ F, V to Lower East Side-Second Ave

It's run-down and ramshackle, but full of history and fueled by the alternative attitude that once permeated the Lower East Side. A holdover from the freewheeling '70s, Bluestockings offers books on a range of radical topics, including gender studies, black liberation theory and plenty more.

☐ BREAKBEAT SCIENCE
☎ 212-995-2592; 181 Orchard St;
🕐 1-8pm Sun-Wed, to 9pm Thu-Sat;
🚇 F, V to Lower East Side-Second Ave

Pick up the equipment and the clothes you'll need to be an effective DJ at this LES shop. It stocks turntables, DJ tees, hoodies and the requisite bling, as well as DJ sling bags, record-cleaner kits and even DJ toy figurines.

☐ ECONOMY CANDY
☎ 212-254-1531; www.economycandy
.com; 108 Rivington at Essex St; 🕐 9am-
6pm Mon-Fri, 10am-5pm Sat; 🚇 F, J, M,
Z to Delancey St-Essex St

Known as the 'Nosher's Paradise of the Lower East Side,' this second-generation family store has an amazing – no, make that astounding – selection of old- and new-style nibbles. Jelly beans, halvah, Pez, Swedish Fish and so much more grace the shelves of this corner candy shop.

☐ ELIZABETH & VINE
☎ 212-941-7943; 253 Elizabeth St;
🕐 11am-10pm Mon-Sat; 🚇 6 to
Bleecker/Lafayette St

Step gingerly in this independently owned liquor store that lacks space but has excellent depth when it comes to wine selection. You can find anything from table plonk to $300 bottles from the world's best vintners. Check out the 'manager's choice' rack in the front that offers insider gems at bargain prices. Chilean and French wines are specialties.

☐ FOLEY + CORINNA
☎ 212-529-5042; 143 Ludlow St at
Stanton St; 🕐 12-8pm; 🚇 F, V to Lower
East Side-Second Ave

This vintage store with a few of its own unique designs is pure girly romance. Delicate dresses, tees, tanks and blouses matched with flirty skirts are the signature style, along with Corinna's unique shoe and jewelry designs.

☐ JUTTA NEUMANN
☎ 212-982-7048; www.juttaneumann
.com; 158 Allen St at Rivington St;
🕐 11am-7pm; 🚇 F, V to Lower East
Side-Second Ave

These handcrafted leather accessories by German-born Neumann get snapped up as soon as they hit the shelves. Wallets, bags, sandals and coats can be custom-made, or given a special design twist just for you (at a price, of course).

☐ MARY ADAMS THE DRESS
☎ 212-473-0237; www.maryadams
thedress.com; 138 Ludlow St; 🕐 1-6pm
Wed-Sat, to 5pm Sun, or by appt; 🚇 F, J,
M, Z to Delancey St-Essex St

You can pick a lacy, romantic Mary Adams off the rack, or ask the designer to make one just for you –

prices start at $1500. Adams' designs are eye-catching and innovative while remaining classically romantic. She's a favorite among those shopping for wedding gowns.

🍴 EAT

🍴 ALIAS *American* $$

☎ 212-505-5011; 76 Clinton St; 🕑 6-11pm Mon-Thu, 6-11:30pm Fri, 11am-3:30pm & 6pm-11:30pm Sat, 11am-4pm & 6pm-10pm Sun; 🚇 F at Delancey St; ♿ 🛗 Ⓥ

The sole survivor of a trio of restaurants that opened up when Clinton St was considered culinary Siberia, Alias continues to deliver delicious, fresh food, heavy on seasonal ingredients with dishes like wild Alaskan black cod, maple-syrup drenched pears with ricotta and tomato braised brisket.

🍴 FREEMAN'S
American (Wild Game) $$$

☎ 212-420-0012; www.freemans restaurant.com; end of Freeman Alley, off Rivington btwn Bowery & Chrystie Sts; 🕑 5-11:30pm daily, 11am-3:30pm Sat & Sun; 🚇 F to Second Ave; Ⓥ

Tucked off the beaten path at the end of a small alley, Freeman's no-reservation policy can translate into long waits, but only because it's become so popular. The delicious, meat-centric dishes (mostly wild game like deer, pheasant and

once even ostrich) are matched with an expensive wine list and airy desserts.

🍴 'INOTECA *Italian* $$

☎ 212-614-0473; 98 Rivington at Ludlow St; 🕑 lunch & dinner daily, brunch Sat & Sun; 🚇 F, V to Lower East Side-Second Ave; ♿ 🛗 Ⓥ

Get in line for one of the square, chunky wooden tables that are always packed at 'inoteca. The tasty bite-sized *panini* and *framezzini* (pressed or regular sandwiches) are wholesome and delicious (try the hollowed out one, filled with egg, truffles and fontina cheese), and deep dishes like eggplant parmigiana, lasagna or *frutti di mare* pasta are famously garlickly and good.

🍴 KATZ'S DELI *Jewish Deli* $

☎ 212-254-2246; www.katzdeli.com; 205 E Houston St; 🕑 breakfast, lunch & dinner; 🚇 F, V to Lower East Side-Second Ave; ♿ 🛗

With sandwiches the size of your arm, come to Katz's teeming deli when you're ready to seriously eat. There's a lightning quick takeout line if you don't want to stay, but the slower table service means more time for people-watching as you tackle that pastrami and rye.

🍴 LITTLE GIANT
Seasonal American $$

☎ 212-226-5047; www.littlegiantnyc .com; 85 Orchard St; 🕑 dinner daily,

brunch Sat & Sun; 🚇 F to Delancey;
♿ V

Fresh ingredients from organic farmers in upstate New York pepper Little Giant's revolving menu, which can carry dishes like chicken liver mousse, maple-roasted brussels sprouts, sticky toffee pudding and a 'swine of the week' dish featuring pork. The 80-bottle wine list proudly offers only local vintners.

🍴 THE ORCHARD Global $$
☎ 212-353-3570; 162 Orchard St;
🕐 dinner Mon-Sat; 🚇 F to Delancey;
♿ V

The perfect restaurant for when you don't know what you're in the mood for, the Orchard claims no allegiance to any one cuisine but instead celebrates them all, from the humble Mexican street taco to tuna *tartare* and seafood risotto. The long, white room gets a glossy lift from candles, but is otherwise pleasantly nondescript.

🍴 SCHILLER'S LIQUOR BAR
Bistro Cuisine $$
☎ 212-673-0330; www.schillersny.com; 131 Rivington St at Norfolk St;
🕐 11am-midnight Mon-Thu, 11am-2am Fri-Sun; ♿ 👶

The combination of the eclectic bistro fare and the warm and homey surroundings is a large part of Schiller's allure – the other

Zucco: Le French Diner

element is the Rivington St location, a great place to sit with a cold beer on a hot day. The wine carafes are generous, portions ample, and the food – steak *frites*, cuban sandwiches, baked chicken and glazed cod – reliably good.

🍴 TENEMENT
American Traditional $$$
☎ 212-598-2130; www.tenement lounge.com; 157 Ludlow St btwn Stanton & Rivington Sts; ❧ 5-11pm; 🚇 F to Second Ave; Ⓥ

The name refers to the past more than the present, because although it's housed in an old tenement (that became a bordello), this restaurant is a slēek and sexy place with gaslights on the walls and pierogies, po'boys, calamari, succulent racks of lamb, duck breast and glazed chicken dishes. The late-night bar menu is even better.

🍴 YONAH SHIMMEL KNISHERY *Knishes* $
☎ 212-477-2858; 137 E Houston St btwn Eldridge & Forsyth Sts; ❧ 9:30am-7pm; 🚇 F, V to Lower East Side-Second Ave; ♿ Ⓥ

Here's how to make a living the old-school way – buy a pushcart c 1890, sell your wife's knishes on Coney Island, save up for a mini storefront on the LES, and turn it into a 92-year-old family business

that still follows the original recipe and uses a century-old dumbwaiter to haul potato, cheese, cabbage and kasha knishes up from your wood-burning stove in the cellar. One bite of a Yonah Shimmel knish and you'll be hooked.

🍴 ZUCCO: LE FRENCH DINER
French $-$$
☎ 212-677-5200; 188 Orchard St near Houston St; ❧ lunch & dinner; 🚇 F to Delancey St; ♿ Ⓥ

Swing by to grab a fresh, crispy sandwich pressed just right, served with white napkins and tiny wineglasses, or savor the deep, meaty flavor of the North African *merguez* lamb sausage. Other French classics, along with the tin-pressed ceiling, include *moules marinières*, and grilled *tuna à la Provençale*.

🍸 DRINK
🍸 THE DELANCEY
☎ 212-254-9920; 168 Delancey St; ❧ 4pm-5am; 🚇 F to Delancey St, J, M, Z to Bowery

Three levels of spacious fun, the main draw being the top-floor roof that's actually got a splashing fountain (of sorts) and the odd shrub or two providing some greenery. Downstairs there's a DJ playing rock (indie and classic) with some new wave, and experimental punk/electronica reign in the basement. No velvet-rope head games to struggle through either – the Delancey's very egalitarian. Wednesday nights are 'Death Disco,' an import from London that has everybody dancing for their lives.

� FONTANA'S
☎ 212-334-6740; www.fontanasnyc
.com; 105 Eldridge St; ☽ 2pm-4am;
Ⓔ F to Delancey St, J, M, Z to Essex St
Kitschy posters on teal-colored walls, and red booths in front of the bar give Fontana's a faded, 1960s appeal that seems to have hit a chord with neighborhood drinkers. The three-level bar packs in the best live bands (in the basement) and the spinning-est DJs (main floor), and a knowledgeable and friendly crowd unassumingly nods along to the beats.

� GOOD WORLD BAR & GRILL
☎ 212-925-9975; www.goodworldbar
.com; 3 Orchard St; ☽ noon-4am Mon-Fri, 10am-4am Sat-Sun; Ⓔ F to East Broadway
Slide on in to this popular hot spot, where late-night revelers heave to DJ sounds and reach for the excellent Swedish meatballs, handed out free when the mood strikes the staff. Gravlax, fish soup, potato pancakes and more are on the late-night menu, but most patrons are more into quaffing the on-tap Stella Artois.

� MAGICIAN
☎ 212-673-7851; 118 Rivington St btwn Essex & Norfolk Sts; Ⓔ F to Delancey St, J, M, Z to Delancey-Essex Sts
Pick out an old classic on the jukebox, take your pick of microbrewed beers or specialty cocktails (mixed with a generous hand) and enjoy the spacious, never-crowded bar at Magician, a low-key neighborhood joint that hasn't been discovered by the 'in' crowd.

� SAPPHIRE LOUNGE
☎ 212-777-5153; www.sapphirenyc
.com; 249 Eldridge St; ☽ 7pm-4am;
Ⓔ F, V to Second Ave
Pile in to what has to be the smallest club in the world and get ready to sweat – you can find a seat on a mini-banquette against the wall, but it's just as easy to get out onto the dance floor. Expect eclectic mixes of hip-hop, dance, reggae and techno, and don't worry if you don't have a partner. At Sapphire, you'll find one.

� SUBTONIC LOUNGE
☎ 212-358-7501; www.tonicnyc.com; 107 Norfolk St; ☽ 10pm-7am Tue-Sun; Ⓔ F to Delancey St, J, M, Z to Essex St
Hidden in the basement of the more famous Tonic lounge, the Subtonic is a hedonistic rave-like dance party that proudly features the best German techno coming

out of Berlin – and sometimes the best guest DJs, too. Friday night's 'Bunker Party' raises the roof as spinmeisters whip the packed dance floor into a frenzy.

▼ THE WHISKEY WARD
☎ 212-477-2998; www.thewhiskey ward.com; 121 Essex St; ⏰ 5pm-4am; ◉ F to Delancey St, J, M, Z to Essex St; ♿

Once upon a time, city officials divided Manhattan into wards – the Lower East Side was the 'Whiskey Ward,' courtesy of its many drinking establishments. Modern owners of the Whiskey Ward apparently appreciate history as much as they adore single malts, rye whiskey, blended Scotch, Irish whiskey and Bourbon. And their patrons, a sleek, and sexy mix of all ages, enjoy the single-mindedness of this brick-walled bar.

PLAY
☆ ABRONS ART CENTER
☎ 212-598-0400; www.henrystreet.org; 466 Grand St; ◉ A, C, E to Canal Street-Sixth Ave; ♿

This venerable cultural hub has three theaters, the largest being the Harry de Jur Playhouse (a national landmark), with its own lobby, fixed seats on a rise, a large, deep stage and good visibility. A mainstay of the downtown Fringe

Festival, Abrons Art Center is also your best bet to catch experimental and community productions. Not afraid of difficult subjects, Abrons sponsors plays and dance and photography exhibits that don't get much play elsewhere.

☆ ARLENE'S GROCERY
☎ 212-358-1633; www.arlenesgrocery .net; 95 Stanton St; ⏰ 6pm-4am daily; ◉ F, V to Lower East Side-Second Ave

Formerly a bodega and butcher shop, Arlene's Grocery now serves up heaping portions of live talent with shows every night. Drinks are cheap and the crowd is good looking – make an impression Monday night with Rock 'n' Roll Karaoke. It's free, and you're backed by a live band. Probably your best shot at getting a groupie.

☆ ART IN ODD PLACES
www.artinoddplaces.org; ◉ F,V to Lower East Side, 6 to Bleecker St & Lafayette

Exploring the boundaries of public space and public art, Art in Odd Places holds an annual 'scavenger hunt' around the Lower East Side, handing out maps with clues that point interested viewers toward installation pieces, like blank sheets of paper stapled to telephone poles that say, 'Draw here.' Check website for dates of upcoming events.

☆ BOWERY BALLROOM

☎ 212-533-2111; www.boweryball room.com; 6 Delancey St; ◉ F to Delancey St, J, M to Bowery

The clue to the Bowery's success, besides its cool location and look, is that it's the kind of place you want to hang in before and after the show, as well as during. Drinks are long and strong, acoustics are grand, and the list of talent is phe-nomenal. Dirty Pretty Things and Ziggy Marley play regularly, and the Losers Lounge nights (the Cure vs the Smiths) sells out instantly.

☆ LANDMARK SUNSHINE CINEMA

☎ 212-358-7709; www.landmark theaters.com; 143 E Houston St; tickets $10; ◉ F, V to Lower East Side-Second Ave; ♿ 🚻

Built in the late 1800s, Sunshine Cinema used to be a Yiddish vaudeville house until it closed in the 1950s. It reopened as a movie theater in 2001 with comfy chairs, great sight lines and a Japanese rock garden. It's a great place to catch a flick, and it leans toward independent and limited-release films, although it will also carry big blockbusters.

☆ THE LIVING ROOM

☎ 212-533-7235; www.livingroomny .com; 154 Ludlow S; no cover, 1 drink minimum; 🕐 6:30pm-2am Sun-Thu, 6:30pm-4am Fri & Sat; ◉ F, V to Lower East Side-Second Ave, J, M, Z to Essex St

There's never a cover at this intimate space, where Norah Jones once played to sold out crowds before winning every Grammy in sight. Most acts are acoustic, but the occasional amplifier will slip in. Look for bands like Mudfunk, Happy Chichester and Julia Darling. If the live music doesn't thrill you, the upstairs lounge features a DJ.

☆ MERCURY LOUNGE

☎ 212-260-4700; www.mercurylounge nyc.com; 217 E Houston St; 🕐 4pm-4am; ◉ F, V to Lower East Side-Second Ave

Some former Mercury Lounge acts have hit the big time, like the Strokes. A few others are on the verge, like Beirut, but this is generally the place to hear bands that are still several leagues away from stardom. That doesn't mean they're not good though. The Mercury's got a good eye (and ear) for talent, so expect to be enter-tained, if not enthralled.

ALTERNATIVE LOWER EAST SIDE

Girls Room (☎ 212-254-5043; 210 Rivington St at Pitt St; ⊖ F to East Broadway) Downtown divas pile in for nights dedicated to karaoke, open mikes and go-go dancers.

Slide/Marquee (☎ 212-420-8885; 356 Bowery; ⊖ F, V to Lower East Side-Second Ave) Guys, gays, girls and trannies come here for movie nights, live-music shows and more; it's connected to the fabulous lounge/restaurant Marion's, serving bistro fare at street level.

⭐ PIANOS

☎ 212-505-3733; www.pianosnyc.com; 106 Norfolk St; ⏱ noon-4am; ⊖ F, V to Lower East Side-Second Ave

Nobody's bothered to change the sign at the door, a leftover from the location's previous incarnation as a piano shop. Now it's a musical mix of genres and styles, leaning more toward pop, punk and new wave, but throwing in some hip-hop and indie bands for good measure.

⭐ SARAH D ROOSEVELT PARK

Houston St at Chrystie St

On weekends this long, thin park gets taken over by local basketball buffs looking to shoot hoops – a far cry from the park's former use as a drug hangout. Reclaimed by local residents, it's now a big part of community life, especially the playground and water fountains toward the back.

>SOHO, NOHO & NOLITA

These three no-man's land neighborhoods have come to represent the zenith of hipness, with movie stars and rock stars taking up residence. It was only a matter of time before Noho – North of Houston – and Nolita followed in Soho's footsteps and became international destinations rather than simply old-style neighborhoods.

Of the three, Soho is still the most visually stunning, with massive, soaring cast-iron-facade buildings and a picturesque skyline.

Nolita now has a similar concentration of pretty shops and eclectic designers but it moves at a slightly slower pace. Where Soho has its galleries and big stores, Nolita has its boutiques and rustic eateries.

On the north side of Houston St, below Astor Pl, is the triangle of Lafayette and Bond Sts. You couldn't pack more treats into a two-block radius – with three standout stores it looms large for shoppers in Manhattan.

SOHO, NOHO & NOLITA

🎥 SEE

Children's Museum of the Arts	1	F6
Drawing Center	2	E6
Merchant's House Museum	3	G1
New York City Fire Musuem	4	B5
St Patrick's Old Cathedral	5	G4

🛍 SHOP

American Apparel	6	F5
Anna Sui	7	E4
Apple Store Soho	8	E4
Bloomingdale Soho	9	F5
Bond 07	10	F2
Bond 09	11	F2
Brooklyn Industries	12	G4
Chelsea Girl	13	D5
Daffy's	14	F6
Housing Works Used Book Café	15	F3
Mayle	16	H3
McNally Robinson	17	G4
Otto Tootsi Plohound	18	G4
Rebecca Taylor	19	G4
Seize Sur Vingt	20	H4
Sigerson Morrison	21	G4

🍴 EAT

24 Prince St	22	H4
Barbossa	23	H4
Bond St	24	F2
Honmura An	25	F3
Kittichai	26	D5
Peasant	27	H5
Public	28	H4
Rice	29	G4
Sparky's	30	G3

🍸 DRINK

C Tabac	31	D6
Chibi's Bar	32	G4
Ear Inn	33	A6
Mercbar	34	F4
Milano's	35	G3
Xicala	36	H5

⭐ PLAY

Angelika Film Center	37	F3
Artists Space	38	E6
Bouwerie Lane Theater	39	H2
Here	40	D5
Louis Meisel Gallery	41	E4
New Museum of Contemporary Art	42	F4
Peter Blum Gallery	43	E4
Spencer Brownstone Gallery	44	E6

Please see over for map

👁 SEE

👁 CHILDREN'S MUSEUM OF THE ARTS

☎ 212-274-0986; www.cmany.org; 182 Lafayette St btwn Broome & Grand Sts; admission $6, suggested donation from 4-6pm Thu; 🕐 noon-5pm Fri-Sun & Wed, noon-6pm Thu; ⦿ 6 to Spring St, N, R to Prince St; ♿

No looking allowed! This is a museum of direct participation. Fabulous multisensory activities are educational, fun, and conducted under the watchful eyes of facilitators, all trained artists themselves. Warning: children will leave knowing how to make Flubber at home.

👁 DRAWING CENTER

☎ 212-219-2166; www.drawingcenter .org; 35 Wooster St; 🕐 10am-6pm Tue-Fri, 11am-6pm Sat; ⦿ A, C, E, 1 to Canal St

A nonprofit center dedicated exclusively to drawings, with examples from the masters, as well as unknown sketchers. You can see work by Michelangelo, James Ensor and Marcel Duchamp, as well as Richard Serra, Ellsworth Kelly and Richard Tuttle.

👁 MERCHANT'S HOUSE MUSEUM

☎ 212-777-1089; www.merchants house.com; 29 E 4th St btwn Lafayette & Bowery; 🕐 noon-5pm Thu-Mon; ⦿ 6 to Bleecker St

Get a glimpse of how wealthy businessmen lived in New York in the 1800s at this local museum. Drug importer Seabury Tredwell lived in this house (built in 1831), and his family has preserved the original furnishings, clothing, and even his kitchen sink. It's a remarkable glimpse into the past.

👁 THE NEW YORK FIRE MUSEUM AND NEW YORK CITY POLICE MUSEUM

Fire Museum (☎ 212-691-1303; www .nycfiremuseum.org; 278 Spring St; 🕐 10am-5pm Tue-Sat, 10am-4pm Sun; ⦿ 1 to Houston, C, E to Spring St; ♿); Police Museum (Map p45; ☎ 212-480-3100; www.nycpolicemuseum.org; 100 Old Slip near South St Seaport; $6 suggested donation; 🕐 10am-5pm Tue-Sat; ⦿ 2, 3 to Wall St; ♿)

Both these museums are bursting with fascinating paraphernalia. The Fire Museum has hand pumps and a mock apartment blaze that kids can try to put out. The Police Museum's got weird bad-guy stuff (Al Capone's tommy gun) and lots of counterfeit money. Informative but exciting tours are offered at both places.

👁 ST PATRICK'S OLD CATHEDRAL

260-264 Prince St at Mott St; ⦿ R, W to Prince St

Before St Patrick's on Fifth Ave stole its thunder, this graceful

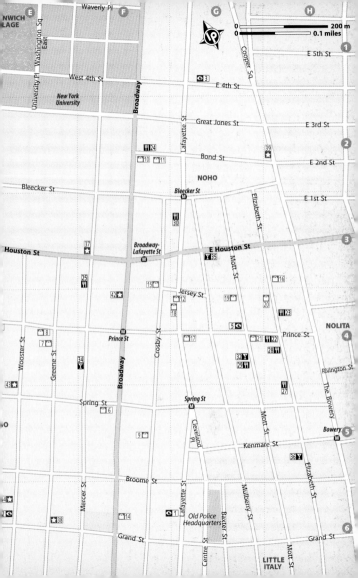

CAST IRON DISTRICT

Soho's nickname comes from its many industrial buildings. Check out the **Singer Building** (561–563 Broadway btwn Prince & Spring Sts) – it used to be the main warehouse for the famous sewing-machine company. The **St Nicholas Hotel** (521–523 Broadway btwn Spring & Broome Sts) that served as the headquarters of Abraham Lincoln's War Department during the Civil War and still has some signage on the current building's marble facade. The **Haughwout Building** (488 Broadway at Broome St) was the first building to put the exotic steam elevator developed by Elisha Otis to use. Known as the 'Parthenon of Cast-Iron Architecture,' the Haughwout is considered a rare structure for its two-sided design; look for the iron clock that sits on the Broadway-facing exterior.

1809 Gothic Revival church was the seat of the Catholic archdiocese in New York. Built by new immigrants mainly from Ireland, it continues to service its diverse community by giving liturgies in English, Spanish and Chinese. Its brick-walled courtyard hides an ancient cemetery, and its mausoleum many a famous New York family.

SHOP

🏠 AMERICAN APPAREL
☎ 212-226-4880; www.americanapparel.net; 121 Spring St btwn Broadway & Mercer St; 🕓 10am-8pm Mon-Thu, 10am-9pm Fri & Sat, 11am-8pm Sun; ⊕ R, W to Prince St

Pick up American classics made with a conscience – no sweatshop labor goes into the making of these clothes. Everything is done with above-board in-house production. Sweats, hoodies, underwear and other apparel available in a range of colors.

🏠 ANNA SUI
☎ 212-941-8406; www.annasui.com; 113 Greene St; 🕓 11:30am-7pm Mon-Sat, noon-6pm Sun; ⊕ R, W to Prince St

Frilly, flimsy and free-flowing, Anna Sui's dresses are must-haves for soigné New York women who like to look sexy but not obvious. The store's a purple-walled curiosity in its own right.

🏠 APPLE STORE SOHO
☎ 212-226-3126; www.apple.com/retail/soho; 103 Prince St; 🕓 10am-8pm Mon-Sat, 11am-7pm Sun; ⊕ N, R, W to Prince St

Always busy, this flagship location attracts visits from the full range of computer users – beginners enjoy the translucent stairway and upstairs walkway as much as the cheery-colored iPods, while tech heads engage the staff in deep discussions. There is free email service at the store, and seminars on computer tips are given for free.

BLOOMINGDALE SOHO
☎ 212-729-5900; 504 Broadway; ⏱ 10am-9pm Mon-Fri, 10am-8pm Sat, 11am-7pm Sun; ⊕ R, W to Prince St
Hipper and younger than the original uptown Bloomies, this downtown outpost eschews housewares to focus solely on fashion, jewelry, makeup and accessories. Everything from clubwear to beachwear hangs on the racks.

BOND 07
☎ 212-677-8487; 7 Bond St; ⏱ 11am-7pm Mon-Sat; noon-7pm Sun; ⊕ R, W to Prince St
Selima Salaun's graceful glasses are the big draw, although Bond 07 also doubles as a chic boutique. Many a celebrity hides their orbs behind her perfectly-tinted, boho chic styles. With more than 100 in stock, she can fit a pair to any face.

BOND 09
☎ 212-228-1940; 9 Bond St; ⏱ 11am-7pm Mon-Sat; ⊕ R, W to Prince St
If you visit New York, you gotta smell like New York – that's the rule at Bond 09. It makes custom

perfumes named after local nabes, like Eau de Noho, Chinatown and Chelsea Flowers. Don't worry – the fragrances actually smell good.

BROOKLYN INDUSTRIES
☎ 212-219-0862; www.brooklynindustries.com; 286 Lafayette St; ☼ 11am-8pm Mon-Sat, noon-7:30pm Sun; ◉ B, D, F, V to Broadway-Lafayette St
Its stores are all over Williamsburg, and this brand of urban chic has cracked Manhattan. Started by two artists who turned their love of fashion into a million-dollar business, these hip clothes, with their catchy Brooklyn skyline label, are comfy, casual and fun.

CHELSEA GIRL
☎ 212-343-1658; www.chelsea-girl.com; 63 Thompson St btwn Spring & Broome Sts; ☼ noon-7pm; ◉ C, E to Spring St
Small but catchy, Chelsea Girl has racks of vintage wear from past decades in all shapes and sizes. You never know what you'll find in the mess; Pucci prints have been pulled from under stacks of old records. It's a browser's dream.

DAFFY'S
☎ 212-334-7444; www.daffys.com; 462 Broadway at Grand St; ☼ 10am-8pm Mon-Sat, noon-7pm Sun; ◉ A, C, E to Canal St

Two floors of designer duds and accessories (and a random handful of housewares) for men, women and children, with prices that can be shockingly low. And the tags – like those at most discount shops – show you the item's suggested retail price, which, at an average of 50 percent off, just gives you more incentive to buy.

HOUSING WORKS USED BOOK CAFE
☎ 212-334-3324; www.housingworks.org/usedbookcafe; 126 Crosby St; ☼ 10am-9pm Mon-Fri, noon-9pm Sat; ◉ B, D, F, V to Broadway-Lafayette St
Relaxed, earthy, and featuring a great selection of fabulous books you can buy for a good cause (proceeds go to the city's HIV-positive and AIDS homeless communities), this spacious café is a great place to head to if you're looking to while away a few quiet afternoon hours.

MAYLE
☎ 212-625-0406; 242 Elizabeth St; ☼ noon-7pm Mon-Sat, noon-6pm Sun; ◉ 6 to Spring St, N to Prince St
Lush fabrics and classic cuts give the clothes at this Nolita hideaway a distinctly vintage feel, but nothing could be further from the truth. They're actually all made on-site with the best in

modern materials. The big, boxy coats, straight wool skirts and tight-waisted frocks are all one-of-a-kind, just like the store.

🏠 MCNALLY ROBINSON
☎ 212-274-1160; www.mcnallyrobin son.com; 52 Prince St; ⏲ 10am-10pm Mon-Sat,10am-8pm Sun; ◎ R, W to Prince St

Zone out in the cozy café (with wi-fi) inside this fully-stacked indie store that has books on every conceivable subject – food, fiction, travel, architecture, LGBT, to name a few – as well as magazines and newspapers from around the world.

🏠 OTTO TOOTSI PLOHOUND
☎ 212-431-7299; 273 Lafayette St; ⏲ 11:30am-7:30pm Mon-Fri, 11am-8pm Sat, noon-7pm Sun; ◎ B, D, F, V to Broadway-Lafayette St

All the labels you love – Miu Miu, Cynthia Rowley, Helmut Lang, Paul Smith and Prada Sport among them – dangle like candy before your eyes. Otto Tootsi's comfy Soho store takes window design to a new level – it's worth stopping by just for the 'wow' factor.

🏠 REBECCA TAYLOR
☎ 212-966-0406; www.rebeccataylor .com; 260 Mott St; ⏲ 11am-7pm Mon-Sat, noon-7pm Sun; ◎ 6 to Bleecker/ Lafayette St, N to Prince St

On a block full of fun and funky clothes, this boutique's peek-a-boo designs stand out. Flirty and girlish frocks, swishy skirts and no-cling pants are big crowd pleasers – half of neighboring Nolita is dressed by Ms Taylor.

🏠 SEIZE SUR VINGT
☎ 212-343-0476; www.16sur20.com; 107 Grand St; ⏲ 11am-7pm Mon-Sat, noon-6pm Sun; ◎ F, V to Broadway-Lafayette St, 6 to Spring St

A Nolita secret, this store turns out stern, classic shirts and suits – they're brightened by high-quality material in flashy and fancy colors. It even custom fits shirts to make sure you get just the right silhouette.

🏠 SIGERSON MORRISON
☎ 212-941-5404; www.sigersonmor rison.com; 242 Mott St & 28 Prince St; ⏲ 11am-7pm Mon-Sat, noon-6pm Sun; ◎ 6 to Spring St, N to Prince St

Innovation combined with surprising practicality (who would have thought we could have high-heeled flip-flops, or designer rubbers to wear in the rain?), plus a love of splashy colors have made Sigerson a hit. The store also carries Belle, a lower-priced line of its signature high-heeled, glamorous styles.

🍴 EAT

🍴 24 PRINCE ST
American Comfort $$

☎ 212-226-8624; 24 Prince St btwn Mott & Elizabeth; 🕑 lunch & dinner; 🚇 6 to Spring St; ♿ 👶 Ⓥ

It's not dishing up anything all that unusual, but 24 Prince has found a recipe for success: serve delectable mac 'n' cheese, burnished chicken, creamed spinach, cornbread and other American favorites in a convivial and casually elegant atmosphere, and everybody leaves happy.

🍴 BARBOSSA
South American $$

☎ 212-625-2340; 232 Elizabeth St; 🕑 11am-11:30pm Tue-Sun; ♿ 👶

A breezy, wide-open front window and the low-level bossa nova in the background give this café a sultry and jazzy feel that's complemented by a light, tropical cuisine, big on salads (mango and peanut and avocado are favorite toppings), delicious soups and a few hearty mains.

🍴 BOND ST
Japanese/Sushi $$$

☎ 212-777-2500; 6 Bond St; 🕑 6pm-10:30pm Sun-Mon, 6pm-11:30pm Tue-Sat; 🚇 6 to Bleecker St; ♿ 👶 Ⓥ

Move over Nobu; this is the new kid in town. Actually, Bond St

has been around awhile, but it's been kept a secret by sushi lovers. The *omakase* tasting menu, $40 to $120 depending on how extravagant you go, is a real winner, but you can't go wrong ordering anything on the menu, from *maki* rolls to sashimi.

🍴 HONMURA AN *Japanese* $$

☎ 212-334-5253; 170 Mercer St btwn Houston & Prince Sts; 🕑 lunch & dinner Wed-Fri, dinner Tue & Sun; 🚇 R, W to Prince St; Ⓥ

Soba and *udon* noodles are served hot or cold and topped with everything from giant prawn tempura to fish cakes and wild Japanese greens. Fresh sashimi and 'soba' gnocchi' are always available, and Honmura An also does small plates of everything for those who can't make up their minds.

🍴 KITTICHAI *Thai* $$

☎ 212-219-2000; www.kittichairestaurant.com; Ground fl, 60 Thompson St btwn Broome & Spring Sts; 🕑 lunch & dinner; 🚇 C, E to Spring St; Ⓥ

Celebrated for its striking decor – bright red silk curtains against dark, carved walls – and creative menu, Kittichai does tapas (limestone tartlet with minced chicken, marinated monkfish in pandan leaves, and more) and mains (roasted red curry with vegetables, braised short ribs in green curry or a rich seared aged sirloin with fermented black bean and whiskey sauce).

🍴 PEASANT *Italian* $$$
☎ 212-965-9511; www.peasantnyc .com; 194 Elizabeth St; 🕙 dinner; 🚇 6 to Spring St, N to Prince St

If a restaurant can garner rave reviews when it's competing on a street like Elizabeth, flush with trendy openings and the latest hot spots, then it's really got something special. Here it's rustic Italian food with poetic names like *polpi i purgatorio*, *quaglie farcite*, and *porchetta arrosto*.

🍴 PUBLIC
Australasian Eclectic $$$
☎ 212-343-7011; 210 Elizabeth btwn Rivington & Stanton Sts; 🕙 lunch & dinner daily, brunch Sat & Sun; 🚇 6 to Spring St

Built to look like a public library or school, with waiters who take your order on a clipboard, Public falls just on the right side of quirky – and that goes for the food, as well. The odd mix of Asian, Australian and New Zealand cooking is heavy on wild game ('roo and ostrich are on the menu), but well-presented and matched with tasty sides like fennel soup and crab cakes.

NEIGHBORHOODS

SOHO, NOHO & NOLITA

🍴 RICE *Asian Fusion* $

☎ 212-226-5775; www.riceny.com; 227 Mott St; 🕐 noon-midnight; 🚇 6 to Spring St; ♿ 🚹 **V**

Nature's most prolific grain is on the menu here, and once you've had a mouthful of the moist green rice (infused with cilantro, parsley and spinach) or the Thai black rice (sticky, tender and steamed in coconut milk) you'll be hooked. The shrimp satay with a warm sauce of roasted almonds is succulent, the lentil stew is flavorful, and the vegetarian meatballs with sesame crunch totally addictive.

🍴 SPARKY'S *Organic Snacks* $

☎ 212-334-3035; 333 Lafayette St at Bleecker St; 🕐 8am-midnight Mon-Fri, 10am-midnight Sat, 10am-10pm Sun; 🚇 6 to Bleecker St; ♿ 🚹 **V**

A pit stop for cheap, tasty, high-quality fast food, Sparky's has soy dogs and beef dogs, real ice cream or Tofutti sandwiches, grilled cheese, hand cut fries and, for breakfast, locally-made yogurts and granola with milk. Everything is organic and family farmed.

🍸 DRINK

🍸 C TABAC

☎ 212-941-1781; 32 Watts St btwn Sixth Ave & Thompson St; 🕐 5pm-2am Sun-Wed, 5pm-4am Thu-Sat; 🚇 A, C, E, 1 to Canal St

Smoking is allowed (and encouraged) at C Tabac, where more than 150 types of smokes are sold. It makes specialty drinks like the Gingersnap (ginger-infused vodka, crystallized ginger and champagne), or you can just grab a beer and hang out in the art deco lounge with its bamboo walls.

🍸 CHIBI'S BAR

☎ 212-274-0025; 238 Mott St btwn Prince & Spring Sts; 🕐 5:30pm-1am Mon-Fri, 3pm-2am Sat, 3pm-midnight Sun; 🚇 6 to Spring St; ♿

This tiny place works its magic through smooth jazz sounds (live on Sundays) and the dangerously delicious flavors of specialty sakes, *saketinis*, Japanese beers and bar treats from *edamame* to salmon caviar. The owner named the place after Chibi, her sweet little bulldog. He sometimes sits outside.

🍸 EAR INN

☎ 212-226-9060; 326 Spring St btwn Greenwich & Washington Sts; 🕐 11:30am-4am; 🚇 C, E to Spring St

A 12-story condo project will tower over this great old dive in a couple of years, but the landmarked Ear Inn, sitting in the 1817 James Brown House (the James Brown, aide to George Washington, not Soul Brother No 1), isn't going anywhere. Patrons range from sanitation workers to bikers and poets – and they all of them love it (as well as the bar's famous shepherd's pie).

MERCBAR
☎ 212-966-2727; 151 Mercer St btwn Houston & Prince Sts; 5pm-2am Sun-Tue, 5pm-4am Wed-Sat; R, W to Prince St

An intimate hideaway where you can actually hold a conversation without having to scream over the soundtrack is a big draw for the after-work publishing crowd, which likes to sip martinis and rub tweedy elbows.

MILANO'S
☎ 212-226-8844; 51 E Houston St btwn Mulberry & Mott Sts; 5pm-4am; B, D, F, V to Broadway-Lafayette St

What it lacks in aesthetic allure, Milano's makes up for with roguish charm. It's a hole in the wall, but a fun one. Belly up for a $3 Pabst beer and have a jaw with the old-timers who can't keep away.

XICALA
☎ 212-219-0599; 151 Elizabeth St; 5pm-2am; 6 at Spring St;

There's a Cuban trio on Wednesday nights that adds to the already festive atmosphere at this quaint, tiny tapas and wine bar. The strawberry sangria is the house signature drink, but the Riojas and Jerez sherries are just as delicious.

 PLAY

ANGELIKA FILM CENTER
☎ 212-995-2000; www.angelikafilm center.com; 18 W Houston St at Mercer St 7-12; daily; B, D, F, V to Broadway-Lafayette St;

Angelika specializes in foreign and independent films and has some quirky charms (the rumble of the subway, long lines and occasionally bad sound). But its roomy café is a great place to meet and the beauty of its Stanford White–designed beaux arts building undeniable.

ARTISTS SPACE
☎ 212-226-3970; www.artistsspace. org; 3rd fl, 38 Greene Street; 11am-6pm Tue-Sun; A, C, E, J, M, N, R, 1, 6 to Canal St

One of the first alternative spaces in New York, Artists Space was founded in 1972 to support contemporary artists working in the visual arts, including video, electronic media, performance, architecture and design. It offers an exhibition space for new art and artists, and tries to foster an appreciation for the role artists play in communities.

⭐ BOUWERIE LANE THEATER

☎ 212-677-0060; www.jeancocteaurep
.org; 330 Bowery; ☽ noon-6pm Mon-Fri
(one hour before curtain for shows); ◉ 6
to Astor Pl

An off-Broadway theatre venue
that is presently inhabited by
the Jean Cocteau Review, the
Bouwerie was designed more
than 100 years ago by Henry
Engelbert. Its cast-iron facade is
a rare standing example of the
French Second Empire style. It
used to be occupied by a bank
and then in the 1960s converted
to a theater, but nonetheless has
great sight lines.

⭐ HERE

☎ 212-647-0202; www.here.org;
145 Sixth Ave btwn Spring and Broome
Sts; ◉ C, E to Canal St

An acclaimed and perpetually
underfunded theater group that
supports the independent, the
innovative, and the experimental,
HERE helped develop Eve Ensler's

The Vagina Monologues; Basil
Twist's *Symphonie Fantastique*;
Hazelle Goodman's *On Edge*; and
Trey Lyford and Geoff Sobelle's *all
wear bowlers*. Production times
and prices vary, but the on-site
café offers a great opportunity to
check things out.

⭐ LOUIS MEISEL GALLERY

☎ 212-677-1340; www.meiselgallery
.com; 141 Prince Street; ☽ 10am-6pm
Tue-Sat, 10am-5pm Tue-Fri; ◉ N, R to
Prince St; ♿

Specializing in photorealism, the
works at this gallery are strikingly
full of color, and the eye-catching
cityscapes of Staten Island and
local fire trucks are among the
best of the bunch.

⭐ NEW MUSEUM OF CONTEMPORARY ART

☎ 212-219-1222; www.newmuseum
.org; 583 Bowery btwn Houston and
Prince Sts; ◉ N, R to Prince St

As of press time this museum was
getting ready to move from its old

NOBU DELIGHTS

Celebrity co-owner Robert DeNiro may be moving on, but hordes of loyal **Nobu** (☎ 212-219-0500;105 Hudson St) fans haven't stirred an inch since the day this Asian/Latin sensation opened. You could wait a lifetime to get into the real deal, or try your luck at the cunningly designed **Nobu Next Door** (☎ 212-334-4445). It serves the same food, is just as glamorous (in a different way) and won't take reservations for groups under six. Come any day other than Saturday, and your chances of getting in after a moderate wait are just as good as anyone else's.

location in the Chelsea Museum (p133) to its new permanent home on the Bowery, where a state-of-the-art facility awaits. Dedicated to global contemporary art, the New Museum likes to focus on multimedia exhibits above all else.

⭐ PETER BLUM GALLERY
☎ 212-343-0441; www.peterblumgallery.com; 99 Wooster St; 🕙 10am-6pm Mon-Fri, closed July/August; 🚇 C to Spring St; ♿
Peter Blum has three galleries spread around town, but his flagship location is at Wooster St, where he's shown Korean artist Kim Sooja and her inspired bedspreads, as well as exhibiting woodcuts, paintings and photography.

⭐ SPENCER BROWNSTONE GALLERY
☎ 212-334-3455; www.spencerbrownstonegallery.com; 39 Wooster St btwn Broome and Grand Sts; 🕙 11am-6pm Tue-Sat; 🚇 C, E to Canal St; ♿
After cutting his teeth as a private art dealer, Spencer Brownstone opened his own space on Wooster St and has never looked back. Dedicated to up-and-coming US and European artists, this gallery shows installations, photography, paintings, sculptures and videos.

>EAST VILLAGE

It's full of punks and anarchists, NYU students and Wall St brokers, professors, philosophers, poets, hustlers, dancers and ditch-diggers – there are layers of class struggle and class-consciousness and revolutionary leanings, and whatever is left of the once vital social energy of the East Village generally gets channeled into its nightlife, which is pretty darn spectacular.

The East Village retains a unique sense of place and purpose. Amid the nightly limo crawls up and down Second Ave and into the LES, people still step into KGB Bar (former Socialist headquarters) for its weekly reading series; they still attend sit-ins and walk-outs and protest rent hikes, and they still fight against high-rise development with all their might. It's refreshing to know that facades may change, but at least in the East Village, the collective spirit remains the same.

EAST VILLAGE

🅒 SEE
6th and B Garden	1	G4
New York Marble Cemetery	2	D6
Russian and Turkish Baths	3	E3
St Mark's in the Bowery	4	C3
Tompkins Sq Park	5	F3
Ukrainian Museum	6	C4

🅗 SHOP
A Cheng	7	E3
Alphabets	8	F4
East Village Music Store	9	D5
Footlight Records	10	B2
Love Saves the Day	11	D4
Other Music	12	B5
St Mark's Bookshop	13	C3
Tokio 7	14	D4
Underdog East	15	E4

🍴 EAT
Angelica Kitchen	16	D2
B&H Dairy	17	C4
Bao 111	18	H4
Boca Chica	19	E6
Caracas Arepas Bar	20	E4
Counter	21	E4
Hearth	22	E2
Il Bagatto	23	F6
Mo Pitkin's	24	F5
Prune	25	D6
S'Mac	26	D2
Veselka	27	D3

🍸 DRINK
11th St Bar	28	F2
Angel's Share	29	C3
B3 Bar	30	G5
Beauty Bar	31	C1
Clubhouse	32	G3
D.B.A.	33	E5

Holiday Cocktail Lounge	34	D3
KGB Bar	35	C5
Odessa Café	36	F4
Rue B	37	G2

⭐ PLAY
Amato Opera House	38	C6
Easternbloc	39	F4
Joseph Papp Public Theater	40	B5
La MaMa ETC	41	C5
Nuyorican Poets Café	42	G5
Orpheum Theater	43	C4
Pyramid	44	F4
Starlight Bar & Lounge	45	F3

Please see over for map

◉ SEE
◉ 6TH AND B GARDEN
**www.6bgarden.org; 6 St & Ave B;
🕙 1-6pm Sat & Sun; ◎ 6 to Astor Pl**
Reclaimed from squalor by local community activists in the 1980s, East Village residents adore this 17,000-sq-ft tangle of plots, vines, sculptures and flowers. Garden members fought long and hard to keep the city from selling the land out from under them; and now it's a city oasis everyone enjoys.

◉ COLONNADE ROW
428-434 Lafayette St btwn Astor Pl & East 4th St; ◎ 6 to Astor Pl
Once there were nine Greek Revival mansions in this row; now there are four. All were built in 1833, out of stone, the work done by prisoners from the upstate Sing Sing prison, and all have ornate, detailed touches on their classic facades.

◉ NEW YORK MARBLE CEMETERY
www.marblecemetery.org; entrance on Second Ave, btwn 2nd & 3rd Sts 🕙 tours 4th Sun of every month, Mar-Nov, other weekends upon request; ◎ F, V to Lower East Side-Second Ave, 6 to Bleecker St/Lafayette St; ♿
Manhattan's first nonsectarian burial spot, dating from the 1800s,

has a wonderful air of history and decay. It's where many prominent New Yorkers are getting their permanent rest.

◉ RUSSIAN AND TURKISH BATHS
☎ 212-473-8806; www.russianturkish baths.com; 268 E 10th St btwn First Ave & Ave A; $25 for 10 visits; 🕙 11am-10pm Mon, Tue, Thu & Fri, 9am-10pm Wed, 7:30am-10pm Sat & Sun; ◎ L to First Ave, 6 to Astor Pl
Since 1892, this has been the place to go for a romp in steam baths, an ice-cold plunge pool, a sauna and a sundeck. All-day access includes the use of lockers, locks, robes, towels and slippers, and an onsite Russian café has fresh juices, potato-olive salad, blintzes and borscht. The spas are women only from 9am to 2pm on Wednesdays and men only from 7:30am to 2pm Saturdays.

◉ ST MARK'S IN THE BOWERY
☎ 212-674-6377; www.stmarkschurch -in-the-bowery.com; 131 E 10th St at Second Ave; 🕙 10am-6pm Mon-Fri; ◎ 6 to Astor Pl, L to Third Ave
Still a working Episcopal church, St Mark's was built in 1799 on farm land owned by Dutch Governor Peter Stuyvesant – he's buried in the crypt below. Sunday services are a big draw, but St Mark's is also revered for its cultural

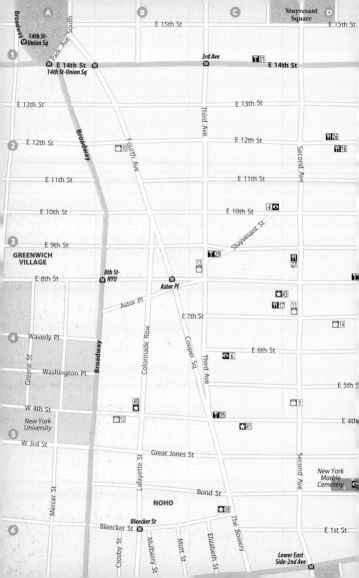

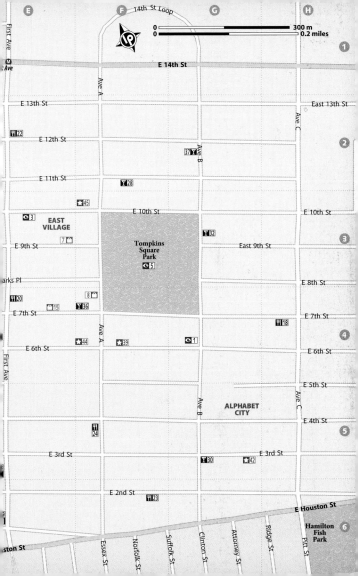

contributions. Regular poetry readings (**Poetry Project**; ☎ 212-674-0910) and dance events (**Danspace**; ☎ 212-674-8194) culminate every New Year's Day in a 24-hour non-stop orgy of poetry, song and performance.

ⓒ TOMPKINS SQ PARK
www.nycgovparks.org; E 7th & 10th Sts, bordered by Aves A & B; ☽ 6am-midnight; ⓞ 6 to Astor Pl; ♿

In 1874, 7000 angry workers took on 1600 police in this leafy enclave, and history's been repeated many times since then – Tompkins Sq Park lies at the heart of every East Village rebellion. This wide, pretty green spot is pastoral by day, communally welcoming at night, and still a bit sketchy in the wee hours.

ⓒ UKRAINIAN MUSEUM
☎ 212-228-0110; www.ukrainianmuseum.org; 222 E 6th St btwn Second & Third Aves; ☽ 11:30am-5pm Wed-Sun; ⓞ F, V to Lower East Side-Second Ave, L to First Ave

Ukrainians have a long history and a strong presence in the East Village, and a visit to this museum explains how and why. The collection of folk art includes ceramics, metalwork and woven textiles, traditional Ukrainian Easter eggs, and offers research tools for visitors to trace their own Ukrainian roots.

Meeting place for dog owners in Tompkins Sq Park

SECRET NEW YORK CITY
In this city, a lot of extraordinary details go unnoticed, and the stories behind the details often go untold. You can tap into an ongoing public dialogue about New York known as Yellow Arrow (http://yellowarrow.net /secretny), which defines itself as a 'Massively Authored Artistic Project.' It involves residents and visitors alike – you can participate by sending in a story of your own, or download podcasts and pictures of other people's New York experiences.

SHOP

A CHENG
☎ 212-979-7324; www.achengshop .com; 443 9th St; 11:30am-8pm Mon-Fri, noon-7pm Sat & Sun; 6 to Astor Pl, L to First Ave
Delicate clothes that fall on just the right side of dainty swing on the racks at Cheng's relaxed East Village shop – a simple but welcoming place that showcases her practical and pretty designs perfectly.

ALPHABETS
☎ 212-475-7250; 115 Ave A btwn 7th St & St Marks; noon-8pm daily; F, V to Lower East Side-Second Ave
A good place to pick up an offbeat souvenir, Alphabets is split down the middle: tees, toys and postcards on one side, and more expensive items like designer tea kettles, Precidio nesting bowls and some menswear on the other.

EAST VILLAGE MUSIC STORE
☎ 212-979-8222; www.evmnyc.com; 85 E 4th St; noon-8pm Mon-Fri, 2-7pm Sun; F, V at Lower East Side-Second Ave
The East Village stop for new and secondhand instruments of all tenors and tones. Repairs are done on-site for most instruments, and you can pick up accessories and sheet music.

FOOTLIGHT RECORDS
☎ 212-533-1572; 113 E 12th St; 11am-7pm Mon-Fri, 10am-6pm Sat, noon-5pm Sun; R, W to 8th St-NYU, 6 to Astor Pl
Home to a well-chosen collection of out-of-print Broadway and foreign-movie soundtracks, Footlight is a must-visit for vinyl hounds, show-tune lovers and anyone searching for a particular version of a hard-to-find cabaret song.

LOVE SAVES THE DAY
☎ 212-228-3802; 119 Second Ave; noon-8pm Mon-Fri, to 9pm Sat & Sun; 6 to Astor Pl
In a city awash with gentrification, it's nice when some things stay

NEIGHBORHOODS

EAST VILLAGE

the same, like this store's campy polyester clothes, fake fur coats, glam-rock spiked boots, Star Wars '77 figurines and other dolls and vintage toys. Not much has changed since Rosanna Arquette bought Madonna's pyramid jacket here in *Desperately Seeking Susan*.

OTHER MUSIC
☎ 212-477-8150; 15 E 4th St; ⏰ noon-9pm Mon-Fri, to 8pm Sat, to 7pm Sun; ⊕ 6 to Bleecker St

An indie-run store that carries new and used offbeat lounge, psychedelic, electronica, indie-rock and more, staffed with helpful, friendly music geeks.

ST MARK'S BOOKSHOP
☎ 212-260-7853; 31 Third Ave; ⏰ 10am-midnight Mon-Sat, 11am-midnight Sun; ⊕ 6 to Astor Pl

Just around the corner from St Marks, this indie bookshop specializes in political literature, poetry, new nonfiction and novels and academic journals. Don't let the slightly antisocial vibe from the staff put you off.

TOKIO 7
☎ 212-353-8443; 64 E 7th St; ⏰ noon-8:30pm Mon-Sat, to 8pm Sun; ⊕ 6 to Astor Pl

This revered, hip consignment shop, down a few steps on a shady stretch of E 7th St, has good-

condition designer labels for men and women at some fairly hefty prices. Best of all is the selection of men's suits – there's nearly always something tip-top worth trying on in the $100 to $150 range.

UNDERDOG EAST
☎ 212-388-0560; 117 E 7th St btwn First Ave & Ave A; ⏰ 2-8pm Tue-Sun; ⊕ 6 to Astor Pl

Most East Village boutiques are all about women, but here, men take center stage. The low-key, exposed-brick space features high-end denim, sweaters, shirts and accessories (including some delicious cashmere hats) from designers like Earnest Sewn, Steven Alan, Filippa K and La Coppola Storta.

🍴 EAT

🍴 ANGELICA KITCHEN
Vegetarian/Vegan $$
☎ 212-228-2909; www.angelickitchen.com; 300 E 12th St; ⏰ 11:30am-10:30pm daily; ⊕ 6 to Astor Pl; ♿ 🚼 V

A much loved vegan eatery with long lines and good (but slightly slow) service, Angelica's has been around for ages. Its famous dragon bowls are stuffed with rice, bean, tofu and sea veggies, and its hot Reuben is one of many tempeh-based sandwiches. Thai Mee Up is all raw foods, and there are some Japanese noodle treats.

B & H DAIRY *Kosher Dairy* $
☎ 212-505-8065; 127 Second Ave btwn St Marks Pl & E 7th St; ✆ breakfast, lunch & dinner; ❻ 6 to Astor Pl; 🚻 🚼 Ⓥ
Fresh, vegetarian, homemade Kosher fare, including six types of soups on offer daily with a big knot of challah bread. Join the crowd at the bar and try to grab someone's attention – you've got to speak up here, or you'll go hungry!

BAO III *Vietnamese* $$
☎ 212-254-7773; www.bao111.com; 111 Ave C; ✆ dinner; ❻ 6 at Astor Pl, F, V at Lower East Side-Second Ave; 🚻 Ⓥ
Phone ahead and make a reservation or you won't get inside

until last call at 2am. Chef Michael Huynh's delicately spiced, super plump summer rolls are known all over town, as are his satay steak on a stick, iron pot chicken and lemongrass-infused hot sake and other specialty cocktails.

BOCA CHICA
Pan-Latin American $-$$
☎ 212-473-0108; 13 First Ave at 1st St; ✆ dinner daily, brunch Sun; ❻ F to Second Ave; 🚻 🚼 Ⓥ
A perennial favorite, this busy, low-ceilinged East Village eatery fills up fast every night of the week. The restaurant doesn't take reservations but people will more than happily queue up for the

One of the fresh Vietnamese dishes at Bao III

COLORS

Opened in 2006 by former employees of Window on the World, **Colors** (☎ 212-777-8443; 417 Lafayette St; ◉ 6 to Astor Pl) is a living tribute to the owners' former coworkers who perished atop the towers on September 11. Run as a worker-owned restaurant co-op, the place transfers that loving vibe into its worldly theme, with many of the international eats inspired by family recipes. Varied fare includes smoked *seitan* with apricot-basil-leaf chutney and a Haitian-style dish of stewed conch with radishes and saffron mayonnaise. A huge map of the world, designed by Maritime Hotel designer Jim Walrod, graces the modern dining room.

killer *mojitos* and rich Latin dishes like *ropa vieja*, deep-fried coconut shrimp and steaming rice and beans.

🍴 CARACAS AREPAS BAR
Arepas/South American $

☎ 212-228-5062; www.caracasarepas bar.com; 93 1/2 E 7th St btwn First Ave & Ave A; ☽ noon-10pm Mon-Sat, noon-11pm Sun; ◉ 6 to Astor Pl; ♿ ♨ Ⓥ

Cram in to this tiny joint and order a crispy, hot *arepa* like the Pepi Queen (chicken and avocado) or La Pelua (beef and cheddar). You can choose from 17 types of *arepas* (plus empanadas and daily specials like ox tail soup), served in baskets with a side of *nata* (sour cream) and fried plantains.

🍴 COUNTER
Vegetarian Eclectic $$

☎ 212-982-5870; 105 First Ave btwn E 6th & E 7th Sts; ☽ lunch & dinner Tue-Sat; ◉ F, V to Lower East Side-Second Ave; ♿ ♨ Ⓥ

Order bar snacks like cashew-kalamata pate at this airy counter serving organic or biodynamic wines and microbrewed beers. Or sit in the roof garden and have some cauliflower risotto, grilled veggie napoleon, *seitan* steak *au poivre* or one of the yummy daily specials.

🍴 HEARTH
American/Italian $$$

☎ 646-602-1300; www.restaurant hearth.com; 403 E 12th St at First Ave; ☽ 6-10pm Fri-Sat, 6-11pm Sun-Thu; ◉ L at First Ave, 4, 5, 6, L, N, Q, R, W at 14th St-Union Sq

Daring eaters and those who like wild game should definitely go for the tasting menu; Hearth doesn't offer a ton of choices, but does its regular dishes – leg of lamb, garlic chicken, tender veal – exceptionally well, and it rotates the sides according to what's in season.

🍴 IL BAGATTO *Italian* $$

☎ 212-228-3703; 192 E 2nd St btwn Aves A & B; ⏰ 5:30-11: 30pm Tue-Sun, takeout & delivery afternoons; 🚇 F, V to Lower East Side-Second Ave; Ⓥ

A bustling yet romantic little nook, this spot has thoroughly delicious Italian creations, plus an excellent wine list and a dedicated sommelier who will let you taste before you decide. Even with a reservation you'll have to wait a few minutes to get seated – it's homey that way. Definitely order dessert – it's fabulous.

🍴 MO PITKINS
Soul Latin Kosher $$$

☎ 212-777-5660; www.mopitkins.com; 34 Ave A btwn 2nd & 3rd Sts; ⏰ 6pm-11pm Fri & Sat, 6pm-midnight Sun-Thu; 🚇 F, V at Lower East Side-Second Ave; Ⓥ

Words really can't do justice to the whacked out, high energy shows that appear at Mo Pitkins, a 'Judeo-Latin' restaurant/cabaret/literary salon. Mo Knows Songwriters is a popular weekly crooner event, but you'll also see acoustic sets and all-out big band swing on other nights. Either way, it's innovative entertainment with some kicking kosher Latin food. Dishes include mac 'n' cheese, garlic fries with *manchego*, fried artichokes, rotis-serie kosher chicken and other delights, like flourless chocolate cake. Monday night is literary night; expect live readings.

🍴 PRUNE
Creative American $$$

☎ 212-677-6221; www.prunerestau rant.com; 54 E 1st St btwn First & Second Aves; ⏰ lunch & dinner daily, brunch Sat & Sun; 🚇 F, V to Lower East Side-Second Ave

Expect lines around the block on the weekend, when the hung over show up to cure their ills with Prune's brunches and excellent **Bloody Marys** (in nine varieties). The small room is always busy as **diners pour in** for roast suckling pig, rich sweetbreads and sausage-studded concoctions.

🍴 S'MAC *American* $

☎ 212-358-7912; www.smacnyc.com; 345 E 12th St at First Ave; ⏰ 1-10pm Mon, 11am-11pm Tue-Thu & Sun, 11am-1am Fri & Sat; 🚇 6 to Astor Pl; 🚼 Ⓥ

If you're only going to do one thing, you've got to do it well – S'Mac has done this, as they've hit the spot with mac 'n' cheese lov-ers. The All-American has cheddar and Vermont jack, with bacon if you like. Or, try the Gruyère mac 'n' cheese and the *manchego* and Cajun macs. Dishes come in four sizes and are served in cast iron skillets.

🍴 VESELKA *Ukrainian/Diner* $

☎ 212-228-9682; www.veselka.com; 144 Second Ave at 9th St; ⏰ 24 hr; 🚇 6 at Astor Pl; ♿ 🚼 Ⓥ

Famous for its delicious burgers, borscht, pirogues and fabulous location, Veselka doesn't stop – it's busy and bustling all day and is a great New York experience.

 # DRINK

11TH ST BAR
☎ 212-982-3929; 510 E 11th St btwn Aves A & B; ⏰ noon-2am; ◎ F, V to Lower East Side-Second Ave
Grab a spot on one of the soft sofas and prepare to be entertained – locals come in throughout the night in a steady stream, each one with a tale to share. It's the adopted watering hole of young reporters from the Daily News too, so it's more like a cozy community room than a bar.

ANGEL'S SHARE
☎ 212-777-5415; 8 Stuyvesant St btwn Third Ave & 9th St, 2nd fl; ⏰ 5pm-midnight; ◎ 6 to Astor Pl
Behind the Japanese restaurant on the same floor, this is a gem of a hideaway, with creative cocktails and well-suited waiters who won't let you stay if there's no table to sit at. This often turns out to be the case, so try to stake your claim early.

B3 BAR
☎ 212-614-9755; 33 Ave B; ⏰ 5pm-11pm Sun-Thu, 5pm-1am Fri-Sat; ◎ F, V at Lower East Side-Second Ave
A pretty, bi-level bistro that opens onto the street, B3 does grand pub fare, and is a good place to sip a *mojito*, listen to the live band and watch the street parade go by.

BEAUTY BAR
☎ 212-539-1389; 531 E 14th St btwn Second & Third Aves; ⏰ 5pm-4am Mon-Fri, 7pm-4am Sat & Sun; ◎ L to Third Ave
A kitschy favorite since the mid-'90s, this homage to old-fashioned beauty parlors pulls in a cool local crowd with its gritty soundtrack, nostalgic vibe and $10 manicures, with a free Blue Rinse margarita thrown in, from Wednesday to Sunday.

CLUBHOUSE
☎ 212-260-7970; 700 E 9th St at Ave C; ⏰ 6pm-3am Sun-Thu, 6pm-4am Fri & Sat; ◎ F, V to Lower East Side-Second Ave
Dance the night away at this straight-but-gay-friendly hotspot that has a rotating cadre of clever DJs and an open, welcoming design with cute nooks to collapse in when the beat has worn you down.

D.B.A
☎ 212-475-5097; www.drinkgoodstuff.com; 41 First Ave; ⏰ 1pm-4am; ◎ F, V at Lower East Side-Second Ave
While you're here, see if you can get owner Ray Deter to tell you if

List of beers on tap at D.B.A.

the name stands for 'doing business as,' 'don't bother asking' or 'drink better ale.' The third choice is the most obvious, since Deter specializes in British-style ales in casks. He's got more than 150 at hand, including microbrews like 'High and Mighty Ale.' Other standouts are the single malts and smooth tequilas. A garden in the back doubles as a beer garden.

☗ HOLIDAY COCKTAIL LOUNGE
☎ 212-777-9637; 75 St Marks Pl btwn First & Second Aves; ✹ 4pm-1am; ◉ 6 to Astor Pl
You want a dive bar? You have got one, right here. This old-school,

battered yet charming place feels as if it's from another era – and with $3 drinks, it might as well be. Expect crotchety service, the never-ending blare of TV shows, and a curious mix of nostalgia seekers, penny-pinching alcoholics and various cheapskates.

☗ KGB BAR
☎ 212-505-3360; 2nd fl, 85 E 4th St; ✹ 7pm-4am; ◉ 6 at Astor Pl, F, V at Lower East Side-Second Ave
Back in the 1940s, this space housed the local headquarters of a Ukrainian socialist party; its dingy red walls and bright yellow propaganda banners are the real thing. KGB reinvented itself as a literary bar a few years ago and hasn't looked back; its readings are marquee events, and the crowd laps up the vodka.

☗ ODESSA CAFÉ
☎ 212-253-1470; 110 Ave A btwn St Marks Pl & E 7th St; ✹ 5pm-4am; ◉ 6 to Astor Pl
This Polish diner-turned-bar, right on Tompkins Sq Park, is classic East Village scruff. Liquor was added into the mix a few years ago, and the tattooed, grungy-fun clientele couldn't have been happier. And, after your $4 cocktail and your plate of rib-sticking pierogi, you'll be right there with them.

�▼ RUE B

☎ 212-358-1700; 188 Ave B btwn 11th & 12th Sts; ⏱ noon-4am Mon-Fri, 11am-4am Sat & Sun; 🚇 L to First Ave, 6 to Union Sq

Mellow out over margaritas and jazz in this elegant, romantic Ave B hangout that's quickly becoming a neighborhood hot spot. You can get snacks like bruschetta and olive pâté at the bar, and the bartenders are renowned for mixing martinis with fanciful ingredients like blood oranges and pear juice.

PLAY

★ AMATO OPERA HOUSE

☎ 212-228-8200; www.amato.org; 319 Bowery; 🚇 6 to Astor Pl; ♿ ♨

After 59 years of no-nonsense opera, Amato still has what it takes to pack in the crowds. Classic shows like *Falstaff*, *Madame Butterfly*, *La Forza del Destino* and *Die Fledermaus* are put on without any of the glitz found in uptown opera houses, but plenty of passion.

★ EASTERNBLOC

☎ 212-420-8885; 505 E 6th St btwn Aves A & B; 🚇 F, V to Lower East Side-Second Ave

The newest gay spot in the 'hood is home to a kitschy iron-curtain theme replete with Bettie Page videos, Communist-era posters and adorable Eastern European–

looking bartenders. The go-go dancers appear Thursday through Saturday.

★ JOSEPH PAPP PUBLIC THEATER

☎ 212-260-2400; www.publictheater .org; 425 Lafayette St; 🚇 N, R to 8th St, 6 to Astor Pl

Every summer the Papp presents its fabulous Shakespeare in the Park productions at Central Park's Delacorte Theater – one of its many contributions to the city's cultural lift. Started by a wealthy progressive more than 50 years ago, Joseph Papp Theater continues to help both beginner and established actors develop their craft through groundbreaking productions.

★ LA MAMA ETC

☎ 212-475-7710; www.lamama.org; 74A East 4th St; 🚇 F, V to Second Ave

A longstanding home for onstage experimentation (the ETC stands for experimental theater club), La MaMa is now a three-theater complex with a café, an art gallery and a separate studio building that features cutting-edge dramas, sketch comedy and readings of all kinds.

★ NUYORICAN POETS CAFÉ

☎ 212-505-8183; www.nuyorican.org; 236 East 3rd St; ⏱ 🚇 F to Second Ave

A legendary club started in 1973 by Miguel Algarín, a Puerto Rican poet, the Nuyorican is home to hip-hop performances, poetry slams, plays, and film and video events. It's a piece of East Village history, but also a vibrant and still-relevant nonprofit arts organization (supported by proceeds from the café).

⭐ ORPHEUM THEATER
☎ 212-477-2477; www.stomponline .com; 126 Second Ave at 8th St; ⊖ F to Second Ave/Houston St; ♿ 🚻
A Yiddish theater in the beginning of the 20th century, the Orpheum feeds off creative East Village energy. Currently it's home to 'Stomp,' a dance-happy beat fest.

⭐ PYRAMID
☎ 212-228-4888; 101 Ave A; ⊖ F, V to Lower East Side-Second Ave
The promoters at Pyramid love a good theme, so sometimes it's punk night and other times it's rock night – the crowd is mainly gay dancers and the straight people who love them. Without a doubt, the favorite night is Friday, '80s night, when you can't help but dance your ass off.

TROMPE L'OEIL
You spotted some sheep moving across the lawn at City Hall Park – perhaps Mayor Bloomberg, so renowned for cutting costs, has found a novel way to trim the grass? No, it's public art, brought to you by the Public Art Fund, a nonprofit organization that goes to great lengths to pepper city streets with engaging works where you least expect them. Locations of the latest installations are available at ☎ 212-980-4575 or www.publicartfund.org.

⭐ STARLIGHT BAR & LOUNGE
☎ 212-475-2172; starlightbarlounge .com; 167 Ave A; 🕐 7pm-3am; ⊖ L to First Ave
A funky mix of Chelsea boys and East Village artistes crosses paths in this pleasantly overcrowded bar, with room to relax in the back lounge. The all-female bartender crew work the crowd and Sunday night ('Starlette') is widely considered one of the best lesbian events in the city. Wednesday is queer comedy night, hosted by funny man Keith Price.

>GREENWICH & WEST VILLAGE

Still charming after all these years, Greenwich Village holds a special place in New Yorkers' hearts. This once flamboyant and progressive toehold became a gentle old lady, albeit one with a decidedly unladylike past.

There's no pleasure equal to exploring this twisty little enclave on a sunny afternoon. Its quaint and quirky streets create oddly-shaped store-fronts and misshapen cafés, and many of its brick buildings are historic landmarks. Edna St Vincent Millay lived at 75 ½ Barrow St for a while; her neighbor was William S Burroughs. They'd sometimes stop for a pint at Ear Inn (p90), or Chumley's (p118).

There are a few old-style cabaret bars and comedy clubs lining Seventh Ave, and some gay icons – the Duplex, the Monster and Stonewall – are still standing. It's easily the most romantic part of Manhattan.

GREENWICH & WEST VILLAGE

Please see over for map

◉ SEE

◉ ABINGDON SQ

Hudson & Banks St at West 12th St; ◉ 2, 3 to 14th St; ♿

Unlike the rest of Greenwich Village, which has seen some shabby days, Abingdon Sq has always been wealthy and well-kept. Once owned by a privileged settler family, it still has its original 1843 perimeter, the Abingdon Memorial (aka the Doughboy) to WW I veterans, and is shaded by immense, stately trees.

◉ CHRISTOPHER ST PIERS/ HUDSON RIVER PARK

Christopher St & West Side Hwy

Like so many places in the Village, the extreme west side was once a derelict eyesore used mostly as a cruising ground for quick, anonymous sex. Now it's a pretty waterside hangout, bisected by the Hudson River Park's slender bike and jogging paths, with great sunset views. It's still a good place to cruise; now it's just much less dangerous.

◉ FORBES COLLECTION

☎ 212-206-5548; www.forbesgalleries .com; 62 Fifth Ave at 12th St; admission free; ◷ 10am-4pm Tue, Wed, Fri & Sat; ◉ L, N, Q, R, W, 4, 5, 6 to 14 St-Union Sq

These galleries house curios from the personal collection of the late publishing magnate Malcolm Forbes. The eclectic mix of objects on display includes Fabergé eggs, toy boats, early versions of Monopoly and tin soldiers.

◉ GRACE CHURCH

800-804 Broadway at 10th St; ◉ R, W to 8th St-NYU, 6 to Astor Pl

Nestled into a surprisingly verdant patch of land not far from Astor Pl, Grace Church's ethereal Gothic Revival design is quite an eye-catcher. Designed by James Renwick Jr, it's made of marble quarried by prisoners in Sing Sing, the prison upstate. It's also a much-sought-after school, and students love the Harry Potter–esque feel of its hidden nooks, stained-glass windows and old libraries.

◉ NEW YORK UNIVERSITY

☎ 212-998-4636; www.nyu.edu; information center at 50 W 4th St

In 1831 Albert Gallatin (buried in the Trinity Church cemetery, p48), Secretary of Treasury under President Thomas Jefferson, founded an intimate center of higher learning open to all students, regardless of race or class. Now it's a mammoth urban campus filled with 50,000 students. Check out the main buildings around Washington Sq Park.

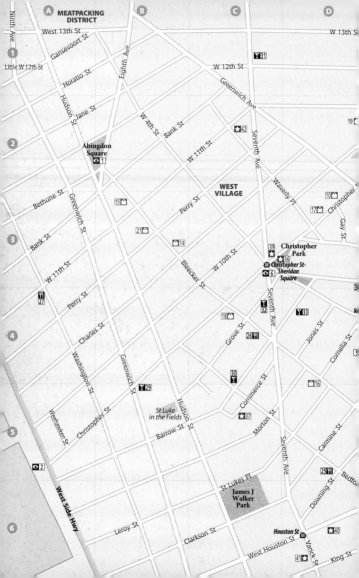

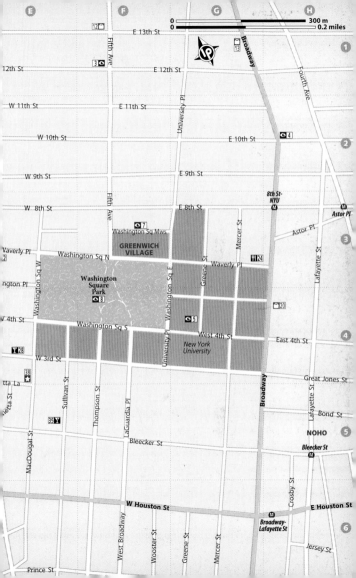

E	
F	
G	
H	

E 13th St
Broadway
Fourth Ave

E 12th St
Fifth Ave
12th St

W 11th St
E 11th St

University Pl
W 10th St
E 10th St

W 9th St
E 9th St

8th St-NYU

W 8th St
E 8th St
Fifth Ave
Astor Pl

Washington Sq Mws
GREENWICH VILLAGE
Mercer St
Astor Pl

Waverly Pl
Waverly Pl

Washington Sq N
Washington Sq W
Washington Sq E
Greene St

Washington Pl
Washington
Square
Park

ngton Pl

W 4th St
Washington Sq S
West 4th St
East 4th St

New York
University

W 3rd St
University Pl

tta La
Broadway
Great Jones St

Lafayette St
Bond St

Sullivan St
Thompson St
LaGuardia Pl
NOHO

Bleecker St
Bleecker St

MacDougal St
etta St

W Houston St
E Houston St

West Broadway
Wooster St
Greene St
Mercer St
Crosby St
Broadway-Lafayette St
Jersey St

Prince St

🅒 SHERIDAN SQ
Christopher St & Seventh Ave

Appropriately the shape of a triangle, Sheridan Sq isn't much more than a few park benches and some trees surrounded by an old-fashioned wrought-iron gate. But its location – the heart of gay Greenwich Village – means it's witnessed every rally, demonstration and uprising that contributed to the gay rights movement. It also holds two sets of slender white statues – one male and one female couple, holding hands and talking. Known as Gay Liberation, they are a tribute to the normalcy of gay life.

🅒 WASHINGTON MEWS
Btwn 5th Ave & University Pl, & 8th St & Washington Sq Park; 🅒 R, W to 8th St; ♿

Private stables converted into homes line one side of the picturesque Washington Mews.

Gaslights and horses have disappeared, but the tiny alley still embodies the essence of old New York. Famous residents include writers Sherwood Anderson and Walter Lippman, and artist Gertrude Vanderbilt Whitney, founder of the Whitney Museum. It's surrounded now by New York University, which owns some of the properties.

🅒 WASHINGTON SQ PARK
www.washingtonsquareparkcouncil.org; 🅒 A, B, C, D, E, F, V to W 4th St, R, W to 8th St-NYU, 6 to Astor Pl

If the world's a stage, then everybody in Washington Sq Park is trying out for a bit part in someone's drama. This crazy place is the heart of what's left of bohemian life in Greenwich Village. But, if the city has its way, the park will undergo a radical redesign: it will have a four-foot fence around it, the famed Garibaldi fountain

---

GAY BARS

Not the center of the city's queer-friendly nightlife (now Chelsea and the Meatpacking District), but the Village still has some good draws. **Henrietta Hudson** (☎ 212-924-3347; 438 Hudson St; 🅒 1 to Houston St) is a sleek lounge with varied DJs, attracting all sorts of cute young lesbians. **Monster** (☎ 212-924-3558; 80 Grove St at Sheridan Sq; 🅒 1 to Christopher St-Sheridan Sq) is old-school gay male-heaven, with a small dancefloor and a piano bar and cabaret space. Theme nights range from Latino parties to drag-queen-hosted soirees. Across the street, DJ Warren Gluck spins flashback songs at **Stonewall** (☎ 212-463-0950; 53 Christopher St; 🅒 1 to Christopher St-Sheridan Sq), the site of riots in 1969 (p120). Young ones are even packing the place since its recent redesign.

Free entertainment in Washington Sq Park

where, rumor has it, Bob Dylan sang his first folk song will be relocated, and the entire site will be raised 4 ft to ground level, disturbing those who were buried underneath it when it was a cemetery and a hanging spot (check out the hanging elm on the northwest corner). Community groups filed a lawsuit and won a stay; the city has appealed, and it will be years before a decision is made. Enjoy it while you can. Regular events are listed on the website. The one not to miss? Quiet Disco on weekend afternoons – 300 people dancing to iPod tunes only they can hear.

WEST 4TH ST BASKETBALL COURTS
Sixth Ave at W 4th St

Don't step into 'the Cage,' as this fenced-in court is called, without bringing your A game; these guys play to win in fierce competitive games. You can have just as much fun watching in the 10-deep crowds that gather, especially on weekends. In summer the W 4th St Summer Pro-Classic League, now in its 26th year, hits the scene.

 # SHOP
AEDES DE VENUSTAS
☎ 212-206-8674; www.aedes.com; 9 Christopher St; ⏱ noon-8pm Mon-Sat,

1-7pm Sun; ⊕ 1 to Christopher St, A, B, C, D, E, F, V to W 4th St
Let your body chemistry do the talking once you get inside the plush, opulent Aedes de Venustas (Temple of Beauty). Amid the red velvet decor a staff person will help design a signature scent based on your own quirky 'skin smell.' Or, take the easy way and grab a bottle of Nirmala or Shalini, sold by the register.

☐ CO BIGELOW CHEMISTS
☎ 212-473-7324; 414 Sixth Ave btwn 8th & 9th Sts; ⏰ 7:30am-9pm Mon-Fri, 8:30am-7pm Sat, 8:30am-5pm Sun; ⊕ A, B, C, D, E, F, V to W 4th St
There are cheaper and more efficient drugstores all over the city, but none have the charm of Bigelow's, America's 'oldest apothecary' if you believe the managers. It's still got a working pharmacy, but it's most famous for its organic beauty products like witch-hazel salves and honey-bee balms.

☐ EAST-WEST BOOKS
☎ 212-243-5994; 78 Fifth Ave; ⏰ 10am-7:30pm Mon-Sat, 11am-6:30pm Sun; ⊕ L, N, Q, R, W, 4, 5, 6 to 14th St-Union Sq
With a calming effect that takes place once entering, this groovy bookstore stocks a wide array of books on Buddhism and Asian philosophies, plus chill-out music,

yoga mats and earthy-crunchy jewelry.

☐ FORBIDDEN PLANET
☎ 212-473-1576; 840 Broadway; ⏰ 10am-10pm Mon-Sat, 11am-8pm Sun; ⊕ L, N, Q, R, W, 4, 5, 6 to 14th St-Union Sq
Card-game lovers match wits and luck in the upstairs room of this sci-fi favorite. It stocks comics, video games and any kind of figurine you could want (Star Wars to William Shatner).

☐ LES PIERRE ANTIQUES
☎ 212-243-7740; www.lespierreinc.com; 369 Bleecker St; ⏰ 10am-6pm Mon-Fri, noon-5pm Sat; ⊕ 1 at Christopher St
You can browse through three floors of beautifully refurbished French furniture, mostly from the 18th and 19th centuries. Mostly heavy wood pieced, the massive armoires and solid dining tables will make you crave a country home.

☐ MARC JACOBS
☎ 212-924-0026; www.marcjacobs.com; 403, 405 & 385 Bleecker St; ⏰ noon-8pm Mon-Sat, noon-7pm Sun; ⊕ 1 to Christopher St
Still going strong, even after years on the scene, Marc Jacobs' monster stores dominate Bleecker St. Bags and accessories at 385, menswear

at 403, and his celebrated women's collection holds court at 405.

🏠 MURRAY'S CHEESE

☎ 212-243-3289; www.murrayscheese .com; 254 Bleecker St; 🕑 8am-8pm Mon-Sat, 9am-6pm Sun; 🚇 1 to Christopher St-Sheridan Sq, A, B, C, D, E, F, V to W 4th St-Washington Sq

Founded in 1914, this is repeatedly hailed as the best cheese shop in the city. Owner Rob Kaufelt is, to put it kindly, obsessed with finding the best *fromage* from all over the world, be it runny, firm, mild, sharp or full of holes. There's a Murray's at Grand Central Terminal, too.

🏠 OSCAR WILDE MEMORIAL BOOKSHOP

☎ 212-255-809; 15 Christopher St; 🕑 11am-7pm; 🚇 1 to Christopher St-Sheridan Sq

The world's oldest bookshop geared to gay and lesbian literature (open since 1967) lives in a lovely red-brick townhouse and stocks new and used books, and a fine range of magazines, rainbow flags, bumper stickers and other gifts. Its founder went on to create the Gay Liberation Movement after the 1969 Stonewall Riots.

🏠 REBEL REBEL

☎ 212-989-0770; 319 Bleecker St; 🕑 noon-8pm Sun-Wed, noon-9pm Thu-Sat; 🚇 1 to Christopher St-Sheridan Sq

This is a tight-fit, tiny music store with CDs and rare vinyl defying the limits of space. Ask for what you don't see as there is loads more in the back, safely out of view.

🏠 RICKY'S

☎ 212-924-3401; 466 Sixth Ave at 11th St; 🕑 9am-11pm Mon-Sat, to 10pm Sun; 🚇 A, C, E to 14th St, L to Eighth Ave

This is one of the few times in life that stocking up on mundane essentials like toothpaste and hair gel is actually fun – Ricky's is a drugstore that likes to think it's a nightclub – expect pounding music, hot-pink toothpaste tubes, and lots of glitter, faux-color, and outrageous hair and wardrobe selections. In the back you'll find sex toys, of course.

🏠 SHAKESPEARE & CO

☎ 212-529-1330; 716 Broadway; 🕑 10am-11pm Sun-Thu, to 11:30pm Fri & Sat 🚇 N, R, W to 8th St, 6 to Astor Pl

A bookstore with branches around the city (and in Paris), Shakespeare & Co does its best to hang on to an indie vibe, even though it's now pretty much a chain. It stocks lots of film and theater books and pays homage to the arts in many ways, including its excellent reading series with local authors.

NEIGHBORHOODS

GREENWICH & WEST VILLAGE

🏠 SUSAN PARRISH ANTIQUES

☎ 212-645-5020; 390 Bleecker St;
🕐 noon-7pm Mon-Sat, or by appt; 🚇 1
to Christopher St

American furniture, textiles, folk
art and paintings are offered at
this well-respected West Village
antiques store. There are early
20th century Amish quilts and
furnishings, as well as 19th
century items in good condition.
Navajo and hooked rugs come
in dozens of floral and geometric
designs.

🍴 EAT

🍴 BABBO Italian $$$

☎ 212-777-0303; www.babbonyc.com;
110 Waverly Pl; 🕐 dinner; 🚇 A, B, C, D,
E, F, V to W 4th St, 1 to Christopher; ♿

Celebrity chef Mario Batali has
multiple restaurants in Manhattan, but everyone has a sneaking
suspicion that this two-level
split townhouse is his favorite.
Whether you order mint love
letters or lamb's brain *francobolli*
or pig's foot *milanese*, you'll find
Batali at the top of his innovative,
eclectic game. Reservations are
in order.

🍴 BLUE HILL

New American $$$

☎ 212-539-1776; www.bluehillnyc.com;
75 Washington Pl; 🕐 dinner; 🚇 A, B, C,
D, E, F, V to W 4th St

They're not kidding with the 'This
Morning's Farm Egg' appetizer.
Everything on the menu is from
upstate, organic growers, so the
'grass-fed lamb' entree is made
from precisely that. Linked to the
Stone Barn estate, an experiment
in growing local, chef Dan Barber
makes the most of every ingredi-
ent's seasonal freshness.

🍴 MANNA BENTO Korean $

☎ 212-473-6162; 289 Mercer St;
🕐 lunch & dinner Mon-Sat; 🚇 N, R to
8th St; ♿ 👶 🅥

There's a constant stream of book-
toting students through Manna
Bento's small front door, which tells
you the food's good, affordable
and a great cure for a hangover.
Plates of rice, kimchi, buckwheat
noodles and spicy hot seafood
soup are generously portioned.

🍴 MAS

NewAmerican/French $$$

☎ 212-255-1790; www.masfarmhouse
.com; 39 Downing St; 🕐 dinner & late-
night dinner Mon-Sat; 🚇 A, B, C, D, E, F, V
at W 4th St; ♿

Chef Galen Zamarra draws heavily from the South of France (in
old Provençal a 'mas' is a traditional stone farmhouse), from the
solid and ornate oak front door
to the earthy menu featuring
beau soleil oysters, braised ribs,
flying pig pork belly and wild

nettle risotto. Also great for late-night dining.

SURYA *Nouvelle Indian* $$
☎ 212-807-7770; www.suryany.com;
302 Bleecker St; dinner Mon-Sat,
boxed lunch noon-3pm daily, buffet
lunch noon-3:25pm Sat & Sun; 1 to
Christopher St;

Sleek and sexy, Surya's cool interior gives way to a trellis-lined patio where you can sip chilled white wine or an excellent bar cocktail while waiting for a fiery vindaloo with spices from India's southwest coast, or a tender *saag* with fresh ginger. Meat and vegetarians options abound.

WALLSE *Austrian* $$
☎ 212-352-2300; www.wallse.com; 344
W 11th St; dinner daily, lunch Sat &
Sun; A, C, E to 14th St, L to Eighth Av,
1 to Christopher St;

Before you start wondering what Austrian food is, try spätzle with braised rabbit, mushrooms and tarragon. It may not answer your question, but you won't care. Pair it with sour cherry strudel and pistachio ice cream, and life is complete. Classic European food tastes best in neighborly places like Wallse.

DRINK
BAR NEXT DOOR
☎ 212-529-5945; 129 MacDougal St
btwn 3rd & 4th Sts; 6pm-2am Sun-

Thu, 6pm-3am Fri-Sat; A, B, C, D, E, F,
V to W 4th St

One of the loveliest boîtes in the neighborhood, the basement of this restored townhouse is all low ceilings, exposed brick and romantic lighting. You'll find mellow, live jazz nightly, as well as the tasty Italian menu of the restaurant next door, La Lanterna di Vittorio.

CHI CHIZ
☎ 212-462-0027; 135 Christopher St;
4pm-4am daily; 1 to Christopher St

A small Christopher St favorite, especially for African American gays, Chi Chiz offers the best drinking deal in the Village: everything half price from 2pm until closing on Sundays. Monday it's karaoke, Tuesday it's bingo, and it's a favorite late-night munchie hangout any day of the week.

LITTLE BRANCH
☎ 212-929-4360; 20 Seventh Ave;
7pm-3am Mon-Fri, 9pm-3am Sun;
1, 2, 3 to 14th St, L to Eighth Av

You might have heard of Milk & Honey, an unmarked Lower East Side bar that famously made patrons call ahead using a secret phone number to gain entry. The same owner Sasha Petraske, a West Village native whose mother worked at *The Village Voice* newspaper alongside Sylvia Plachy for years, just opened his third bar. The homey, welcoming Little

Branch serves perfectly mixed cocktails; be nice to the bartender and he may be able to give you the secret digits to Sasha's other bars.

▼ MARIE'S CRISIS
☎ 212-243-9323; 59 Grove St btwn Seventh Ave & Bleecker St; 🕑 4pm-4am; 🚇 1 to Christopher St-Sheridan Sq
Aging Broadway queens, wide-eyed out-of-town gay boys, giggly tourist girls and various other fans of musical theater assemble around the piano here and take turns belting out campy numbers, often joined by the entire crowd. It's old-school fun that'll put a spring in your step, no matter how jaded you were when you walked in.

▼ ONE IF BY LAND, TWO IF BY SEA
☎ 212-255-8649; 17 Barrow St; 🕑 dinner; 🚇 1 at Christopher St-Sheridan Sq, A, B, C, D, E, F, V to W 4th St-Washington Sq
Famous for its beef Wellington and graceful, aged location in Aaron Burr's old carriage house, this is quite possibly New York's favorite date restaurant. But it's even better as a quiet watering hole, perfect for a cocktail hour or late-night libation for those who need a break from the harried streets.

▼ STONED CROW
☎ 212-677-4022; 85 Washington Pl btwn Washington Sq West & Sixth Ave; 🕑 4pm-4am Mon-Fri, 2pm-4am Sat & Sun; 🚇 A, B, C, D, E, F, V to W 4th St
A divey but fun jukebox joint located in a basement, Stoned Crow's semi-claustrophobic vibe seems to appeal to students hiding from homework and midterm exams. Its big pitchers of beer

CHUMLEY'S
You could get a headache trying to find the entrance to this old speakeasy at 86 Bedford St on the corner with Barrow St; the door's unmarked and easy to miss. Once you find it though, you'll slip inside and into another time. Chumley's, which gets packed with a loud crowd later in the evenings, is a great place for an afternoon drink. You can commune with old patrons – among them F. Scott Fitzgerald, Ernest Hemingway, William Burroughs and Norman Mailer – and you may be joined by the bar's very first owner, Henrietta Chumley, who reportedly likes to return to her favorite seat by the fireplace and drink Manhattans. Chumley's has a long and varied history of hauntings, including the current owner's belief that the 12 firefighters he employed part-time (all from the nearby firehouse), who died when the Twin Towers collapsed on September 11, return to play songs on the jukebox when the mood strikes them.

and regulation pool tables add to the allure as well.

SULLIVAN ROOM
☎ 212-252-2151; 218 Sullivan St btwn Bleecker & W 3rd Sts; 🕙 9pm-5am Wed-Sat; ⊖ A, B, C, D, E, F, V to W 4th St
You'll have to look hard to find the entrance to this below-ground hangout, which attracts its share of the beautiful people with DJ-hosted dance parties, a foreign beer collection and generous mixed cocktails. Best after 1am.

PLAY

55 BAR
☎ 212-929-9883; www.55bar.com; 55 Christopher St; cover $3-15, 2 drink minimum; 🕙 1pm-4am; ⊖ 1 to Christopher St/Sheridan Sq, A, B, C, D, E, F to W 4th St
An unpretentious basement gem favoring jazz and blues driven by funky, guitar-laden combos that will get your feet tapping, 55 Bar has a glow all of its own. Spilling music onto a historic corner of the Village (it's next to Stonewall) at all hours, 55 features local artists and international players.

CHERRY LANE THEATER
☎ 212-989-2020; www.cherrylane theater.com; 38 Commerce St; ⊖ 1 to Christopher St
A theater with a distinctive charm hidden in the West Village, Cherry Lane has a long and distinguished

history. It was started by poet Edna St Vincent Millay and has given a voice to numerous play-wrights and actors over the years. It remains true to its mission of creating 'live' theater that's accessible to the public. Readings, plays and spoken-word performances rotate frequently.

COMEDY CELLAR
☎ 212-254-3480; www.comedycellar .com; 117 MacDougal St; admission $15 🕙 shows start at 9pm Sun-Fri, 7:30pm Sat; ⊖ A, C, E, F, V, S to W 4th St
A Greenwich Village staple for decades, the Comedy Cellar has seen quite a few careers come and go over the years, and is still filled nightly with wannabes, has-beens and hot-for-the-moment comics. Celebrity drop-ins are pretty frequent; keep an eye out for Jon Lovitz or Colin Quinn.

THE DUPLEX
☎ 212-255-5438; www.theduplex.com; 61 Christopher St; 🕙 4pm-4am; ⊖ 1 to Christopher St
Pictures of Joan Rivers, apparently the patron saint of the Duplex, adorn the campy walls of this West Village townhouse. It offers up great cabaret in the small back room, as well as open mike opportunities after 9pm in the front room. If you don't like war-bling, you can dance to jukebox tunes upstairs.

STONEWALL

The decrepit-looking building at 55 Christopher St, across from Sheridan Sq, is the infamous Stonewall Inn, birthplace of the gay civil rights movement, thanks to a police raid just after 1am on June 28, 1969. As the story goes, many lesbian, transgendered and gay patrons were in the bar mourning the passing of gay icon Judy Garland. Police showed up, someone threw a bottle, a crowd gathered, a woman getting hustled into a cop car put up a fight, and things suddenly got very ugly. The eight officers barricaded themselves inside the bar and the riots continued for three days. At its peak, more than 200,000 people surged into the Village to participate in the 'Stonewall Rebellion.' When it was all over, the Gay Liberation Movement had officially been formed.

★ FILM FORUM

☎ 212-727-8110; www.filmforum.com; 209 W Houston St; tickets $12; ⊙ daily; ◉ 1 to Houston St; ♿ ♿

Frequently showing retrospectives of particular artists, like Fellini or Truffaut, and consistently bringing great movies back from the grave, Film Forum is a favorite place for celluloid buffs. Its annual summer new wave series is always a sellout. In general, tickets – even to the most obscure flicks – tend to go fast. Buy in advance when possible.

★ SOBS

☎ 212-243-4940; www.sobs.com; 204 Varick; ⊙ 6:30pm-3am daily; ◉ 1 to Houston St; ♿

SOBs – aka Sounds of Brazil – means lots of people shaking it to samba, Afro-Cuban rumba, salsa, reggae and more. The cheery (if kitschy) decor and decent food make it a popular choice for after-work parties; real dancing

doesn't start until 2am. Check out the weekly Basement Bhangra, a six-year-old party that's become a mecca for the growing number of Asian-hip-hop fanatics, and La Tropica on Monday nights for some seriously old-school Latin moves.

★ VILLAGE VANGUARD

☎ 212-255-4037; www.villagevanguard .com; 178 Seventh Ave; cover $15-40, 2 drink minimum ⊙ 7pm-1am; ◉ 1 to Christopher St

Possibly the city's most prestigious jazz club, the Vanguard has hosted literally every major star of the past 50 years. It started as a home to spoken word performances and occasionally harkens to its roots, but most of the time it's just smooth, sweet jazz all night long. Mind your step on the steep stairs, and close your eyes to the signs of wear and tear – acoustically, you're in one of the greatest venues in the world.

Petar Marchev,
Pedicab driver, Staten Island (from Ukraine originally)

What's your favorite season in the city? Definitely fall – with all the colors it's magnificent! **What's the best thing about your neighborhood?** The Staten Island Ferry is the best commute in NYC. **Do you have a favorite landmark in NYC?** Probably Coney Island and the Brighton Beach area. I don't know if it's a landmark but I love the boardwalk. **Do you have any 'only in New York' moments to share?** About a thousand, usually involving some cabbie shaking a fist at me. **Favorite NYC book?** I don't know if I have a favorite book set in New York City, but one of my favorite authors to read in the city is Maxim Gorky; he just seems like he fits here somehow. **What's your favorite thing about being a pedicab driver in NYC?** I get to mainly work in Central Park, and I think overall, that's the best thing in the city.

>MEATPACKING DISTRICT

The Meatpacking District is all about shopping, eating and drinking – and if you enjoy all three, this neighborhood will be nirvana for you.

As you explore this district's wide cobblestone streets, check out two hotels that helped moved this part of town from stodgy to fabulous: the Hotel Gansevoort and the Maritime Hotel. Be sure to stroll the nabe's most famous byway, Gansevoort St, which used to be a Dutch market, and then a slaughterhouse. It also did a brisk business in prostitution, mostly plied by transsexual or gay men. A holdover from that time is the Lesbian, Gay, Transgender and Bisexual Community Center (p246), which played a crucial role in forcing discussion of the AIDS epidemic in the 1980s and '90s.

The district's far less rough-and-ready these days. With the advent of the High Line, and more incursions from restaurants, galleries and high-end boutiques, this is one neighborhood that's not looking back.

MEATPACKING DISTRICT

◉ SEE
Hotel Gansevoort **1**   D3
LGBT Community
Center **2**   G3
Maritime Hotel **3**   D1

🏠 SHOP
Alexander McQueen ...**4**   C2
An Earnest Cut & Sew..**5**   C4
B8 Couture **6**   C3
Buckler **7**   E3
Carlos Miele **8**   D2
Catherine Malandrino **9**   D3
Chocolate Bar **10** F3

Destination **11** C3
Jeffrey New York **12** B2

🍴 EAT
Markt **13** D2
Mi Cocina **14** E4
Paradou **15** C3
Pastis **16** C3
Sascha **17** D3
Son Cubano **18** D2
Soy Luck Club **19** F3
Spice Market **20** C3
Spotted Pig **21** E6

🍸 DRINK
Brass Monkey **22** C5
Double Seven **23** C2
Plunge **24** D3

★ PLAY
Cielo **25** C3
Level V **26** D2
Movida **27** G3

Please see over for map

SHOP

ALEXANDER MCQUEEN
☎ 212-645-1797; www.alexandermc
queen.com; 417 West 14th St; 🕙 11am-
7pm Mon-Sat, noon-6pm Sun; ◉ A, C, E,
1, 2, 3 to 14th St, L to Eighth Ave
Assuming you don't get lost
among the sloping, white-walled
sections of this circular store,
you're in for a treat. Sunglasses,
accessories, menswear and
shoes are sold here, but it's the
brocaded, cutting-edge, heavily
constructed women's clothes that
steal the show.

AN EARNEST CUT & SEW
☎ 212-242-3414; www.earnestsewn
.com; 821 Washington St; 🕙 11am-7pm
Mon-Fri, 11am-8pm Sat, 11am-7pm
Sun; ◉ A, C, E, 1, 2, 3 to 14th St, L to
Eighth Ave
Ok, so you finally found the perfect pair of jeans…but they're two
inches too long. No worries –
at Earnest Cut & Sew, custom
alterations are done on the spot.
Custom-sewn jeans can also be
had, for (ahem) a price. This
industrial-themed shop still clings
to the frontier aesthetic of denim,
liking it to look a little rough and
ready to work, but in a nod to the
modern taste, they insist it fit like
a glove.

B8 COUTURE
☎ 866-623-5545; 27 Little W 12th St;
🕙 10am-9pm daily; ◉ A, C, E, 1, 2, 3 to
14th St, L to Eighth Ave
Lots of looks and styles, mostly
big name European designers
with some token Americans, are
featured here. The magic is in how
you mix collections – a girlish skirt
from McFadden with a top from
Gaultier.

BUCKLER
☎ 212-255-1596; www.bucklershow
room.com; 13 Gansevoort St; 🕙 11am-
7pm Mon-Sat, noon-6pm Sun; ◉ A, C, E,
1, 2, 3 to 14th St, L to 8th Ave
Producing cult menswear that
blends 'roguish American icons
with British edge,' Buckler's
famous for its selection of brash
and boyish denim designs. If you
like the way Lenny Kravitz and
Iggy Pop dress, you've found the
perfect store.

CARLOS MIELE
☎ 646-336-6642; www.carlosmiele
.com.br; 408 W 14th St; 🕙 noon-7pm;
◉ A, C, E to 14th St, L to Eighth Ave
A bright store for bold shoppers,
the design of Miele's flagship
boutique is almost as eye-catching
as his sexy, sultry, Carnaval-
inspired Brazilian dresses. Great for
glamorous gowns that leave you
room to dance.

NEIGHBORHOODS

MEATPACKING DISTRICT

CHELSEA

Chelsea Market

MEATPACKING DISTRICT

W 16th St
W 15th St
Tenth Ave
Eleventh Ave
W 14th St
Ninth Ave
W 13th St
Little W 12th St
Gansevoort St
Gansevoort St
Greenwich St
Washington St
Horatio St
West Side Hwy
West 12th St
Bethune St
Hudson River

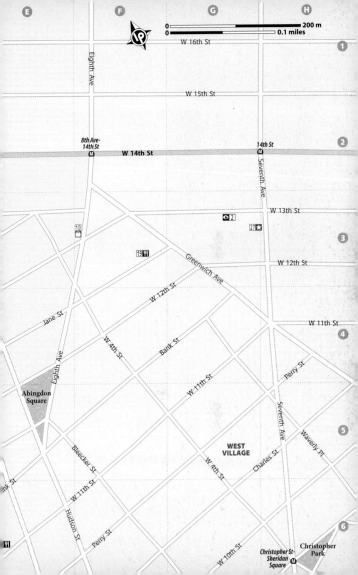

Window shopping at Carlos Miele (p123)

CATHERINE MALANDRINO
☎ 212-929-8710; www.catherinemalan
drino.com; 652 Hudson St; 🕙 11am-8pm
Mon-Sat, noon-6pm Sun; 🚇 A, C, E, 1, 2,
3 to 14th St, L to Eighth Ave
Fun, refreshing looks that make
the most of curves are the watch-
word at Malandrino's two stores –
one in the Meatpacking District
and the other in Soho. Her breezy
blouses and feminine spaghetti-
strap sundresses are must-have
items for a summer in the city.

CHOCOLATE BAR
☎ 212-367-7181; 48 Eighth Ave at W
13th St; 🕙 11am-8pm Tue-Sun; 🚇 A, C,
E to 14th St, L to Eighth Ave

It's all chocolate all the time at
this tiny storefront. You can create
custom gift boxes of fancy artistic
chocolates (flavors from chocolate
mint tea to pistachio marzipan)
by Brooklyn Willy Wonka Jacques
Torres (p224), stock up on rich
bricks of the stuff or simply hover
over a steaming cup of some of
the best hot cocoa ever.

DESTINATION
☎ 212-727-2031; www.destinationny
.net; 32-36 Little W 12th St at Washington St; 🕙 11am-8:30pm Tue-Sun; 🚇 A,
C, E to 14th St, L to Eighth Ave
The eclectic merchandise provides
the color in this vast, all-white
space. You'll find hard-to-get
jewelry from European designers
including Les Bijoux de Sophie,
Serge Thoraval and Corpus Chris-
tie. Then there are the military
chic fashion pieces – funky leather
boots with buckles by Gianni Bar-
bato, sailor-inspired pants by John
Rocha, cargo bags by Orca –
all mixed in with whimsical vests
and jackets, bags from Mik, and
Comptoirs de Trikitrixa shoes (with
scented soles, no less!).

JEFFREY NEW YORK
☎ 212-206-1272; www.jeffreynewyork
.com; 449 W 14th St; 🕙 10am-8pm
Mon-Wed,10am-9pm Thu, 10am-7pm
Sat, 12:30-6pm Sun; 🚇 A, C, E to 14th St,
L to Eigth Ave

Come to the store that started it all – Jeffrey's was one of the first major design emporiums to brave the Meatpacking District's cobblestone streets, and it stays on top of trends to this day. Valencia, Prada and more sold here, with some cosmetics.

⚕ EAT

ⵀ MARKT *Belgian* $$
☎ 212-727-3314; 401 W 14th St at Ninth Ave; 🕒 lunch & dinner; 🚇 L to Eighth Ave, A, C, E to 14th St; ♿ ♿ V

Its big red awnings have dominated the nabe's center square for years now, and it remains one of the best places in town for a Hoegaarden or another foreign beer alongside some mussels and fries.

ⵀ MI COCINA *Mexican* $$
☎ 212-627-8273; 57 Jane at Hudson St; 🕒 dinner daily, lunch Sat & Sun; 🚇 A, C, E to 14th St, L to Eighth Ave; ♿ V

Delicious veggie enchiladas are stuffed with Swiss chard and roasted-tomato-chipotle sauce, while a roasted-zucchini-corn casserole is flavored with roasted tomatoes and cilantro. Usuals like grilled chicken and roasted shrimp get jazzed up with Mexican oregano, white wine and artistic dabs of guacamole and sour cream. Top-shelf tequilas make for amazing cocktails, and sinful desserts make for dreamy endings.

ⵀ PARADOU *French Bistro* $$
☎ 212-463-8345; 8 Little W 12th St btwn Ninth Ave & Washington St; 🕒 dinner; 🚇 A, C, E to 14th St, L to Eighth Ave; V

The hydrangea-heavy garden out the back is a mini-miracle in springtime and is the perfect place for buckwheat crepes, *panini,* and grilled fish dishes. The wine list is stellar, with plenty of affordable options and by-the-glass pours served in individual mini-carafes.

ⵀ PASTIS *French Bistro* $$
☎ 212-929-4844; 9 Ninth Ave at Little W 12th St; 🕒 breakfast, lunch & dinner; 🚇 A, C, E to 14th St, L to Eighth Ave; V

Yes, it's crowded, and yes, most New Yorkers consider the 'buzz' gone from Pastis, although a few still nip in for early-morning coffee. It may no longer be as trendy as it was, but that's fine – it's still a comfort-food bistro for the ages, a bit of working-class Paris brought back to life with skirt steak, fried artichokes and hearty glazed duck dishes that are not super fancy, but do hit the spot.

ⵀ SASCHA *American/Belgian* $$
☎ 212-989-1920; 55 Gansevoort St near Ninth Ave; 🕒 9am-midnight daily; 🚇 L to Eighth Ave, A, C, E to 14th St; ♿ V

There's a swanky restaurant upstairs and an attractive bar/bistro

NEIGHBORHOODS

MEATPACKING DISTRICT

downstairs, but the best part of Sascha is its on-site bakery. Fresh brioche, croissants, and *paninis* washed down with fresh hot chocolate while you sit in the sunshine at Sascha's outdoor tables.

SON CUBANO
Latin American/Tapas/Soul $$

☎ 212-366-1640; 405 W 14th St; ☽ lunch & dinner; Ⓐ A, C, E to 14th St, L to Eighth Ave; ♿

Bringing a touch of Little Havana to the West Side, with *mojitos*, conga drummers and spicy tapas, Son Cubano is a popular after-work and weekend drinking, dining and dancing establishment. Dishes include grilled *pulp*o with a smoky sauce, plantains and a daily seviche.

SOY LUCK CLUB
Healthy Cafe $

☎ 212-229-9191; 115 Greenwich Ave at Jane St; ☽ 7am-10pm Mon-Fri, 9am-10pm Sat & Sun; Ⓐ A, C, E to 14th St, L to Eighth Ave; Ⓥ

Lots of the menu items are indeed soy-based – the soy chicken and fontina (wheat-free) crepe, the tofu salad and avocado sandwich, and the mesclun, *edamame* and soy-nut salad, just for starters – but there's plenty here too for the soy-phobic. *Panini,* salads and brunch items, some even containing meat, abound.

Son Cubano

🍴 SPICE MARKET

Southeast Asian $$-$$$

☎ 212-675-2322; www.jean-georges
.com; 403 W 13th St; 🕑 lunch & dinner;
🚇 A, C, E to 14th St, L at Eighth Ave; ♿

You can easily get lost wandering among the beautiful pagodas and Buddha-filled corners of Spice Market, yet another innovation from Jean-Georges Vongerichten, who's now got six restaurants in the city. Expect Asian street food taken up a notch: satay on a stick, mussels in lemongrass, chicken samosas and pork vindaloo. A night at the bar downing an assortment of appetizers is just as fun as (some say better than) the table experience.

🍴 THE SPOTTED PIG

Pub Fare $$-$$$

☎ 212-620-0393; www.thespottedpig
.com; 314 W 11th St; 🕑 lunch & dinner to
2am; 🚇 A, C, E to 14th St, L to Eighth Ave;
♿ 🚼 V

When you belly up for a drink at this bar, don't expect bowls of peanuts. Pub fare here means chicken liver toast, mozzarella with fava bean bruschetta, duck egg with tuna *bottarga* and much, much more. Busy at night, much better for children in the day, and with at least two vegan options daily, the Spotted Pig's got something for everyone.

🍸 DRINK

🍸 BRASS MONKEY

☎ 212-675-6686; 55 Little W 12th St at
Washington; 🕑 11:30am-4am; 🚇 A, C, E
to 14th St, L to Eighth Ave

While most Meatpacking District bars tend toward chic, the Monkey is down-to-earth, appealing to folks who put more thought into their favorite beer than which shoes to wear. The small, stripped-wood facade is comforting, and the interior just keeps putting you at ease: low, wood-beam ceilings, friendly bartenders and a nice long list of beer and scotch. A small bar menu offers snacks from mussels to bangers and mash.

🍸 DOUBLE SEVEN

☎ 212-981-9099; 418 W 14th St btwn
Ninth & Tenth Aves; 🕑 6pm-4am Mon-
Fri, 8pm-4am Sat; 🚇 A, C, E to 14th St, L
to Eighth Ave

The owner of hipster Lotus (p145) has added a haven for more mature audiences (read: 30s) right across the street. This small cocktail lounge is an intimate den with high, cushiony leather stools, filled with sophisticates who don't mind doling out close to twenty bucks for a single drink – probably because they're uncommonly delicious, and come with a side of designer chocolates.

NEIGHBORHOODS

MEATPACKING DISTRICT

Drinks at Plunge.

▼ PLUNGE

☎ 212-206-6700; Gansevoort Hotel, 18 Ninth Ave at 13th St; ⏲ 11am-3am; ⊖ A, C, E to 14th St, L to Eighth Ave

Located in the 15th-floor penthouse of the hopelessly trendy Gansevoort Hotel, this star affords great views of the Hudson River and New Jersey, best seen in the glow of sunset. It helps tremendously to get here early – and on a weeknight, to boot – or else you'll risk being packed in like well dressed sardines with hordes of scenester-searching wanna-bes. And don't even think about plunging into the lounge's pool – it's for guests only, and the security crew will not be fooled.

★ PLAY

☆ CIELO

☎ 212-645-5700; 18 Little W 12th St; admission $15-25; ⏲ 10:30pm-5am Mon-Sat; ⊖ A, C, E to 14th St, L to Eighth Ave

House music lovers of the world unite! Thanks to your support Cielo is still here, pulling in its regulars with fantastic 'Deep House' Monday nights and monthly 'Turntables on the Hudson' dance-athons. Regular DJs include Willie Graff and the celebrated François K; their alluring, hypnotic sounds draw everyone, sooner or later, to the dancefloor.

⭐ LEVEL V

☎ 212-699-2410; 675 Hudson St;
🕐 8pm-4am; Ⓜ A, C, E to 14th St, L to
Eighth Ave

Waaay underground, in all senses
of the word, Level V is actually
hidden beneath Vento Trattoria, a
fine-looking Italian restaurant on
Hudson St. If you can manage
to get past the doorman, you'll
descend into a super-cool, dun-
geon-like club, with beckoning
bright red puffy couches, sexy
bartenders (men and women) and
a DJ that works the dancefloor all
night long.

⭐ MOVIDA

☎ 212-206-9600; www.movidanyc.com;
28 Seventh Ave; 🕐 10pm-4am Tue-Sat;
Ⓜ A, C, E to 14th St, L at Eighth Ave

Meant to look like a luxury yacht,
and succeeding fairly well, Movida's a strange brew of glitz and
bonhomie. Liberal entrance policies, a relaxed, hip crowd, and an
affinity for retro punk, post-punk,
rock and electro have put Movida
on the downtown map. The Robot
Rock party on Saturday night is
a favorite; a second happy hour
when drinks are half-price runs
from 2am to 3am nightly.

>CHELSEA

There's a lot of excitement in Chelsea these days, as art galleries and collectives push into the neighborhood, expanding and raising its profile.

The latest pioneer, gallery group, turned a derelict old nightclub into a block-long assemblage of artist studios, the first horizontal breakthrough in an otherwise vertical neighborhood. It's an interesting marriage because Chelsea is known primarily for two things – gallery hopping and clubbing, and there's ample opportunity to do both.

Despite crackdown from NYPD, the neighborhood's west side from 26th St up to approximately 29th St is peppered with discos and dance clubs, some of them gay oriented as Chelsea is the city's center of gay life now. But generally, anything goes – gays, straights, whomever is welcome, as long as they can get past the bouncer at the front door. Chelsea can look a little cold, with its wide, sweeping streets and long blocks, but once you're comfortable amid the art and the clubbing, you'll love the nabe.

CHELSEA

SEE
Barbara Gladstone Gallery 1 C3
Cheim & Read 2 B2
Chelsea Art Museum .. 3 B3
Chelsea Hotel 4 F3
Chelsea Piers Complex 5 B4
Gagosian 6 B3
Lehmann Maupin 7 B2
Matthew Marks 8 C3
Mitchell-Innes & Nash 9 C2
Museum at FIT 10 F2
Paul Kasmin 11 C1
Rubin Museum of Art . 12 F5

SHOP
192 Books 13 C4
Balducci's 14 E6
Balenciaga 15 B3
Barney's Co-op 16 F5
Books of Wonder 17 H5
Chelsea Market 18 D5
Giraudon 19 E5
Housing Works Thrift Shop 20 G5

EAT
Amuse 21 G5
Better Burger 22 E4
Blossom 23 D4
Elmo 24 F4
Empire Diner 25 C3
La Taza de Oro 26 E6
Matsuri 27 E5
Tía Pol 28 C3

DRINK
Chelsea Brewing Company 29 A4

Eagle 30 B1
Gym 31 E5
Half King 32 C3
Peter McManus Tavern 33 F4
Serena 34 F3
Splash Bar 35 H5
West Side Tavern 36 E3

PLAY
718 Sessions 37 H3
Cain 38 C2
Hiro 39 E5
Joyce Theater 40 E4
Lotus 41 C6
Marquee 42 C2
Roxy 43 C5

Please see over for map

👁 SEE

👁 BARBARA GLADSTONE GALLERY

☎ 212-206-9300; www.gladstonegal lery.com; 515 W 24th St btwn 10th & 11th Aves; 🕑 10am-6:00pm Tue-Sat, closed weekends Jul & Aug; 🔵 C, E, 1 to 23rd St; ♿

The curator of this eponymous gallery has learned a thing or two after 27 years in the Manhattan art world. Ms Gladstone consistently puts together the most talked-about and well-critiqued displays, and artists such as Shirin Neshat, Magnus von Plessen and Anish Kapoor are frequently shown.

👁 CHEIM & READ

☎ 212-242-7727; www.cheimread .com; 547 W 25th St btwn 10th & 11th Aves; 🕑 10am-6pm Tue-Sat; 🔵 C, E to 23rd St; ♿

Sculptures of every shape, size and material abound at Cheim & Read, and monthly changes keep the exhibits fresh. If the timing is right, you might catch William Eggleston's bouncy color photographs hanging on the wall, or a Jenny Holzer light installation blazing over the front door.

👁 CHELSEA ART MUSEUM

☎ 212-255-0719; www.chelseaartmu seum.org; 556 W 22nd St; 🕑 noon-6pm Tue, Wed, Fri & Sat, noon-8pm Thu; 🔵 C, E to 23rd St; ♿

One of many new additions to the art scene here, this museum occupies a three-story red brick building dating from 1850, and stands on land once owned by writer Clement Clarke Moore. Its focus is on post-war abstract expressionism, especially by national and international artists; its permanent collection includes works by Antonio Corpora, Laszlo Lakner and sculptor Bernar Venet. It's also the headquarters of the Miotte Foundation, dedicated to archiving the works of Jean Miotte, a Soho-based artist who has played a big role in the genre of Informel (Informal Art).

👁 CHELSEA HOTEL

☎ 212-243-3700; 222 W 23rd St btwn Seventh & Eighth Aves; 🔵 1, 2, C, E to 23rd St

The prime sight on noisy 23rd St is a redbrick hotel with ornate iron balconies and no fewer than seven plaques declaring its literary land-mark status. Even before the Sex Pistols' Sid Vicious murdered girl-friend Nancy Spungeon here, the hotel was famous as a hangout for the likes of Mark Twain, Thomas Wolfe, Dylan Thomas and Arthur Miller. Jack Kerouac allegedly crafted *On the Road* during one marathon session here. Musicians have long favored the Chelsea, and it counts many of the local eccentrics among its permanent

A

B

C

D

W 30th St

W 29th St

W 28th St

Twelfth Ave (West Side Hwy)

Eleventh Ave

Y30

★88

11

9 ★42

7

2

6

1

Y82

Hudson River Park

W 23rd St

3 8

15

Y25 5

Chelsea Piers

Hudson River

25**Y1**

13

Y128

23**Y1**

W 27th St

W 26th St

W 25th St

W 24th St

Chelsea Park

London Tce Gardens

Tenth Ave

Ninth Ave

W 22nd St

W 20th St

W 19th St

W 17th St

W 15th St

W 13th St

Tenth Ave

Eleventh Ave

Ninth Ave

Washington St

★43

18

★41

1

2

3

4

5

6

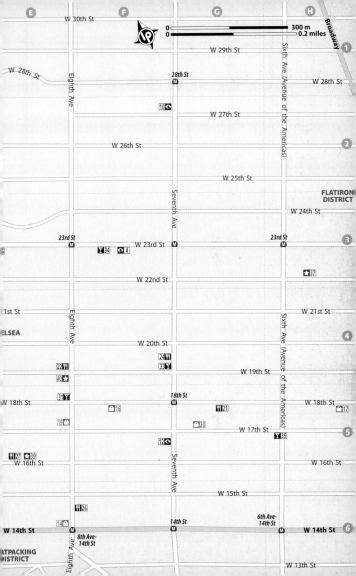

residents. Its basement lounge bar, Serena (p143), is a sexy, low-lit spot for a martini.

☉ CHELSEA PIERS COMPLEX
☎ 212-336-6000; www.chelseapiers .com; Hudson River at end of 23rd St; ◉ C, E to 23rd St

This massive waterfront sports center caters to the athlete in everyone. You can set out to hit a bucket of golf balls at the four-level driving range, ice skate in the complex's indoor rink or rent in-line skates to cruise down to Battery Park along the new Hudson Park waterfront bike path. There's a jazzy bowling alley, Hoop City for basketball, a sailing school for kids, batting cages, a huge gym facility with an indoor pool (day passes for nonmembers are $50), indoor rock-climbing walls – the works. Kayaks are loaned out free at the Downtown Boathouse just north of Pier 64. There's even waterfront dining and drinking at the Chelsea Brewing Company (p142), which serves great pub fare and delicious home brews. Though the Piers are somewhat cut off by the busy West Side Hwy, the wide array of attractions here brings in the crowds; the M23 crosstown bus, which goes right to its main entrance, saves you the long, four-avenue trek from the subway.

☉ GAGOSIAN
www.gagosian.com; Chelsea (☎ 212-741-1111; 555 W 24th St; ☼ 10am-6pm Sat; ◉ C, E, to 23rd St; ♿); Uptown (☎ 212-741-1111; 980 Madison Ave; ☼ 10am-6pm Tue-Sat; ◉ 6 to 77th St-Lexington Ave; ♿)

International works dot the walls at both the Gagosian in Chelsea and uptown. The ever-revolving exhibits feature greats like Julian Schnabel, William de Kooning, Andy Warhol and Basquiat.

☉ LEHMANN MAUPIN

☎ 212-255-2923; www.lehmann
maupin.com; 540 W 26th St; ⏲ 11am-
6pm Tue-Sat; ⊘ C, E to 23rd St; ♿
Still one of the most influential
galleries around, Lehmann Maupin
shows Korean sculptor Do-Ho Suh,
as well as British bad girl Tracey
Emin, David Salle and many others.

☉ MATTHEW MARKS
GALLERY

☎ 212-243-0200; www.matthewmarks
.com; 522 W 22nd St at Tenth Ave & 523 W
24th St; ⏲ 10am-6pm Mon-Fri; ⊘ C, E
to 23rd St; ♿
The trendsetter that started the
push into Chelsea, Matthew Marks'
two galleries were once factories.
Now they are high-falutin' art
houses with shows by the likes of
Nan Goldin and Andreas Gursky.

☉ MITCHELL-INNES & NASH

www.miandn.com; Chelsea (☎ 212-
744-7400; 534 W 26th St near 10th
Ave; ⏲ 10am-6pm Mon-Fri; ⊘ C,
E to 23rd St); Uptown (1018 Madison
Ave; ⏲ 10am-5pm Mon-Fri; ⊘ 6 to
77th St)
The married couple behind these
galleries started their careers at
Sotheby's, and their appreciation
of the past infuses their spaces –
while they feature the best of
cutting-edge artists, they also
mount lovingly researched retrospectives.

☉ MUSEUM AT FIT

☎ 212-217-5800; www.fitnyc.edu;
Seventh Ave at 27th St; admission
free; ⏲ noon-8pm Tue-Fri, 10am-5pm
Sat; ⊘ 1 to 28th St
The Fashion Institute of Technology is a fashion, design and fine
arts school located on the edge
of Manhattan's Fashion District.
The best way for a visitor to access
its unique riches is to visit its museum, which showcases rotating
exhibits on fashion and style, including works by students. Its new
permanent collection, opened
in late 2005, is the country's first
gallery of fashion and textile history; it showcases rotating items
from its collection of more than
50,000 garments and accessories
dating from the 18th century to
the present.

☉ PAUL KASMIN

☎ 212-563-4474; www.paulkasmingal
lery.com; 293 Tenth Ave at 27th St &
511 W 27th St; ⏲ 10am-6pm Tue-Sat,
9am-5pm Mon-Fri July & Aug; ⊘ C, E to
23rd St; ♿
Expect the unexpected at Paul
Kasmin. After all, the gallery does
represent the legendary Frank
Stella. All media are accepted
here – collages, paintings, photography, sculptures and more.
Shows at this gallery are wide-
ranging, expansive and thought-
provoking.

V

◉ RUBIN MUSEUM OF ART
☎ 212-620-5000; www.rmanyc.org; 150 W 17th St at Seventh Ave; 11am-7pm Mon & Sat, 11am-5pm Wed, 11am-9pm Thu & Fri, 11am-6pm Sun; 1 to 18th St

One of the newest museums in the city, the Rubin, opened in 2004. It's the first museum in the Western world dedicating itself to art of the Himalayas and surrounding regions. Impressive collections include embroidered textiles from China, metal sculptures from Tibet, Pakistani stone sculptures, intricate Bhutanese paintings and ritual objects and dance masks from various Tibetan regions, spanning from the 2nd to 19th centuries.

SHOP
☐ 192 BOOKS
☎ 212-255-4022; 192 Tenth Ave btwn 21st & 22nd Sts; 11am-7pm Tue-Sat, noon-6pm Sun & Mon; C, E to 23rd St

This small indie bookstore is located right in the gallery district, with sections on literature, history, travel, art and criticism. The rotating art exhibits, during which the owners organize special displays of books which relate, thematically, to the featured show or artist are a special treat.

☐ BALDUCCI'S
☎ 212-741-3700; 81 Eighth Ave at 14th St; 9am-10pm; A, C, E to 14th St, L to Eighth Ave

Housed in a landmark, turn-of-the-century bank building, this new Balducci's shop (which had reigned for years just south of here, in the Village) came to Chelsea recently, bringing with it its highest quality gourmet produce, international cheeses, olives, bakery goods, fresh roasted coffee and packaged items from around the globe.

☐ BALENCIAGA
☎ 212-206-0872; 522 W 22nd St at Eleventh Ave; 10am to 7pm Mon-Sat, noon-5pm Sun; C, E to 23rd St

Come and graze at this cool, gray, Zen-like space. It's the gallery-district's showcase, appropriately enough, for the artistic, post-apocalypse avant-garde styles of this French fashion house. Expect strange lines, goth patterns and pants for very skinny (and deep-pocketed) gals.

BARNEY'S CO-OP
☎ 212-593-7800; 236 W 18th St;
🕑 11am-8pm Mon-Fri, to 7pm Sat,
noon-6pm Sun; ◉ 1 to 18th St

The edgier, younger, less expensive version of Barneys (p161) has (relatively) affordable deals. At this expansive, loft-like space, with a spare, very selective inventory of clothing for men and women, plus shoes and cosmetics, the biannual warehouse sale (February and August) packs the place, both with endless merchandise and mobs of customers.

BOOKS OF WONDER
☎ 212-989-3270; www.booksofwonder .com; 16 W 18th St; 🕑 11am-7pm Mon-Sat, 11:45am-6pm Sun; ◉ L, N, R, 4, 5, 6 to 14th St-Union Sq

It's never too early to infect your children with book fever – and this is the place to do it. Among the first-edition signed Maurice Sendaks you'll find all the most popular kid-lit of the day, with options for even the youngest kids. It's a hands-on environment with patient and informed staff.

CHELSEA MARKET
www.chelseamarket.com; 75 Ninth Ave btwn 15th & 16th Sts; 🕑 7am-9pm Mon-Sat, 10am-8pm Sun; ◉ A, C, E to 14th St, L to Eighth Ave

Gourmet food fans will think they've entered the pearly gates

once they've stepped into this 800ft-long shopping concourse bursting with some of the freshest eats in town. But it's part of a larger, million-sq-ft space that occupies a full city block, home to the Nabisco cookie factory in the 1930s (which created the Oreo cookie), and current home to the Food Network, Oxygen Network and the local NY1 news channel. The prime draw for locals are the more-than-25 market food shops, including Amy's Bread, Fat Witch Brownies, the Lobster Place, Hale & Hearty Soup, Ronnybrook Farm Dairy and Frank's butcher shop.

GIRAUDON
☎ 212-633-0999; 152 Eighth Ave btwn 17th & 18th Sts; 🕑 11:30am-7:30pm Mon-Wed & Fri-Sun, to 11pm Thu; ◉ A, C, E to 14th St, L to Eighth Ave

This small shoe boutique has been selling finely made leather foot sculptures since way before the 'hood was hip. The designs are classic with a touch of edginess, with both casual and glamorous options. It's a tiny space, but rarely crowded. The staffers are friendly and encouraging.

HOUSING WORKS THRIFT SHOP
☎ 212-366-0820; 143 W 17th St;
🕑 10am-6pm Mon-Sat, noon-5pm Sun;
◉ 1 to 18th St

This thrift shop, with its swank window displays, looks more boutique than thrift, and its selections of clothes, accessories, furniture and books are great value. All proceeds benefit the charity serving the city's HIV-positive and AIDS homeless communities.

🍴 EAT

🍴 AMUSE *American* $$
☎ 212-929-9755; 108 W 18th St; ☽ lunch & dinner; ⊕ 1 to 18th St; ⛫ ⚹ Ⓥ

You'll love grazing on the small plates of Amuse Fries (served with chipotle and aioli), olive poached tuna, braised beets or roasted shiitake mushrooms (to name but a few). To try it all, get the *prix-fixe* sampler.

🍴 BETTER BURGER
Organic Burgers $
☎ 212-989-6688; www.betterburger .nyc.com; 178 Eighth Ave at W 19th St; ☽ lunch & dinner; ⊕ A, C, E to 14th St, 1 to 18th St; ⛫ ⚹ Ⓥ

Catering to the muscled, protein-loving boys in the 'hood, this is a brilliant take on the tired old burger. It's a sleek, bright fast-food joint that offers organic, hormone-free burgers made from your choice of beef, ostrich, turkey, chicken, tuna, soy or mashed veggies. All come on homemade whole-wheat buns and are topped

with homemade 'tomato zest,' a more sophisticated version of ketchup. To really treat yourself, add an order of the air-baked 'fries,' which are so delicious you'll swear they were dunked in grease, and one of several smoothies or bottled beers. Find other outposts of the fast-growing local chain in Midtown, Murray Hill and the Upper East Side; check the website for locations.

🍴 BLOSSOM *Vegetarian* $$
☎ 212-627-1144; 187 Ninth Ave btwn W 21st & W 22nd Sts; ☽ lunch & dinner; ⊕ C, E to 23rd St; Ⓥ

Chelsea, brimming with Americana spots that love to get creative with meat, is not known for being particularly vegetarian friendly. Enter Blossom, a fresh new addition to the 'hood that's hoping to turn that beat around. The sweet spot, housed in a Chelsea townhouse and owned by a healthy but creative husband-and-wife team, offers a casual juice-bar vibe by day and ambient, candle-lit, fireplace-warmed dining room by night. That's when its best charms come out, as the dinner-menu items span the globe and enliven the taste buds. Try the delicately sweet pumpkin gnocchi with wild mushrooms or tofu *fra diablo*, which pairs bean curd with spicy tomato sauce and broccoli rabe. Chocolate ganache tortes or

pineapple crepes are the perfect way to finish.

🍴 ELMO American $$

☎ 212-337-8000; 156 Seventh Ave btwn W 19th & W 20th St; 🕑 11am-11pm; 🚇 1 to 18th St; V

An epicenter for Chelsea boys who need to refuel after clubbing and before working out (or vice versa), Elmo is on the big bandwagon of diners sporting a nightclub vibe (and it's got an actual clubby lounge, with a rotating performance schedule, in its basement). It's a sexy scene with high ceilings, low lighting, cushy banquettes and a garage door–like facade that's opened to the street come

spring and summer. The simple, comfort-food favorites – meatloaf, fried chicken, baked mac 'n' cheese (with added fontina and Gruyère), mussels (steamed in tequila) and big fresh salads – are consistently delicious. And so are the lovely looking waitstaff and clientele.

🍴 EMPIRE DINER Diner $-$$

☎ 212-243-2736; www.theempirediner .com; 210 Tenth Ave; 🕑 24hr; 🚇 C, E to 23rd St; ♿ V

Housed in a restored silver Pullman car, Empire Diner has a lot of wacky charm, mostly thanks to the occasional odd character who sits at the counter eating pie. Can't really blame 'em – the pie, burgers, salads and heaping, fat omelettes are delicious, and all types swing by for a bite.

🍴 LA TAZA DE ORO
Puerto Rican $-$$
☎ 212-243-9946; 96 Eighth Ave; 🕐 breakfast, lunch, dinner Mon-Sat; 🚇 1, A, C, E to 14th St; 🚻 🚼

Keeping it real for more than three decades, La Taza de Oro has a long, functional countertop with barstools and plain tables that won't win any design awards. But the decor goes with the stomach-filling cheap eats like rice-and-beans, *lechón asado*, flan and more. Unpretentious, and very satisfying.

🍴 MATSURI
Japanese Sushi $$-$$$
☎ 212-243-6400; The Maritime Hotel, 369 W 16th St; 🕐 dinner Tue-Sat; 🚇 L to Eighth Ave; A, C, E to 14th St; 🚻 Ⓥ

People pay so much attention to the decor – the ceiling looks just like the hull of an overturned samurai ship – that the food plays second fiddle. That's a shame, because with fresh rice grains flown in daily from Japan, and staples like fluke sashimi with red pepper and *ponzu*, sake black cod and yellowtail sashimi with ginger vinegar sauce, it merits your full attention.

🍴 TÍA POL
Spanish Tapas $$
☎ 212-675-8805; 205 Tenth Ave btwn W 22nd & W 23rd Sts; 🕐 dinner Tue-Sun; 🚇 C, E to 23rd St; Ⓥ

This closet-sized, authentic, romantic Spanish tapas bar is the real deal – and the hordes of locals who crowd into the front-bar waiting area to get one of six teeny tables filled with massive doses of deliciousness know it. Come on the early side and you may get seated in under a half-hour. It's a wait well worth its weight in red wine and Spanish tortillas as both are beyond splendid here. So is just about everything else on the menu, from the fresh salad topped with tuna to the lima-bean-puree bruschetta and sautéed cockles with razor clams.

🍸 DRINK
🍸 CHELSEA BREWING COMPANY
☎ 212-336-6440; Chelsea Piers, Pier 59, West Side Highway at 23rd St; 🕐 noon-midnight; 🚇 C, E to 23rd St

Enjoy a quality microbrew, waterside, in the expansive outdoor area of this way-west beer haven – a perfect place to re-enter the world after a day of swimming, golfing or rock climbing as a guest at the Chelsea Piers Complex (p136).

▼ EAGLE

☎ 646-473-1866; www.eaglenyc.com; 554 W 28th St; 🕙 10pm-4am Mon-Sat, 5pm-4am Sun; ◉ C, E to 23rd St

Leather- and Levi-clad men descend on the Eagle for cruisey fun and thematic nights that include live S&M action. Come summertime, its open-air roof deck is the place to be.

▼ GYM

☎ 212-337-2439; 167 Eighth Ave at 18th St; 🕙 4pm-2am Mon-Thu, 4pm-4am Fri, 1pm-4am Sat, 1pm-2am Sun; ◉ A, C, E to 14th St, L to Eighth Ave

This sports bar for men is nothing like the rowdy straight sports bars that pepper Midtown side streets. Here the decor is classy – wide-plank wooden floors, high ceilings and a sleek bar – the men are polite, and ice-skating championships are as popular as basketball playoffs (which are beloved thanks to the hot players' booties).

▼ HALF KING

☎ 212-462-4300; 505 W 23rd St at Tenth Ave; ◉ C, E to 23rd St

A unique marriage of cozy pub and sophisticated writers' lair, you'll often experience top-notch literary readings in this wood-accented, candlelit watering hole. Its myriad seating-area options are bound to provide one that will seduce you – particularly during

warm weather, when a front side-walk café, main indoor room, cozy back section and mellow backyard patio are all open for business.

▼ PETER MCMANUS TAVERN

☎ 212-929-6196; 152 Seventh Ave at 19th St; 🕙 11am-4am Mon-Sat, noon-4am Sun; ◉ 1 at 18th St

James 'Jamo' McManus, the founder's grandson, still tends bar when he can. This family-run business has been around since the early 1900s, and it's got the paraphernalia to prove it – Tiffany glass windows, wooden phone booths and more.

▼ SERENA

☎ 212-255-4646; www.serenanyc.com; 222 W 23rd St; 🕙 6pm-4am Mon-Fri, 8pm-4am Sat; ◉ C, E to 23rd St, 1 to 23rd St

Tucked into the basement below the quirky Chelsea Hotel, Serena's is a former speakeasy that looks more like a bordello – pink satin and black couches with white filigree lanterns make for a sexy space. The crowd is upscale and relaxed, and the multi-cushioned couches deeply inviting.

▼ SPLASH BAR

☎ 212-691-0073; 50 W 17th St; 🕙 5pm-4am Wed-Sat; ◉ L to 6th Ave, F, V to 14th St

First it was Splash, then SBNY, and now Splash Bar. Still, not much has changed (a good thing) at this Chelsea staple, a multilevel spot that is part lounge, part club, and home to some of the hottest, most scantily-clad bartenders around. Sunday's Trannyshack is a popular drag-queen party.

🍸 WEST SIDE TAVERN
☎ 212-366-3738; 360 W 23rd St btwn Eighth & Ninth Aves; ⏱ 2pm-2am; ⓜ C, E to 23rd St

Talk about normal! This beer-soaked tavern has an old-fashioned vibe, loud classic rock and a popular pool table, along with decent pub fare and some roomy tables alongside its lengthy bar. It's filled with regular Joes, and the occasional girlfriend, and on alternating Fridays, the high (for Chelsea) straight-boy content is especially obvious, as the small basement is packed with some of the hottest

THE HIGH LINE
It was a 75-year-old elevated subway track that stood 30 feet above ground, starting in the Meatpacking District and running west. Slated for demolition in 2000, it was salvaged by a group of preservationists who formed Friends of the High Line. Now the 1.5-mile structure's being transformed into an above-ground public park. As of press time, the project was nearing completion. For details on its progress go to www.thehighline.org.

men in the 'hood for Snaxx, a DJ-driven lounge soiree that pulls in a big crowd based on buzz alone.

⭐ PLAY
⭐ 718 SESSIONS
☎ 212-229-2000;16 W 22nd St btwn Fifth & Sixth Aves; ⏱ 11pm-4am Tue-Sat; ⓜ F, V, R, W to 23rd St (W Sat & Sun only)

This monthly party, held at an otherwise unremarkable club space, is a riot of old-school dancing to deep, soulful house from DJ Danny Krivit and occasional live performers, like the recent New Year's Eve show from Joi Cardwell. House parties rage on Fridays with DJ Marc Anthony.

⭐ CAIN
☎ 212-947-8000; www.cainnyc.com; 544 W 27th St; ⏱ 10pm-4am Mon-Sat; ⓜ C, E at 23rd St

Plenty of wanna-be partiers would commit fratricide for a glimpse of the safari-themed interior of Cain, known for its rather hoity-toity entrance policies as much as for its wild dancing, a DJ booth carved out of a boulder, and live drummers accompanying the funk, house and rock music. Don't miss a Tuesday night if you're a fan of celeb sightings, but be prepared to work some magic at the door if you want to get in.

★ HIRO
☎ 212-727-0212; www.maritimehotel
.com; 371 W 16th St; ⏰ 10pm-4am daily,
closed Wed ⦿ A, C, E to 14th St, L to
Eighth Ave

The decor is urban Japanese chic
with a touch of yachting flavor, so
skip Hiro if you have an aversion
to hanging red lanterns, bamboo
wall dividers and low-slung banquettes with pretty appliqués.
But, if you like sleek lines and eye-
catching accessories – and we're
talking about the crowd now –
Hiro's a great choice, especially on
Thursday and Sunday nights when
a gay crowd from surrounding
Chelsea hits the sprawling dance
floor.

★ JOYCE THEATER
☎ 212-242-0800; www.joyce.org; 175
Eighth Ave; ⦿ C, E to 23rd St, A, C, E at
14th St, 1 to 18th St

An offbeat, intimate venue in
Chelsea with clean sight lines
from every corner, the Joyce is
blessed with annual visits from
Merce Cunningham and Pilobolus
dance companies, comfortably
seen from any of the renovated
theater's 470 seats.

★ LOTUS
☎ 212-243-4420; 409 W 14th St btwn
Ninth & Tenth Aves; cover $10-20; ⏰ 7-
11pm Tue-Sat; ⦿ A, C, E to 14th St, L to
Eighth Ave

The big night at this slick, VIP-
crowd club is Friday, when GBH
(not to be confused with GHB)
rocks the house with a fresh mix
of house, disco and garage for
groovy downtown hipsters.

★ MARQUEE
☎ 646-473-0202; 289 Tenth Ave btwn
26th & 27th Sts; ⏰ 10pm-4am Tue-
Sat; ⦿ C, E to 23rd St

Glamorous masses and a fair share
of A-listers try to slip past the velvet ropes to get inside, where DJs
spin electronica, house and funk
all night long.

★ ROXY
☎ 212-627-0404; 515 W 18th St btwn
Tenth & Eleventh Aves; admission $15-25;
⏰ 8pm-2am Wed, 11pm-4am Fri &
Sat; ⦿ A, C, E to 14th St, L to Eighth Ave

This legendary megaclub keeps
the good times rolling with the
freewheeling Wednesday roller
disco. John Blair promotes the
big, ever-popular Saturday-night
bash, a Circuit Party–like massive
gathering of shirtless gay men,
humping to the sounds of big
names from Manny Lehman to
Junior Vasquez. The boys are
still talking about how Madonna
herself made an appearance here
to promote *Confessions on a Dance
Floor* in late 2005.

>UNION SQ/FLATIRON DISTRICT/GRAMERCY PARK

There's a mismatch of energy between bustling, busy Union Sq and inclusive, tony Gramercy Park. Union Sq is an open square, home to green markets, community demonstrations, bike rallies and more, while Gramercy is dominated by a lush, beautiful park that is gated to keep out people who don't live in the soaring townhouses directly on its perimeter.

But Gramercy does have its good points, namely the intersection of great restaurants and clubs around Irving Plaza, on the east side, and the sedate Pierpont Library that affords rare glimpses into a past life.

The Flatiron District just to the north of Union Sq is heavy with traffic and big name department stores, like Home Depot and ABC Home Carpets.

The three of them together form a practical and yet wealthy neighborhood that has more than its share of big and expensive restaurants.

UNION SQ/FLATIRON DISTRICT/GRAMERCY PARK

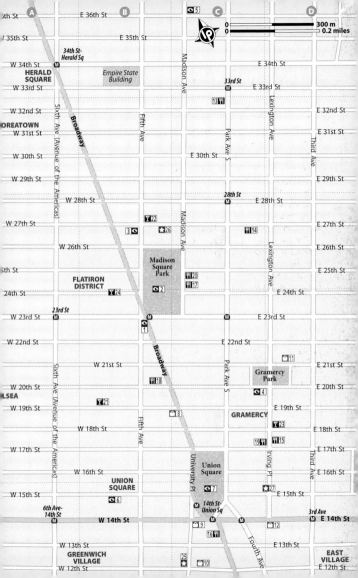

◉ SEE

◉ FLATIRON BUILDING
Broadway, Fifth Ave & 23rd St; ◉ **N, R, 6 to 23rd St**
Skeptical residents who doubted Daniel Burnham's 21-story limestone and terra-cotta building would stay up nicknamed this building 'Burnham's Folly.' Six feet across at its narrowest point, it's now the defining landmark of the neighborhood.

◉ MADISON SQ PARK
www.nycgovparks.org; 23rd to 26th Sts btwn Broadway & Madison Ave; ◔ **6am-1am;** ◉ **N, R, 6 to 23rd St;** ♿
You can visit this cute little spot in the Flatiron District for the elegant statues, free summer art programs, and the playground for kids. Or you can be like everyone else and come for the Shake Shack, an environmentally-friendly food kiosk that's turned the park's south end into a dining hot spot.

◉ MUSEUM OF SEX
☎ **212-689-6337; www.museumofsex .com; 233 Fifth Ave at 27th St; adults/ seniors & students $14.50/13.50;** ◔ **11am-6:30pm Sun-Fri, 11am-8pm Sat (last ticket sold 45min before closing);** ◉ **N, R, 6 to 28th St**
Starting with its groundbreaking exhibit, 'How New York City Transformed Sex in America,' this museum has sought to inform, educate and gently titillate the world. Its permanent collections showcase America's various sexual revolutions, from burlesque to gay rights, and it sells top-of-the-line sex toys in the museum gift store.

◉ NATIONAL ARTS CLUB
☎ **212-475-3424; 15 Gramercy Park South;** ◉ **6 to 23rd St**
This exclusive club boasts a beautiful, vaulted, stained-glass ceiling above its wooden bar. Calvert Vaux, who was one of the creators of Central Park, designed the building. The space does hold art exhibitions, ranging from sculpture to photography, that sometimes open to the public from 1pm to 5pm.

◉ PIERPONT MORGAN LIBRARY
☎ **212-685-0610; www.morganlibrary .org; 29 E 36th St at Madison Ave;** ◔ **10:30am-5pm Tue-Thu, 10:30am-9pm Fri, 10am-6pm Sat, 11am-6pm Sun, closed Mon;** ◉ **6 to 33rd St**
This library, recently reopened after beautiful, extensive renovations, is part of the 45-room mansion owned by steel magnate JP Morgan. His collection features a phenomenal array of manuscripts, tapestries and books (with no fewer than three Gutenberg Bibles), a study filled with Italian

Renaissance artwork, a marble rotunda and the three-tiered East Room main library. The rotating art exhibitions here are really top notch.

◎ TIBET HOUSE
☎ 212-807-0563; www.tibethouse.org; 22 W 15th St btwn Fifth & Sixth Aves; ⏱ noon-5pm Tue-Fri; ⊕ F to 14th St, L to Sixth Ave
With the Dalai Lama at the head of its board, this nonprofit cultural space is dedicated to presenting Tibet's ancient traditions through art exhibits, a research library and publications, and programs which include educational workshops, open meditations, retreat weekends and docent-led tours around the globe.

◎ UNION SQ
17th St btwn Broadway & Park Ave; ⊕ L, N, Q, R, W, 4, 5, 6 to 14th St-Union Sq
Opened in 1831, this park quickly became the central gathering place for surrounding mansions and grand concert halls. The later explosion of high-end shops gave the area its nickname of Ladies' Mile. Then, from the start of the Civil War, well into the 20th century, this became the site for protests of all kinds – for union workers as well as political activists. By WWI, the area had become neglected and depressed. It

A Christmas market in Union Sq

DEAD MAN'S CURVE

Electronic cable cars once barreled through Union Sq at nine miles an hour to avoid stalling at a particularly sharp turn on the park's western edge. So few conductors did it without striking pedestrians that the spot was nicknamed 'Dead Man's Curve,' although it seems women and horses bore the brunt of the punishment.

eventually became home to all sorts of working-class headquarters, including the American Civil Liberties Union, the Communist and Socialist parties and the Ladies' Garment Workers Union.

 ## SHOP

☐ ABC CARPET & HOME

☎ 212-473-3000; 888 Broadway; ⏱ 10am-8pm Mon-Thu, to 6:30pm Fri & Sat, noon-6pm Sun; ☺ L, N, Q, R, W, 4, 5, 6 to 14th St-Union Sq

Home designers and decorators stroll over here to brainstorm. Set up like a museum on six floors, ABC is filled with all sorts of furnishings, small and large, including easy-to-pack knick-knacks, designer jewelry, global gifts and more bulky antique furnishings and carpets. Come Christmas season, the shop is a joy to behold, as the decorators go all out with lights and other wondrous touches.

☐ FILENE'S BASEMENT

☎ 212-348-0169; 4 Union Sq; ⏱ 9am-10pm Mon-Sat, 11am-8pm Sun; ☺ L, N, Q, R, W, 4, 5, 6 to 14th St-Union Sq

This outpost of the Boston-based chain is not actually in a basement, but three flights up, with a tremendous view of Union Sq. You'll find labels at up to 70 percent less than regular retail outlet prices. Like similar discount department stores, it's got clothing, shoes, jewelry, accessories, cosmetics and some housewares (like bedding). Fashionistas willing to go on painstaking searches could unearth treasures, including apparel from Dolce & Gabbana, Michael Kors, Versace and more.

☐ KENTSHIRE GALLERIES

☎ 212-673-6644; www.kentshire.com; 37 E 12th St; ⏱ 9am-5pm Mon-Fri, 10am-3pm Sat in Oct, Nov and January; ☺ 4, 5, 6, L, N, R, Q, W to 14th St-Union Sq

There are three floors of 18th- and 19th-century Georgian and Regency period pieces at Kentshire, but the real must-see items are in the jewelry collection. Check out the vintage Van Cleef & Arpels' gold watches, and delicate drop-pearl Edwardian earrings.

☐ STARDUST ANTIQUES

☎ 212-677-2590; www.stardustantiques.com; 38 Gramercy Park; ⏱ noon-

7pm Mon-Sat, noon-6pm Sun; N, R, 6 to 23rd St

A rambling, eclectic shop with enchanting rooms, Stardust Antiques has myriad paintings, furnishings and accessories. It's particularly known for its early 19th century, Edwardian and art deco wedding bands and engagement rings. If you're romantic enough to pop the question at the top of the Empire State Building, you'll want a ring from here.

TRADER JOE'S

☎ 212-529-4612; 142 E 14 St; ⏰ 9am-10pm daily; 4, 5, 6, L, N, Q, R, W at 14th St-Union Sq

If you like fair-trade coffee and organic produce, beef and poultry, and have a hankering for exotic ingredients not stocked in most stores, Trader Joe's wants to talk to you. A Whole Foods competitor, this chain came to New York in 2005 and is holding its own so far.

�ঁ EAT

ঁ ARTISANAL *French* $$$

☎ 212-725-8585; 2 Park Ave; ⏰ lunch & dinner daily; 6 at 33rd St; ♿ V

For those who live, love and dream *fromage*, Artisanal is a must-eat. More than 250 varieties of cheese, from stinky to sweet, are on the menu. Along with classic French entrees like steak *au poivre*, you can sample four types of fondue (including chocolate) and *gougères* (little servings) of everything from Brie to Ossau-Iraty.

ঁ BLUE SMOKE
Southern/BBQ $$

☎ 212-447-7733; www.bluesmoke.com; 116 E 27th St; ⏰ lunch & dinner; 6 to 28th St; ♿ ঁ

Purists may eschew northern-style BBQ, but Blue Smoke's got a few recipes that rival those of the deep South. Beer ribs, salt-and-pepper ribs, baby-back ribs, pulled pork sandwiches and killer mac 'n' cheese are the menu standouts.

ঁ CASA MONO
Spanish Tapas $$

☎ 212-253-2773; 52 Irving Pl; ⏰ noon-midnight; any train to Union Sq; ♿ V

Another winner from Mario Batali and chef Andy Nusser, Casa Mono's got a great, long bar where you can sit and watch your *pez espada a la plancha* and *gambas al ajillo* take a grilling. Or grab one of the wooded tables and nosh on tapas with *jerez* (sherry) from the bottles lining the walls. For a cheese dessert, hop next door to Bar Jamon, also owned by Batali; you may have to squeeze in – the place is communal and fun.

🍴 CHOCOLATE BY THE BALD MAN *American Eclectic* $-$$

☎ 212-388-0030; www.maxbrenner .com; 841 Broadway; 🕑 8am-midnight Mon-Wed, 8am-2am Thu-Sat, 9am-midnight Sun; ◉ any train to 14th St-Union Sq

Sweet-toothed Aussie Max Brenner brought his chocolate empire to Union Sq, and his wildly popular café-cum-chocolate-bar, looking from the outside like a gingerbread house, is all the rage. Besides the sweets he's got a full menu (great breakfast) and also does low-cal variations mixed by hand on the spot. Divine!

🍴 ELEVEN MADISON PARK *French* $$$$

☎ 212-889-0905; www.elevenmadison park.com; 11 Madison Ave; 🕑 lunch & dinner; ◉ 6, N, R to 23rd St; ♿ 👶

An art deco wonder that's often overlooked in this star-studded town, Eleven Madison Park is welcoming enough to bring children into for fine dining, and delicious enough to please even the most discerning diner. Dishes include muscovy duck with honey sauce, wild salmon with horseradish crust and fennel risotto, halibut *mi-cuit* with carrots, and seasonal surprises.

🍴 FLEUR DE SEL *French* $$$

☎ 212-460-9100; www.fleurdeselres taurant.com; 5 E 20th St; 🕑 lunch & dinner; ◉ R, W to 23rd St

With the sea-scented aura of Brittany, where chef Cyril Renaud was born and raised, Fleur de Sel is a sensuous delight. Extensive wine choices and a wide selection of daily, seasonal dishes add depth and originality to the menu. Expect braised rabbit leg, sautéed fluke, almond-crusted halibut and a gorgeous ganache for dessert.

🍴 PURE FOOD & WINE *Raw Food/Vegetarian* $$

☎ 212-477-1010; 54 Irving Pl btwn E 17th & E 18th Sts; 🕑 dinner; ◉ L, N, Q, R, W, 4, 5, 6 to 14th St-Union Sq; 🅥

The 'chef' (there's no oven in the kitchen) at this gem achieves the impossible, churning out delicious, artful concoctions made completely from raw organics. Dishes include tomato-zucchini lasagna (sans cheese and pasta); mushroom, avocado and ginger sushi rolls; and the chanterelle, olive and 'ricotta' ravioli with pistachio oil and macadamia cream sauce. In warmer months, don't miss a chance to settle into a table in the shady, oasis-like backyard.

🍴 TABLA *Indian-American Fusion* $$

☎ 212-889-0667; 11 Madison Ave; 🕑 lunch Mon-Fri, dinner; ◉ R, W 6 to 23rd St; 👶 🅥

At first glance you'll wonder if you're reading the menu wrong – could lobster and *haricot verts* be Indian? Only in the hands of Goa-born and France-raised chef Floyd Cardoz, who masterfully blends American produce with his native staples. If you can't get in to the second-floor Tabla, or you're just in a relaxed mood, stay downstairs at Cardoz' more casual Bread Bar. Order a Tablatini with your tandoori steak and watch the endless parade of street traffic.

DRINK

FLATIRON LOUNGE
☎ 212-727-7741; 37 W 19th St btwn Fifth & Sixth Aves; ⏰ 5pm-2am Sun-Wed, 5pm-4am Thu-Sat; ◉ F, N, R, V, W to 23rd St

A simple nook with a classic vibe, this mahogany bar from 1927 serves up specialty cocktails made with fresh, seasonal ingredients – pomegranate, Granny Smith apples, mint, lychee nuts – in a setting that's historic and retro, decorated with red leather booths and stained-glass lamps. The dramatic entrance, a low-lit archway, only adds to the elegant excitement.

GALLERY AT THE GERSHWIN
☎ 212-447-5700; Gershwin Hotel, 7 E 27th St btwn Fifth & Madison Aves; ⏰ 6pm-midnight daily; ◉ F, N, R, V, W to 23rd St

A convenient perk for those bedding down at this hip, budget hotel, it's a pretty cool destination for anyone, solo travelers especially as it's a sure bet you'll meet other globetrotters here. Either way, stop in and relax on one of the high-backed red banquettes and enjoy the vibe – artistic (huge paintings grace the walls), mellow (lounge DJs set the vibe) and clever, with cocktails named after luminaries from Pablo Neruda to Jean-Michel Basquiat.

PETE'S TAVERN
☎ 212-473-7676; 129 E 18th St at Irving Pl; ⏰ noon-2am; ◉ L, N, Q, R, W, 4, 5, 6 to 14th St-Union Sq

Pete's Tavern

This dark and atmospheric watering hole is a New York classic – all pressed tin and carved wood with an air of literary history. You can get a respectable burger here, and choose from more than 15 draft beers. The crowd draws in everyone from post-theater couples and Irish expats to no-nonsense NYU students.

▼ SAPA
☎ 212-929-1800; 43 W 24th St btwn Fifth & Sixth Aves; 🕑 11:30am-2:30pm and 5:30-11:30pm Mon-Fri, 6pm-midnight Sat, 5:30pm-10:30pm Sun; 🚇 N, R, W, 6 to 23rd St

Thanks to an inspired and modern look by award-winning designers, the stylish bar at this French-Vietnamese eatery has become a Flatiron hotspot, drawing not only local professionals and destination diners, but the occasional clutch of celebs. Enjoy the slim walnut bar, whisper-thin scrims and work-of-art lighting schemes. Cocktails make creative use of mint, mulberry syrup, homemade infusions and all things muddled, though you can also get a quality bottle of beer or glass of wine.

 # PLAY

☆ BOWLMOR LANES
☎ 212-255-8188; www.bowlmor.com; 110 University Pl; per person per game before 5pm/per person per game after 5pm $7.95/8.95; 🕑 11am-6pm all ages, after 6pm 21 & over only; 🚇 any train to Union Sq; 🚻

It will set you back some change, but this is a perfect activity for a rainy day. Bowlmor Lanes has neon pins, lightweight balls for little hands, lots of hip music and, very frequently, celebrity clients. Kids love the whole scene, starting with the elevator ride to get to the 2nd floor lanes.

☆ HAPPY VALLEY
☎ 212-481-2628; 14 E 27th St; admission $20 if not on the list; 🕑 10:30pm-4am Tue, Fri & Sat; 🚇 N, R, W to 23rd St

If you can't get into Tuesday night hotspot Cain (p144), Happy Valley's the next best thing. You may not get in here either, but with three pulsating floors to fill, your chances are better. Come dressed to impress, but remember, this club is anything but staid – it's got go-go dancers, disco balls, mirrored ceilings and an electro-pop sensibility.

⭐ IRVING PLAZA

☎ 212-777-6800; 17 Irving Pl at 15th St; admission $12-35; ⏱ 7pm-midnight Tue-Sat; ⊕ 4, 5, 6, L, N, Q, R, W to 14th St-Union Sq

An old-time hall, Irving Plaza shows run the gamut, from classic hard rock to emo to punk – sometimes in the same night, depending on who's opening for whom. U2, Prince, Rufus Wainwright and others have played here. A nonprofit organization hands out free condoms at the door, and proceeds from ticket sales go toward AIDS initiatives in developing nations.

>MIDTOWN EAST

A fluid space encompassing many worlds, Midtown East has instantly recognizable landmarks – Trump Tower, opulent Fifth Ave and the beautiful stretch of Park Ave that touches the Waldorf Astoria Hotel. It can be overwhelming and crowded, but very exciting. The energy here is classic New York and pretty intoxicating.

Aside from Fifth Ave and the Rockefeller Center, including the Top of the Rock, Midtown East has two good areas for exploring: Little Korea, home to karaoke bars and Korean eateries, and the ritzy Sutton Pl, with homes running parallel to First Ave from 54th to 59th Sts. The views of the Queensboro Bridge and the East River are amazing.

The Theater District overlaps Sixth Ave and a few lone production houses and performance spaces spill onto the streets around 40th St.

MIDTOWN EAST

◎ SEE
Bridgemarket	1	D1
Chrysler Building	2	C4
Empire State Building	3	A6
Grand Central Terminal	4	B4
MoMA	5	A2
New York Public Library	6	A5
Rockefeller Center	7	A3
St Patrick's Cathedral	8	B3
United Nations	9	D4

⌂ SHOP
Barneys	10	B1
Bergdorf Goodman	11	A1
Bloomingdale's	12	C1
Conran Shop	13	D1
FAO Schwarz	14	A1
Ghurka	15	B1
Henri Bendel	16	A2
Jimmy Choo	17	A3
Joon New York	18	B1
Takashimaya	19	A2

🍴 EAT
Al Bustan	20	C3
Alcala	21	C4
BLT Steak	22	B2
Dawat	23	C1
L'Atelier	24	B2

▼ DRINK
Campbell Apartment	25	B4
Ginger Man	26	A5
Manchester Pub	27	C3

★ PLAY
Bryant Park	28	A5
Little Korea	29	A6

👁 SEE

🅢 BRIDGEMARKET
☎ 212-980-2455; 409 E 59th St at First Ave; ⏱ 9am-8pm; ⓢ E, F, 6 to 59th St-Lexington Ave

After decades of restoration, Bridgemarket – the vaulted, Guastavino-tiled space under the 59th St Bridge that served as a farmers market in the early 20th century – was brought back to life in 1999 by design guru Sir Terence Conran. Now it's a thriving retail and dining complex, anchored by the Conran Shop (p162), alive with ingenious modern design accessories, and Guastavino's, a former restaurant (now reserved for private functions) that's worth peeking into.

🅒 CHRYSLER BUILDING
405 Lexington Ave at 42nd St; ⏱ lobby 9am-7pm; ⓢ any train to 42nd St-Grand Central Terminal

Feast your eyes on the gorgeous silver spire that most New Yorkers identify as their favorite city symbol. No observation deck here, but the iconic Chrysler Building's art deco lobby and chic wood elevators are sights unto themselves.

🅔 EMPIRE STATE BUILDING
☎ 212-736-3100; www.esbnyc.com; 350 Fifth Ave at 34th St; over 18 yr/under 18

yr $18/16 ⏱ 9:30am-midnight; ⓢ B, D, F, N, Q, R, V, W to 34th St-Herald Sq

Since 1976 the building's top 30 floors have been floodlit in seasonal and holiday colors (eg green for St Patrick's Day in March, black for World AIDS Day on December 1, red and green for Christmas, lavender for Gay Pride weekend in June; visit the website for each day's lighting scheme and meaning). The views from the 102nd-floor Observatory Deck are best at sunset.

🅒 GRAND CENTRAL TERMINAL
☎ 212-340-2210; www.grandcentralterminal.com; Park Ave at 42nd St; ⏱ 5:30am-1:30am; ⓢ any train to 42nd St-Grand Central Terminal

The world's largest and busiest train station (76 acres; 500,000 commuters and subway riders daily) is also a gorgeous feat of engineering and architecture. Take in the theatrical beaux art facade from E 42nd St, particularly luminous at night, and then head inside to marvel at gold-veined marble arches and the bright blue domed ceiling, decorated with twinkling fiber-optic constellations. Don't miss the tiny unrenovated corner of the original ceiling, left alone to acknowledge the size of the job. For a glimpse of how the unfinished ceiling looks underneath all the celestial glitter, find the northwest corner amid the 88,000-sq-ft ceiling, at the very end of the meridian line, and you'll see a small black patch that designers deliberately left there for contrast.

MOMA
☎ 212-708-9400; www.moma.org; 11 W 53rd St btwn Fifth & Sixth Aves; adult/student $20/16, 4-8pm Fri free; ☽ 10:30am-5:30pm Sat-Mon & Wed-Thu, 10:30am-8pm Fri
Its grand reopening in 2004, following the most extensive renovation project in its 75-year history, created a veritable art universe of more than 100,000 pieces. You could easily hole up

for a couple of days and still not properly see it all. Most of the big hitters – Matisse, Picasso, Cézanne, Rothko, Pollock – are housed in the central five-story atrium, where peaceful, airy galleries contain works from the departments of Painting and Sculpture, Architecture and Design, Drawings, Prints and Illustrated Books, and Film and Media. The museum's sculpture garden – returned to its original, larger vision of the early '50s by Philip Johnson – is a joy to sit in.

NEW YORK PUBLIC LIBRARY
☎ 212-930-0800; www.nypl.org; Fifth Ave at 42nd St; ☽ 11am-7:30pm Tue-

NEIGHBORHOODS

MIDTOWN EAST

Wed, 10am-6pm Thu-Sat; 🚇 any train to Grand Central Station or 42nd St-Times Sq; ♿

Wave hello to Patience and Fortitude, the two great lions who greet you as you walk up the steps of the white marble beaux arts New York Public Library. Filled with books, it also has architectural delights such as curved bay windows, molded ceilings, ancient staircases and more. The NYPL has frequent exhibits of rare or out-of-print books that attract bibliophiles from around the world.

🄶 ROCKEFELLER CENTER

☎ 212-632-3975; www.rockefeller center.com; btwn Fifth & Sixth Aves & 48th & 51st Sts; 🕐 24hr, times vary for individual stores; 🚇 B, D, F, V to 47th-50th Sts-Rockefeller Center

Built in the 1930s, during the height of the Great Depression in the United States, the 22-acre center gave jobs to 70,000 workers over nine years. Rockefeller Center was also the first project to combine retail, entertainment and office space in what is often referred to as a 'city within a city.' The biggest news here as of late has been the late-2005 reopening of the long-shuttered Top of the Rock (p12) observation deck, which affords stunning views of the city.

ST PATRICK'S CATHEDRAL

☎ 212-753-2261; www.ny-archdiocese
.org/pastoral/cathedral_about.html;
Fifth Ave btwn 50th & 51st Sts; 🕐 7am-
8:45pm; 🚇 V to Fifth Ave-53rd St, 4, 6 to
53rd St-Lexington Ave; 🚹

Check out the 330 ft spires that
dwarf everything in the Midtown
neighborhood surrounding St
Patrick's, including nearby Rockefeller Center. This graceful cathedral, done in Gothic Revival style,
is the seat of New York's Roman
Catholic Archdiocese, and is used
for every major city ceremony.

UNITED NATIONS

☎ 212-963-8687; www.un.org; 46th St
& First Ave; 🕐 free tours every 20min
from 9:45am-4:45pm, for tours in other
languages call the number above; 🚇 any
train to 42nd St-Grand Central Station; 🚹

Enjoy the aura of international in-
trigue as you stride the East River
promenade and stare up at the
green-glass Le Corbusier buildings
built in 1953. A tour inside is even
better – a thousand languages
and everyone talking at once.

SHOP

BARNEYS

☎ 212-826-8900; www.barneys.com;
660 Madison Ave; 🕐 10am-8pm Mon-Fri,
10am-7pm Sat, 11am-6pm Sun; 🚇 N, R,
W to Fifth Ave-59th St

No true shopper could skip a visit
to this revered institution. The best
department store in town carries
the best of today's designers – Marc
Jacobs, Miu Miu, Prada and more.
Bargains (comparatively speaking)
are on the 7th and 8th floors; or try
the Co-Op Barneys on the Upper
West Side, in Soho and Chelsea.

BERGDORF GOODMAN

☎ 212-753-7300; www.bergdorfgood
man.com; 754 Fifth Ave; 🕐 10am-7pm
Mon-Wed & Fri, 10am-8pm Thu, noon-
8pm Sun; 🚇 N, R, W to Fifth Ave, F to
57th St

There's no experience akin to stepping into the otherworldly Bergdorf's. Fabulous collections for women – Pucci, Moschino, Dolce & Gabbana – and separate floors for jewels, fragrance, handbags, menswear, shoes and more give you room to browse unhurriedly.

BLOOMINGDALE'S
☎ 212-705-2000; www.bloomingdales.com; 1000 Third Ave at 59th St; 10am-8:30pm Mon-Thu, 9am-10pm Fri & Sat, 11am-7pm Sun; ④ 4, 5, 6 to 59th St, N, R, W to Lexington Ave-59th St
It's big and brash and full of attitude – beloved Bloomie's is where New Yorkers go to get a major shopping fix. While the store carries plenty of high-end names, it also likes to bring in new designers and right-off-the-runway collections that won't break the bank.

CONRAN SHOP
☎ 212-755-9079; 407 E 59th St at First Ave; 11am-8pm Mon-Fri, 10am-7pm Sat, noon-6pm Sun; ④ 4, 5, 6 to 59th St
Find slick kitchenware and tableware, linens, furniture and home accessories at this sleek emporium, nestled in a marvelous space under the Queensboro Bridge, from British design king Terence Conran. Browse through streamlined sofas, Missoni china, Ducati pens, retro Jacob Jensen alarm clocks, Rob Brandt tumblers,

Mandarina Duck luggage, Lucite photo frames and much more.

FAO SCHWARZ
☎ 212-644-9400; 767 Fifth Ave; noon-7pm Mon-Wed, to 8pm Thu-Sat, 11am-6pm Sun; ④ 4, 5, 6 to 59th St, N, R, W to Fifth Ave-59th St
The toy-store giant, where Tom Hanks played footsie piano in the movie *Big*, is number one on the NYC wish list of most visiting kids. Why not indulge them? The magical (over-the-top consumerist) wonderland, with dolls up for 'adoption,' life-size stuffed animals, gas-powered kiddie convertibles, air-hockey sets and much more, might even thrill you, too.

GHURKA
☎ 212-826-8300; www.ghurka.com; 683 Madison Ave; 10am-6pm Mon-Wed, Fri & Sat, 10am-7pm Thu, noon-5pm Sun; ④ 4, 5, 6 to 59th St
Take the hassle out of buying luggage with a visit to this specialty store that crafts carry-on and full-sized bags out of high-quality leather and other materials. Most bags also have nifty rollers that pop out of nowhere and other thoughtful additions that make organizing a breeze.

HENRI BENDEL
☎ 212-247-1100; www.henribendel.com; 712 Fifth Ave; 10am-7pm Mon-

Wed & Fri-Sun, 10am-8pm Thu; ⊕ E,
V to Fifth Ave-53rd St, N, R, W to Fifth
Ave-59th St

The lovely Lalique windows in
Henri Bendel frame its quaint little
tearoom perfectly; it makes you feel
like you're shopping in someone's
home. Wandering about the Fifth
Ave townhouse is a treat – avant-
garde European collections and
classics like Chanel sit side by side.

⬚ JIMMY CHOO

☎ 212-593-0800; www.jimmychoo.com;
645 Fifth Ave; ⏰ 10am-6pm Mon-Sat,
noon-5pm Sun; ⊕ E, V to Fifth Ave-53rd
St, 6 to 51st St

To understand the appeal of
Jimmy Choo, you've got to like sky-
high heels (even the sandals have
stilettos). You can find thick leather
boots, closed-toe pumps and
ethereal, flirty sling backs in satin
or leather at this uptown store.

⬚ JOON NEW YORK

☎ 212-935-1007; www.joon.com; 795
Lexington Ave; ⏰ 9:30am-6:30pm Mon-
Fri, 10am-6pm Sat; ⊕ 4, 5, 6 to 59th St

Blotch-free pens from Cartier, Mont-
blanc, Namiki and Carter are the
bread-and-butter of this long-time
local chain, with shops in Trump
Tower and Grand Central Station.

⬚ TAKASHIMAYA

☎ 212-350-0100; www.nytakashimaya
.com; 693 Fifth Ave; ⏰ 10am-7pm

MALL OF MANHATTAN

The closest thing to a big suburban
mall in this town is the **Time Warner
Center** (p172; ☎ 212-823-6300;
www.shopsatcolumbuscircle.com)
at Columbus Circle. The first few floors
of the massive building contain largely
upscale shops, including Williams-
Sonoma, Coach, Hugo Boss, Sephora,
Armani Exchange and Thomas Pink.
You can also take care of more mundane needs in the Whole Foods grocery in the basement; the café inside
is a popular place to come down off a
shopping high.

Mon-Sat, noon-5pm Sun; ⊕ E, V to Fifth
Ave-53rd St

Forty-two types of tea are sold
at the refreshing Tea Box café in
the basement of this stunner of
a store. Each of its seven stories
has something different, from
beauty products and a day spa
(top floor), to clothes, accessories,
home design and floral bouquets
(bottom floor).

🍴 EAT

🍴 AL BUSTAN

Lebanese/Middle Eastern $$

☎ 212-759-5933; 827 Third Ave;
⏰ lunch & dinner; ⊕ 6 to 51st St, E, V
to Lexington Av-53rd St; ♿ Ⓥ ☻

Al Bustan does a brisk trade in
delicious hummus and baba
ganoush, as well as *moudardarah*

(green lentils and rice pilaf), grilled lamb chops, ovals of ground beef stuffed with cracked wheat that are deep-fried, and other Middle Eastern fare. Its meze – the best way for a group to eat – is one of the most succulent in the city.

🍴 ALCALA
Spanish/Basque $$$
☎ 212-370-1866; 342 E 46th St; 🕒 lunch & dinner Mon-Fri, dinner Sat-Sun; 🚇 S, 4, 5, 6, 7 to 42nd St-Grand Central; 🚻 ♿
A well-kept secret near the UN; you won't find a quieter backyard anywhere. It'd be a shame not to try the excellent Basque wines – they go so well with dishes like salted codfish salad with black olives, baby squid, meat cannelloni with truffle and béchamel sauce, and the obligatory seafood paella.

🍴 BLT STEAK
Steakhouse/American $$$
☎ 212-752-7470; www.bltsteak.com; 106 E 57th St; 🕒 lunch & dinner Mon-Sat; 🚇 4, 5, 6 to 59th St, N, R, W to Fifth Av-59th St; ♿
Any steakhouse that sets aside part of its menu just for mushrooms has a lot more going for it than meat – BLT pays as much attention to its sides as it does the main attraction. The bar is a buzzy, playful place, and the warmly hued restaurant very

relaxing; perfect to digest your slab of porterhouse or big Kobe burger.

🍴 DAWAT *Indian* $$
☎ 212-355-7555; 210 E 58th St btwn Second & Third Aves; 🕒 dinner daily, lunch Mon-Sat; 🚇 N, R, W to Lexington Ave-59th St; ♿ V 🚻
Famed chef, cookbook author and actress Madhur Jaffrey runs this outpost of Nirvana, transforming Indian favorites, including spinach *bhajia* (fritter) and fish curries, into exotic masterpieces served with fancy flourishes. Sea bass and lamb chops get royal treatments with marinades made of various blends of yogurt, mustard seeds, saffron and ginger, and charming, ardamom-flecked desserts cool your palate. The dining room is formal and subdued and the crowd is a bit on the stuffy side (it comes with the territory in this part of town), but none of it'll matter after your first bite of heaven.

🍴 L'ATELIER DE JOEL ROBUCHON
Japanese/Sushi, French $$$
☎ 212-350-6658; 57 E 57th St near Park Ave; 🕒 11:30am-2pm & 6-11pm; 🚇 4, 5, 6 to 59th St; V
If you've eaten at any of Robuchon's celebrated restaurants in Paris, Tokyo, London or Las Vegas,

Reuven Blau,
Brooklyn, Journalism student at Columbia University

Have you had any 'only in New York' moments? I was checking out the site of an independent band I'd discovered and realized they had a gig scheduled in Manhattan later that night. I bought tickets and caught an amazing concert at a great local place in the Village. **How has New York changed in the past five years?** It's become increasingly difficult for middle-class residents to find affordable housing. **Any guilty NYC pleasures?** I love people-watching at restaurants and busy locations. **What's a tourist trap worth the trip?** The View Restaurant and Lounge at the New York Marriott Marquis, Times Sq. **Where can you get affordable food between classes?** I keep kosher, so it's not easy. When I have time, I make a run to H&H Bagels on 81st St. They're the best in the city, cheap and kosher!

NEIGHBORHOODS

MIDTOWN EAST

you know what to expect – a smorgasbord of flavors in tiny bites. Taking small plates and *omakase* (chef's choice) to a whole new level, L'Atelier's frog-legs croquettes, hangar steak, caramelized free-range quail stuffed with foie gras and served with potato puree, and litchi desserts are divine. Sit at the counter, if you can.

DRINK

CAMPBELL APARTMENT
☎ 212-953-0409; 15 Vanderbilt Ave at 43rd St; ⏰ 3pm-1am Mon-Sat, 3-11pm Sun; ⊕ S, 4, 5, 6, 7 to Grand Central
Take the lift beside the Oyster Bar, or the stairs to the West Balcony, and head out the doors to the left to reach this sublime cocktail spot. This used to be the apartment of a landed railroad magnate and has the velvet, mahogany and murals to prove it. Cigars are welcome, but sneakers and jeans are not. The Apartment is a great way to enjoy the grandeur of the train station, martini in hand.

GINGER MAN
☎ 212-532-3740; 11 E 36th St; ⏰ 11:30am-2am Mon-Wed, 11:30am-4am Thu & Fri, 12:30pm-4am Sat, 3pm-midnight Sun; ⊕ 6 to 33rd St
The most exciting watering hole to hit Midtown in a while, this high-ceilinged, handsome pub is heaven to those who take their

suds seriously. Based in Texas (with three locations in that state and just one in these parts), Ginger Man will thrill beer connoisseurs, as it's got an extensive selection of global bottles and drafts, not to mention a range of scotches, wines and even cigars. The pub fare – Guinness beef stew or bratwurst sandwiches – is serious, too.

MANCHESTER PUB
☎ 212-935-8901; 920 Second Ave at 49th St; ⏰ 11am-4am; ⊕ E, V, 6 to Lexington Ave-53rd St
Thirsty for a taste of England? Head to this popular, cozy pub then, where you'll find solid pub grub, icy pints (Guinness included, natch) and a really cool internet jukebox that lets you download any song you fancy. Get here early, though, as local fans mob the place by 9pm.

PLAY

BRYANT PARK
☎ 212-768-4242; www.bryantpark.org; Sixth Ave btwn E 40th & 42nd Sts; ⏰ 7am-11pm Mon-Fri, 7am-8pm Sat & Sun in summer, 7am-7pm Jan-Apr & Sep-Dec; ⊕ F, V, B, D to 42nd St-Bryant Park, 7 to Fifth Ave; ♿
Fashion Week, free films, Latin dancing, concerts and Broadway shows (plus ice-skating in winter): there's always something going on in this grassy haven behind the New York Public Library. With

free wi-fi and a cute coffee bar, it's everyone's favorite satellite office. Come early for free films in summer – blankets suggested.

⭐ LITTLE KOREA
Broadway & Fifth Ave & 31st & 36th Sts; Ⓢ B, D, F, N, Q, R, V, W to 34th St-Herald Sq
Herald Sq is a bit on the tasteless side when it comes to finding foodie treats; luckily, you can head for quality refueling at nearby Little Korea, a small enclave of Korean-owned restaurants, shops, salons and spas. Over the past few years this neighborhood has seen an explosion of eateries serving Korean fare, with authentic Korean BBQ available around the clock at many of the all-night spots on 32nd St, some with the added treat of karaoke.

>MIDTOWN WEST

Referring to a collection of neighborhoods including the far-west reaches of Hell's Kitchen, and the office-worker crush of food carts and harried suit-wearers along Sixth Ave and Columbus Circle, Midtown West is a cornucopia of tempos and options.

You'll find Brazilian BBQ and hear Portuguese conversation and samba music in Little Brazil. Or, head to the frenzied Diamond District, packed with newly engaged couples shopping for rings and a slew of folks in the biz buying wholesale. Then there's the famed Garment District, home to designers' offices, and wholesale and retail shops. Visit the Fashion Center information kiosk for maps and details. The tip of this area is Columbus Circle, the gateway to both the Upper West Side and Central Park, and home to the gleaming Time Warner Center.

MIDTOWN WEST

👁 SEE

International Center of Photography	**1**	C4
Museum of Television & Radio	**2**	D2
Times Square	**3**	C3

📷 SHOP

B & H Photo-Video	**4**	A6
Colony	**5**	C3
Drama Bookshop	**6**	B5
Gotham Book Mart	**7**	D4
Macy's	**8**	C6
Manny's Music	**9**	C3
Rizzoli's	**10**	D1
Time Warner Center	**11**	B1
Wear Me Out	**12**	B4

🍴 EAT

Burger Joint	**13**	C1
Cho Dang Goi	**14**	D6
DB Bistro Moderne	**15**	C4
Eatery	**16**	A2
Market Café	**17**	A5
Taboon	**18**	A2
Town	**19**	D2
Virgil's Real Barbecue	**20**	B4

🍸 DRINK

Ava Lounge	**21**	C2
Bellevue Bar	**22**	A5
Morrell Wine Bar & Café	**23**	D3
Single Room Occupancy	**24**	B2

⭐ PLAY

Ambassador Theater	**25**	B3
Biltmore Theater	**26**	B3
Birdland	**27**	B4
City Center	**28**	C2
Loews 42nd St - E Walk Theater	**29**	B4
Majestic Theater	**30**	B4
New Amsterdam Theater	**31**	C5
New Victory Theater	**32**	B4
The Oak Room	**33**	D4
Town Hall	**34**	C4

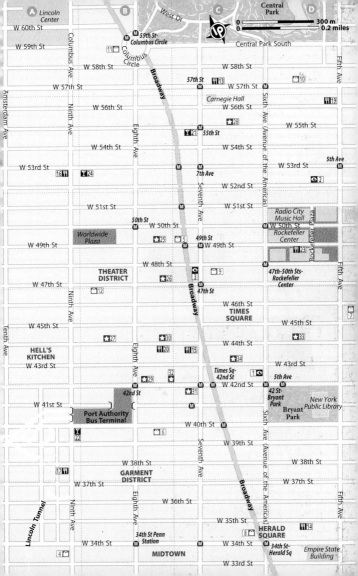

A Lincoln Center

West Dr

B

Central Park

C

D

W 60th St

W 59th St

59th St-
Columbus Circle

11

Columbus Circle

W 58th St

Central Park South

W 58th St

10

W 57th St

57th St

13

W 57th St

Carnegie Hall

Columbus Ave

W 56th St

W 56th St

19

Ninth Ave

Amsterdam Ave

W 55th St

28

W 55th St

21 55th St

W 54th St

W 54th St

Eighth Ave

W 53rd St

16

24

7th Ave

W 53rd St

5th Ave

2

W 52nd St

W 51st St

W 51st St

Radio City
Music Hall

50th St

W 50th St

25 5

49th St

Worldwide
Plaza

W 49th St

W 49th St

23

Rockefeller
Center

Rockefeller Plaza

Seventh Ave

THEATER
DISTRICT

W 48th St

3

9

47th-50th Sts-
Rockefeller
Center

W 47th St

26

Broadway

47th St

W 47th St

12

W 46th St

TIMES
SQUARE

7

W 45th St

W 45th St

33

HELL'S
KITCHEN

27

30

W 44th St

20 15

34

W 43rd St

W 43rd St

Tenth Ave

29

32

Times Sq-
42nd St

1

5th Ave

42nd St

31

W 42nd St

42 St-
Bryant
Park

New York
Public Library

W 41st St

Port Authority
Bus Terminal

Bryant
Park

Sixth Ave (Avenue of the Americas)

W 40th St

6

W 39th St

W 39th St

22

W 38th St

W 38th St

17

GARMENT
DISTRICT

W 37th St

W 37th St

W 36th St

W 36th St

Lincoln Tunnel

Ninth Ave

Eighth Ave

W 35th St

W 35th St

34th St Penn
Station

8

HERALD
SQUARE

14

4

W 34th St

MIDTOWN

W 34th St

34th St-
Herald Sq

Empire State
Building

W 33rd St

Fifth Ave

0   300 m
0   0.2 miles

◉ SEE

◉ HERALD SQUARE

◉ B, D, F, N, Q, R, V, W to 34th St-Herald Sq

This crowded convergence of Broadway, Sixth Ave and 34th St is best known as the home of Macy's department store (p172), where you can still ride some of the remaining original wooden elevators. The busy square gets its name from a long-defunct newspaper, the *Herald*, and the small, leafy park here bustles during business hours thanks to a recent and much-needed face-lift. Don't bother with the two indoor malls south of Macy's on Sixth Ave, where you'll find a boring and suburban array of chain stores (with the exception of Daffy's, which offers great discounts on big labels).

◉ INTERNATIONAL CENTER OF PHOTOGRAPHY

☎ 212-857-0000; www.icp.org; 1133 Sixth Ave at 43rd St; admission $10, voluntary contributions from 5-8pm Friday ; ◷ 10am-6pm Tue-Thu, Sat & Sun, 10am-8pm Fri; ◉ B, D, F, V to 42nd St-Bryant Park

Past exhibitions have included work by Henri Cartier-Bresson, Man Ray, Matthew Brady, Weegee and Robert Capa, and have explored a wide range of themes through

creative shows such as the recent *Che! Revolution and Commerce* and *The Body at Risk: Photography of Disorder, Illness and Healing*. It's also a photography school, offering coursework for credit as well as a public-lecture series. Its gift shop is an excellent place to stock up on quality photo books or quirky, photo-themed gifts.

MUSEUM OF TELEVISION & RADIO

☎ 212-621-6800; www.mtr.org; 25 W 52nd St; adult/child under 14 yr/senior & student/$10/free/$8; ☽ noon-6pm Tue-Sun; ⊙ E, V to Fifth Ave, 53 St, N, R, W to 49 St & Seventh Ave, 1 to 50 St & Broadway, B, D, F, or V to 47th-50th Sts-Rockefeller Center; ⛪

If you've been saying that *Star Trek* merits its own retrospective, someone's finally listened to you. This museum is dedicated to small screen scenes and classic radio moments, and if Bob Hope and Lucille Ball aren't enough to bring you in, there's plenty of Spock and Captain Kirk.

RADIO CITY MUSIC HALL

☎ 212-247-4777; www.radiocity.com; 51st St at Sixth Ave; admission to hall free, shows $15-40; ⊙ B, D, F, V to 47th-50th Sts-Rockefeller Center

This 6000-seat art deco movie palace had a triumphant restoration, returning the velvet seats and furnishings to their original

1932 state. Concerts here sell out quickly, and tickets to the annual Christmas spectacular featuring the hokey but enjoyable Rockette dancers now cost up to $70. You can see the interior by taking a tour, which leaves every half-hour between 11am and 3pm Monday to Sunday. Tickets are sold on a first-come, first-served basis.

SHOP

B & H PHOTO-VIDEO

☎ 212-502-6200; www.bhphotovideo .com; 420 Ninth Ave; ☽ 9am-7pm Mon-Thu, 9am-1pm Fri, 10am-5pm Sun; ⊙ A, C, E to 34th St-Penn Station

A trip here is an experience unto itself – it's big, buzzy and bristling with every piece of camera, video or DVD equipment you could ever want.

COLONY

☎ 212-265-2050; www.colonymusic .com; 1619 Broadway; ☽ 9:30am-midnight Mon-Sat, 10am-midnight Sun; ⊙ R, W to 49th St

Do you dream of hearing Frank Sinatra sing live? Well, that's not going to happen, but you can buy a real ticket to one of Old Blue Eyes' shows here – the rock memorabilia and posters round out what could be the world's largest collection of sheet music anywhere. Charlie Parker and Miles Davis used to shop here, as did the Beatles.

🎭 DRAMA BOOKSHOP
☎ 212-944-0595; www.dramabook
shop.com; 250 W 40th St; ⏲ 10am-8pm
Mon-Sat, noon-6pm Sun; Ⓜ A, C, E to
42nd St-Port Authority Bus Terminal
Broadway fans will find treasures
in print at this expansive bookstore, which has taken its theater
(plays and musicals) seriously
since 1917. Staffers are good at
recommending worthy selections. Check out the website for
regular events, such as talks with
playwrights.

📖 GOTHAM BOOK MART
☎ 212-719-4448; 16 E 46th St btwn Fifth
& Madison Aves; ⏲ 9:30am-6:30pm
Mon-Fri, 9:30am-6pm Sat; Ⓜ B, D, F, V
to 47th-50th Sts-Rockefeller Center
Overflowing with choice lit since
1920, the Gotham Book Mart is
just how a bookstore is meant to
be. It's historic, too (despite having
recently moved a block from its
original location). Frances Stelof
(who died in 1989) founded the
James Joyce Society here in 1947,
and snuck some of his books, and
other naughty ones such as Henry
Miller's *Tropic of Cancer,* past US
obscenity laws.

🏬 MACY'S
☎ 212-695-4400; www.macys.com;
151 W 34th St at Broadway; ⏲ 10am-
8:30pm Mon-Sat, 11am-7pm Sun; Ⓜ B,
D, F, N, Q, R, V, W to 34th St-Herald Sq

Mind your fingers on the old
wooden elevators, a highlight of
a Macy's trip. The store's goods,
mainly linens, clothing, furniture,
kitchenware, shoes and more, are
affordable and basic. You can lose
yourself for hours here, the world's
largest department store.

🎸 MANNY'S MUSIC
☎ 212-819-0576; www.mannysmusic
.com; 156 W 48th St; ⏲ 10am-7pm Mon-
Sat, noon-6pm Sun; Ⓜ N, R, W to 49th St
Manny's sells musical instruments,
not music, but if you take your
licks seriously you'll want to see
where Jimi Hendrix had his (right-
handed) Stratocasters re-strung.
Everyone from Dizzy Gillespie to
the Beatles shopped here, leaving
behind pictures to prove it.

📕 RIZZOLI'S
☎ 212-759-2424; 31 W 57th St;
⏲ 10am-7:30pm Mon-Fri, 10:30am-7pm
Sat, 11am-7pm Sun; Ⓜ F to 57th St
This handsome store of the Italian
bookstore and publisher sells
great art, architecture and design
books (as well as general-interest
titles). There's also a good collection of foreign newspapers and
magazines onsite.

🏢 TIME WARNER CENTER
☎ 212-484-8000; www.timewarner
.com; 1 Time Warner Center; Ⓜ A, B, C,
D, 1 to 59th St-Columbus Circle; ♿

Shop 'til you drop in Manhattan's glossy urban mall, built to look like a glass-covered mountain and home to more than 40 stores, an organic market, a couple of clubs and theaters, as well as tony residences and $500-a-meal restaurants (p204).

☐ WEAR ME OUT
☎ 212-333-3047; 358 W 47th St btwn Eighth & Ninth Aves; 🕑 11:30am-8pm; ◉ C, E to 50th St

A fun little boutique for 'Hellsea boys' needing the perfect outfit to wear to Roxy (p145) this weekend, Wear Me Out is a friendly place that's great for picking up a pec-promoting tight tee, a pair of sexy Energie jeans, provocative undies and various types of jewelry. The fun, flirtatious staff is full of encouragement, too.

🍴 EAT
🍴 BURGER JOINT Burgers $
☎ 212-708-7414; Le Parker Meridien, 118 W 57th St; 🕑 lunch & dinner; ◉ F, N, Q, R, W to 57th St; 🚻 🚼

Like the name says, this joint serves one thing, and one thing only. Well, you can get fries and a shake with your order, but burgers are the specialty of the house. They're juicy, tender and just the right size. It's hard to find Burger Joint – you have to enter

Le Parker Meridien hotel and ask around. Moving from the stylized lobby to this greasy spoonish place adds another dimension to its charm.

🍴 CHO DANG GOI *Korean* $$
☎ 212-695-8222; 55 W 35th St; 🕑 lunch & dinner; 🚇 B, D, F, N, Q, R, W to 34th St-Herald Sq; Ⓥ 🏃

Right in the heart of Koreatown, Cho Dang Goi does a brisk business in traditional *bibimbops* (vegetables with rice and spicy sauce), sticky-rice dishes and pork stews, which are all among the best in the area. You'll also get tiny plates of kimchi surprises (including a pile of teensy dried fish, eyes intact) right before your meal begins.

🍴 DB BISTRO MODERNE
French $$$
☎ 212-391-2400; 55 W 44th St; 🕑 lunch & dinner Mon-Sat, closed Sat lunch in summer; 🚇 any train to 42nd St; 🏃

A sophisticated standout in neon-filled Times Sq, sleek and modern DB Moderne saves its flashiness for the food – chilled fennel velouté, bacon-veiled salmon, snail fricassee, coq au vin and of course, the DB Burger, stuffed with truffles, foie gras and braised short ribs.

🍴 EATERY *American* $
☎ 212-765-7080; www.eaterynyc.com; 798 Ninth Ave at 53rd St; 🕑 lunch &

dinner; 🚇 C, E at 50th St, 1, A, B, C, D at 59th St-Columbus Circle; 🏃 Ⓥ 🏃

Come and hang out at the bar, even if you don't feel like eating – you'll have a really hard time not ordering something as soon as the plates of edamame, ginger calamari, black mussels in curry broth and big juicy burgers start coming by. Maybe if you try to fix your attention on the DJ spinning cool tunes in the corner, you can resist the amazing food – but why try?

🍴 MARKET CAFÉ
American/French $-$$
☎ 212-564-7350; 496 Ninth Ave; 🕑 lunch & dinner Mon-Sat; 🚇 A, C, E to 34th St; 🏃

An oldie but a goodie, Market Café is still a favorite local choice for the far West Side. Its plain Formica tables and plastic booths don't exactly scream high-end, but stick around for the warm service, cool music and grilled gravlax, Atlantic cod, steak frites and pizzas and you'll see why it's a hipster hangout.

🍴 TABOON *Middle Eastern/ Mediterranean* $$
☎ 212-713-0271; 773 Tenth Ave; 🕑 dinner; 🚇 C, E at 50th St; 🏃 Ⓥ 🏃

A white-domed oven grabs the eye as you enter this airy, stone-floored and brick-walled eatery, and if you watch it carefully, you'll see some crisp, sage-rubbed bread taken out and brought to your table as you're seated. The food is a fusion from both sides of the Mediterranean: shrimp in shredded pastry, haloumi salad, lamb kabobs, various grilled fish dishes and lots of variations on hummus. Live flamenco Monday nights.

🍴 TOWN
American/French $$$$
☎ 212-582-4445; www.townrestaurant .com; 15 W 56th St; breakfast, lunch & dinner; F at 57th St, E, V at Fifth Ave-53rd St, N, R, W at Fifth Av-59th St; &
There are just so many choices at Town! Start your day with creamy eggs benedict, balanced with wobbly perfection on lobster hash, or drop in for a midday snack of diver scallops with sausage and ginger lettuce. And then there's dinner – quail with citrus arugula and foie gras fritters, duck steak with endive and soba buckwheat pilaf, a bounty of rich risottos, for dessert beautiful chocolate beignets.

🍴 VIRGIL'S REAL BARBECUE
American BBQ $$
☎ 212-921-9494; 152 W 44th St btwn Broadway & Eighth Ave; lunch & dinner; N, R, S, W, 1, 2, 3, 7 to Times Sq-42nd St
Rather than specializing in one specific style of BBQ (styles vary in sauce type and meat base throughout the US), Virgil's celebrates them all. Menu items cover the entire BBQ map, with Oklahoma State Fair corndogs, pulled Carolina pork and smoked Maryland ham sandwiches, and platters of sliced Texas beef brisket and Georgia chicken-fried steak. Meats are smoked with a combo of hickory, oak and fruitwoods, keepin' it all real.

SWING 46
A former Hell's Kitchen speakeasy, **Swing 46** (☎ 212-262-9554; www.swing46.com; 349 W 46th St; cover $10; noon-midnight daily; any train to 42nd St-Times Sq; & &) occupies a special place in the heart of many a Broadway hoofer. Its pleasantly shabby rooms are thrown open every night for free dance lessons – swing, Latin, tap and more – with live music from local bands and often a surprise dance performance by a celebrity drop in. Sundays from 1-5pm are a family favorite; tap aficionados from the city and beyond show up and let it rip. Former luminaries like Jimmy Slyde host, sometimes aided by the divine Savion Glover.

V

NEIGHBORHOODS

MIDTOWN WEST

♚ DRINK

♙ AVA LOUNGE

☎ 212-956-7020; Majestic Hotel, 210 W 55th St btwn Seventh Ave & Broadway; ⏱ 6pm-2am Sun, 5pm-2am Mon-Tue, 5pm-3am Wed, 5pm-4am Thu-Fri, 6pm-4am Sat; Ⓜ N, Q, R, W to 57th St

The modern, palm-studded rooftop lounge of the Majestic Hotel is a high-up Midtown gem, bringing pleasure and joy to balmy nights in the city with its stellar views of the sparkling skyline around you. Once inside the lounge, sink into a sumptuous ottoman and enjoy the retro-modern, honey-hued decor and stylish crowd. It's oh so South Beach, right in NYC.

♙ BELLEVUE BAR

538 Ninth Ave; ⏱ 11am-4am; Ⓜ A, C, E at 42nd St-Port Authority Bus Terminal, 1, 2, 3, 7, N, Q, R, S, W to Times Sq-42nd St, B, D, F, V to 42nd St-Bryant Park; ♿

It ain't pretty, but the Bellevue Bar sure is fun! Despite being something of a local dive, Bellevue is one of the most popular places in this rapidly-gentrifying neighborhood – could be the blues music on Mondays, $1 sandwiches, daily 11am-to-7pm two-for-one happy hour and $3 margaritas, or the interesting mix of youngish newcomers and graybeard Hell's Kitchen residents.

♙ MORRELL WINE BAR & CAFÉ

☎ 212-262-7700; 1 Rockefeller Plaza, W 47th St btwn Fifth & Sixth Aves; ⏱ 11:30am-11pm Mon-Sat, noon-6pm Sun; Ⓜ B, D, F, V 49th-50th Sts-Rockefeller Center

This mega grape-geeks' haven was one of the pioneers of the wine-bar craze that swept through NYC. There are over 2000 bottles of wine to choose from, and there are a whopping 150 wines available by the glass. The airy, split-level room, right across from the famous skating rink at Rockefeller Center, is as lovely as the vino.

♙ SINGLE ROOM OCCUPANCY

☎ 212-765-6299; 360 W 53rd St btwn Eighth & Ninth Aves; ⏱ 7:30pm-4am Mon-Sat, closed Sun; Ⓜ C, E to 50th St

Just one of a growing number of places that make you do a bit of work to get in – here you have to know to ring the doorbell – SRO is one spot that's worth it. It's got a speakeasy vibe in the air, and a nice selection of wine and beer on the menu. But, it's very small and kind of cave-like, so claustrophobic tipplers best not apply. Most others should find it titillating.

PLAY

⭐ AMBASSADOR THEATER

☎ ticket inquiries 800-927-2770, ext 4148; www.ambassadortheater.com; 219 W 49th St; 🚇 C, E to 50th St; ♿ 🚻
Classically horseshoe shaped, the Ambassador's one of the most intimate large-sized venues on Broadway. If you're in town while *Chicago* is still playing, you'll feel every kick and hear every note Roxie Hart hits, even if you're in the cheap seats in the back.

⭐ BILTMORE THEATER

☎ 212-399-3000; biltmoretheater.net; 261 W 47th St; 🚇 1 at 50th St, C, E at 50th St; ♿ 🚻
Pockmarked in the 1980s by arson and vandalism, the once-grand Biltmore seemed destined for the wrecking ball, despite its landmarked interior. A face-lift and fresh infusion of cash revived it in the 1990s, and now it's one of the premiere theaters on Broadway. Home to the Manhattan Theater Club, it covers American and European works.

⭐ BIRDLAND

☎ 212-581-3080; www.birdlandjazz .com; 315 W 44th St; admission $10-40; 🚇 A, C, E to 42nd St-Port Authority
Named for Charlie Parker, or 'Bird,' this jazz club has been turning out big-name acts since 1949 when Thelonious Monk, Miles Davis, Stan Getz and others made music and cut records in front of a live audience. Today you're likely to catch big names from European festivals, like Montreux, North Sea Jazz, and other up-and-coming local talent. Regular performers include the Chico O'Farrill Afro-Cuban Jazz Big Band, Barry Harris and David Berger's Sultans of Swing.

⭐ CITY CENTER

☎ 212-581-1212; www.citycenter.org; 131 W 55th St; 🚇 N, Q, R, W to 57th St; ♿ 🚻
This red-domed wonder almost went the way of the wrecking ball in 1943, but was saved by preservationists, only to face extinction again when its major ballet companies departed for Lincoln Center. Today, this overlooked treasure hosts the Paul Taylor Dance Company, Alvin Ailey and American Ballet Theater, as well as the New York Flamenco Festival in February and other dance performances.

⭐ LOEWS 42ND ST-E WALK THEATER

☎ 212-505-6397; 42nd St btwn Seventh & Eighth Aves; admission $9-13; 🚇 any train to 42nd St; ♿ 🚻
As if there wasn't enough escapism in Times Sq, now you have a 13-screen megaplex to duck

NEIGHBORHOODS

MIDTOWN WEST

into when you need a break from 'reality.' Catch the latest from Hollywood in luxe surroundings.

⭐ MAJESTIC THEATER
☎ 212-239-6200; www.majestic-theater.net; 247 W 44th St; ⊕ any train to 42nd St

A fabled performance house that saw the likes of Angela Lansbury, Julie Andrews and several Barrymores on its stage, the Majestic is still (still!) selling out every night for *Phantom of the Opera*, 20 years after Andrew Lloyd Webber's creation debuted.

⭐ NEW AMSTERDAM THEATER
☎ 212-282-2900; www.newamsterdamtheater.net; 214 W 42nd St; ⊕ any train to 42nd St; ♿ 🚻

If your kids are into theater, watch their eyes pop as they pass through the art deco entrance, into the art nouveau interior of carved and painted plaster, stone, wood, murals and tiles – all of which evoke early-20th-century theater-going – on their way to see *Mary Poppins*, the musical.

⭐ NEW VICTORY THEATER
☎ 646-223-3020; www.newvictory.org; 209 W 42nd St; ⊕ any train to 42nd St-Times Sq; ♿ 🚻

Budding thespians and dancers alike flock to the upbeat energy of this kid-focused theater. New Victory puts on comedy, dance, music, puppetry and drama shows for the 12 and under set, and a range of offerings for the older folk (teenagers). Adults aren't forgotten either – in between 'Hip-Hop Legends' and 'Speedmouse,' there's also *The Bluest Eye,* an adaptation of a novel by Pulitzer Prize winner Toni Morrison.

⭐ THE OAK ROOM
☎ 212-840-6800; www.algonquinhotel.com; 59 W 44th St; ⊕ D, F, V to 42nd St-Bryant Park; ♿

Let the excellent martinis loosen your tongue and channel all the wicked Dorothy Parker energy palpably careening around the Oak Room. Soon though your barbs and bon mots will be hushed by the tinkle of the Baby Grand piano – expect talent along the lines of Barbara Carroll and Andrea Marcovicci (who has an annual holiday show through New Year's), with a Harry Connick Jr sighting always possible.

⭐ TOWN HALL
☎ 212-840-2824; www.the-townhall-nyc.org; 123 W 43rd St; 🕐 closed Aug; ⊕ any train to 42nd St-Times Sq; ♿ 🚻

When Town Hall was designed in the early 1900s, it was done so with democratic principles in mind – box seats and those with partially obstructed views were eliminated (not a bad seat in the house) and the acoustics stunned everyone when first heard. Tours on its history and famous performances are given daily and are well worth the time. Performances range from jazz to blues to classic singers and everything else in between.

>CENTRAL PARK

All kinds of characters make this stunning sequence of rolling hills home, including Pale Male and Lola, red-tailed hawks that have lived on a Fifth Ave buttress for more than 10 years. It's a glimpse of just how wild this park can be, for all of its intense human activity.

There are big swaths of land, mostly in the northern section, left untouched so visitors might have the pleasure of an ever-changing landscape. The southern acres were shaped with a firmer hand, but still created with the public in mind. The farm that's next to Central Park's still-working carousel was an actual dairy in the late 1800s. Designers Olmsted and Vaux put it there thinking that poor children, after a long and dusty walk, would welcome a cool glass of milk.

Ballfields and tennis courts come alive in summer, and numerous statues, fountains and plazas are a delight to behold. It's practically impossible to get lost in the park, although you can go for stretches without seeing anyone. Sometimes that is the best treat of all.

CENTRAL PARK

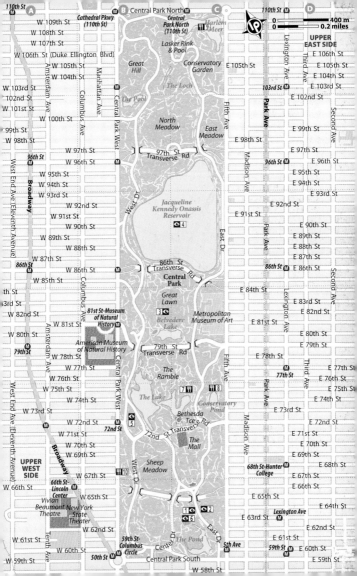

SEE

ARSENAL

Built between 1847 and 1851 as
a munitions supply depot for the
New York State National Guard,
this landmark brick building (at E
64th St) was designed to look like
a medieval castle, and its construction predates the actual park.
Today the building houses the
City of New York Parks & Recrea-
tion and the Central Park Wildlife
Center. The reason to visit here is
not to see the building, though,
but to view Olmsted's original
blueprint for the park, treasured
here under glass in a 3rd-floor
conference room.

CENTRAL PARK WILDLIFE CENTER

☎ 212-861-6030; www.centralparknyc
.org; 64th St at Fifth Ave; ⏱ 10am-5pm
The penguins are the main attraction at this modern zoo, though
you'll find more than two dozen
other species to visit, including
polar bears and the endangered
tamarin monkeys and red pandas.
Feeding times are especially
rowdy, fun times to stroll through:
watch the sea lions chow down
at 11:30am, 2pm and 4pm and
see the penguins gobble fish at
10:30am and 2:30pm. The Tisch
Children's Zoo, between 65th
and 66th Sts, is perfect for smaller
children.

GREAT LAWN

Located between 72nd and 86th
Sts, this massive emerald carpet
was created in 1931 by filling in a
former reservoir. It is the place for
outdoor concerts (this is where
Paul Simon played his famous
comeback show, and where you
can catch the New York Philharmonic Orchestra each summer),
and there are eight softball fields,
basketball courts and a canopy
of London plane trees. Not far
from the actual lawn are several
other big sites: the Delacorte
Theater, home to the annual
Shakespeare in the Park festival,
and its lush Shakespeare Garden;
the panoramic Belvedere Castle;
the leafy Ramble, the epicenter

PARK STATUES

Scattered among the many natural sculptures, otherwise known as trees is a host of wonderful, freestanding, crafted works of art. Check out the **Maine Monument** (at the Merchant's Gate at Columbus Circle), a tribute to the sailors killed in the mysterious explosion in Havana Harbor in 1898 that sparked the Spanish American War. Further east, toward the Seventh Ave entrance, there are statues of Latin America's greatest liberators, including **José Martí**, 'The Apostle of Cuban Independence.' Further east still at the Scholar's Gate (Fifth Ave at 60th St), there's a small plaza dedicated to **Doris Chanin Freedman**, the founder of the Public Art Fund, where you can see a new sculpture every six months or so.

The iconic **Angel of the Waters** sits atop Bethesda Fountain, and the Literary Walk between Bethesda Fountain and the 65th St Transverse is lined with statues, including the requisite **Christopher Columbus**, and literati such as **Robert Burns** and **Shakespeare**. At Conservatory Water, where model sailboats drift lazily by, kids crawl over the giant toadstools of the **Alice in Wonderland** statue. Replete with Alice of flowing hair and dress, a dapper Mad Hatter and mischievous Cheshire Cat, this is a Central Park treasure and a favorite of kids of all ages. Nearby is the **Hans Christian Andersen** statue, where Saturday story hour (11am June to September) is an entertaining draw.

At the northeastern extent of the park is the soaring **Duke Ellington** statue, depicting the man and his piano. An oft-overlooked site because of its northern location (at 110th St), this stunning tribute to the jazz master, featuring a 25ft bronze tableau, was unveiled in 1997 and conceived and funded by the late Bobby Short.

of both birding and gay-male cruising; and the Loeb Boathouse, where you can rent rowboats for a romantic float in the middle of this urban paradise.

◎ JACQUELINE KENNEDY ONASSIS RESERVOIR

Don't miss your chance to run or walk around this 1.58-mile track, which draws a slew of joggers in the warmer months. The 106-acre body of water no longer distributes drinking water to residents, but serves as a gorgeous reflecting pool for the surrounding

skyline and flowering trees. The most beautiful time to be here is at sunset, when you can watch the sky turn from brilliant shades of pink and orange to cobalt blue, just as the city's lights slowly flicker on.

◎ STRAWBERRY FIELDS

Standing just across from the famous Dakota building – where *Rosemary's Baby* was filmed in 1967, and where John Lennon was fatefully shot in 1980 – is this poignant, tear-shaped garden, a memorial to the slain star. It's the

Impromptu concert in Strawberry Fields.

most visited spot in Central Park, and maintained with some help from a $1 million grant from Lennon's widow Yoko Ono, who still resides at the Dakota. The peaceful spot contains a grove of stately elms and a tiled mosaic that's often strewn with rose petals from visitors. It says, simply, 'Imagine.'

WOLLMAN SKATING RINK
☎ 212-439-6900; btwn 62nd & 63rd Sts;
🕙 Nov-Mar
Located on the park's east side, this is a romantic and popular skating rink at which to strap on rented ice skates and glide around, especially around the holidays, when it's lit by flickering Christmas lights.

🍽 EAT
🍽 CENTRAL PARK BOATHOUSE
Seafood/American Traditional $$$
☎ 212-517-2233, E 72nd St at Park Dr N; 🕙 noon-4pm Mon-Fri, 9:30am-4pm Sat & Sun Nov 4-Apr 14, noon-4pm & 5:30-9:30pm Mon-Fri, 9:30am-4pm & 6-9:30pm Sat & Sun Apr 15-Nov 3; V
After a recent makeover and refinancing, Central Park Boathouse shed its reputation as a restaurant that only cared about communing with nature and became a culinary delight. The roasted duck and delicate salmon

Christian Larsen,
Senior Curatorial Assistant, Architecture & Design, The Museum of Modern Art

What's your job like? I have a hand in putting together exhibitions, hunting down and buying new pieces for the collection and going through our archived material – we've got many an object accumulated in storage. **What's a tourist trap that's worth the trip?** I went up to Top of the Rock the other day with my brother and I have to say it was spectacular. You see everything for 360 degrees, and into the boroughs. **What's your favorite place to hang in at MoMA?** I love the view from the Sculpture Garden into the gallery wing on Friday afternoons; people come because it's free and it looks like an ant farm, you see people moving across the bridges through the clear glass, circulating through the galleries. **What's great about the MoMA that not everybody sees?** The Ferrari hanging on the wall in the education building.

tartare are on par with some of the city's best, and it still has that gorgeous waterfront spot.

🍴 KIOSKS SNACKS

Sandwiches/Snacks $

76th St near Conservatory Pond & 108th St near Harlem Meer; 🕑 **11am-8pm Jun-Sep;** Ⓥ

There are a number of snack spots that pop up in the park during the warmer months, but these two are particularly popular. They both sit right on the edge of small ponds, so you can grab a pretzel on a nice day and then watch the ducks swim your way (hoping you'll share) while you eat.

🍴 TAVERN ON THE GREEN

American Traditional $$$

☎ **212-873-3200; Central Park West at 67th St;** 🕑 **lunch & dinner;** Ⓜ **1 at 66th St-Lincoln Center, B, C at 72nd St**

Everything about Tavern on the Green screams romance – its location, its quiet ambience, its bejeweled and bedecked gardens with sweeping views. It's a unique experience to dine here, but don't go expecting great cuisine. The menu's been the same forever it seems, and the kitchen's apparently just lost interest. But, don't let that fact spoil your view.

 PLAY

Several of Central Park's most celebrated arts events happen in the summer: Shakespeare in the Park (p106) and Summerstage are the two big ones. If you miss those, there are plenty of year-round activities to enjoy.

⭐ BOWLING LAWNS

You'll find two 15,000-sq-ft bowling lawns, north of Sheep Meadow at 69th St – one for croquet and one for lawn bowling, where members of the 80-year-old New York Lawn Bowling Club still mix it up with tournaments from May to October.

⭐ GO CAMPING

☎ **866 NYC-HAWK; www.nycgovpark .org/sub_about/parks_divisions ('schedule of upcoming events' in the 'Urban Park Ranger programs' section)**

It's news to most New Yorkers, but it's true: the Urban Park Rangers, a division of the NYC Parks Department, lead overnight camping excursions. These happen in various parks, including this one, throughout the summer.

⭐ HORSEBACK RIDING

☎ **212-724-5100; per 30min $58**

Claremont Riding Academy in the park will give you a private horseback-riding lesson, or take you out on a group tour. Viewing the park from the back of a stately horse definitely changes your perspective.

⭐ ROCK CLIMBING
In New York, the urban rock-climbing community flocks to Worthless Boulder (a 10ft-tall rock at the park's north end) near Harlem Meer. Some scaling skills of your own can be harnessed at the supervised Climbing Wall (North Meadow Recreation Area just north of 97th St).

⭐ SAFARI PLAYGROUND
W 91st St
For kids, there's Safari Playground, a jungle-themed play area featuring 13 hippo sculptures, a tree house and a kiddie jogging path.

⭐ SENECA VILLAGE
btwn 81st & 89th Sts
Marked by a simple plaque, Seneca Village was home to Manhattan's first prominent community of African American property owners (c 1840).

UPPER EAST SIDE

Known as New York's 'Gold Coast,' and only half in jest, these moneyed blocks stretch from the lower edge of Central Park to 96th St. The stores and homes along Fifth Ave, Madison Ave and Park Ave are among the most expensive in the world.

The rest of the neighborhood isn't too shabby either. Traces of its past remain in the crumbly (but ornate) buildings that pop up as you head east, but its notorious drug-dealing days are long gone. It's now filled with preppy college students, young couples and families, with a big dose of single thirty-somethings.

The nightlife focuses on Central Park's free summer events, eating out in the delicious restaurants, and grabbing a few beers at old-school pubs and wine bars. For dancing and clubbing, go downtown, but for an evening of adult drinking, dining and discussion, the Upper East Side does just fine.

UPPER EAST SIDE

◉ SEE
Frick Collection **1**	A5	
Metropolitan Museum of Art **2**	A2	
Neue Galerie..............**3**	A2	
Solomon R Guggenheim Museum**4**	A1	
Temple Emanu-El.......**5**	A6	
Whitney Museum of American Art..............**6**	B4	

⬒ SHOP
Luca Luca...................**7**	B3	
Nellie M Boutique **8**	B1	
Ralph Lauren **9**	B4	

🍴 EAT
Andre's Patisserie......**10**	D2	
Beyoglu **11**	C3	
Cafe Sabarsky............**12**	A2	
Candle Café **13**	C4	
Daniel **14**	B5	
David Burke & Donatella.................**15**	B6	
Jo Jo.........................**16**	B6	
Maya Mexican **17**	D6	

⭐ PLAY
92nd St Y **21**	B1	
Café Carlyle **22**	B3	

▼ DRINK
Bar East **18**	D1	
Bemelmans Bar..........**19**	B3	
Subway Inn **20**	B6	

SEE

◉ FRICK COLLECTION

☎ 212-288-0700; www.frick.org; 1 E 70th St at Fifth Ave; admission $12; ⏱ 10am-6pm Tue-Thu & Sat, 10am-9pm Fri, 1-6pm Sun; ⬤ 6 to 68th St-Hunter College

This spectacular collection sits in a mansion built by businessman Henry Clay Frick in 1914, one of the many such residences that made up 'Millionaires' Row.' Most of these mansions proved too expensive for succeeding generations and were eventually destroyed, but the wily and very wealthy Frick, a Pittsburgh steel magnate, established a trust to open his private art collection as a museum. Look for Jean-Antoine Houdon's stunning figure *Diana the Huntress*; works by Titian and Vermeer, and portraits by Gilbert Stuart, El Greco, Goya and John Constable. An audio tour is included in the price of admission. Perhaps the best asset here is that it's never crowded.

◉ METROPOLITAN MUSEUM OF ART

☎ 212-535-7710; www.metmuseum .org; Fifth Ave at 82nd St; admission by

Home of the Frick Collection

Metropolitan Museum of Art

suggested donation; 🕐 9:30am-5:30pm Tue-Thu & Sun, 9:30am-9pm Fri & Sat; 🚇 4, 5, 6 to 86th St

What can you say about this gorgeous behemoth? Its size, and the depth and breadth of its collection, simply overwhelms. More than five million come a year for special exhibits, or just to see the cavernous Great Hall entrance, the Temple of Dendur, the Tiffany windows in the American Wing, the collection of African, Oceanian and other works, as well as the famed European Collection on the 2nd floor – it's a city within a city, really, and it's easier to get lost here than in Central Park outside.

Avoid rainy Sundays in summer if you don't like crowds. But, during horrible winter weather, you might find the 17-acre museum deserted at night – a real NYC experience. The rooftop garden is also a find, especially in the summer, when it becomes a wine bar on weekend evenings.

🄲 NEUE GALERIE

☎ 212-628-6200; www.neuegalerie .org; 1048 Fifth Ave at 86th St; admission $15, child under 12yr not admitted; 🕐 11am-6pm Sat-Mon & Thu, 11am-9pm Fri; 🚇 4, 5, 6 to 86th St

This showcase for German and Austrian art is a relative newcomer to the museum strip (it opened in 2000), but it stood out as a star right away. The intimate but well-hung collection, housed in a former Rockefeller mansion, features impressive works by Gustav Klimt, Paul Klee and Egon Schiele. It boasts a lovely street-level eatery, Cafe Sabarsky (p194), serving Viennese meals, pastries and drinks. And, because of its no-children policy, you'll never encounter noisy stroller blockades.

◉ SOLOMON R GUGGENHEIM MUSEUM

☎ 212-423-3500; www.guggenheim .org; 1071 Fifth Ave at 89th St; adult/child under 12 yr/senior & student/ $18/free/ $15; ⌚ 10am-5:45pm Sat-Wed, 10am-7:45pm Fri; ⊕ 4, 5, 6 to 86th St; ♿

MUSEUM MILE

Imagine Fifth Ave devoid of traffic and filled with colors of a thousand canvases – such is **Museum Mile** (☎ 212-606-2296; www.museummilefestival .org; Fifth Ave btwn 82nd & 104th Sts; admission free; ⌚ 6-9pm; ⊕ 4, 5, 6 to 86th St, 6 to 103rd St; ♿), an annual event that takes place every June. Fifth Ave is closed to traffic from 82nd to 105th St and museums are free. Thousands turn out to enjoy the street art, music and incredible cultural richness of Manhattan.

The Guggenheim is one of Manhattan's premier museums, as much for its white-ribbon cylindrical design as its fabulous displays of art. Dedicated to showcasing the avant-garde, the curving walls hold plenty of Piet Mondrians, Wassily Kandinskys and more.

◉ TEMPLE EMANU-EL

☎ 212-744-1400; www.emanuelnyc .org; 1 E 65th St; ⌚ 9am-7pm; ⊕ 6 to 68th St-Hunter College; Once part of the Jewish Community on the Lower East Side, Temple Emanu-El houses a renowned collection of Judaica, and tells the story of its transformation into a ritzy Upper East Side house of worship with murals on the walls.

◉ WHITNEY MUSEUM OF AMERICAN ART

☎ 212-570-3676; www.whitney.org; 945 Madison Ave at 75th St; adult/ child under 12 yr/senior & student, $15/free/$10, suggested donation 6-9pm Fri; ⌚ 11am-6pm Wed-Thu, Sat & Sun, 1-9pm Fri; ⊕ 6 to 77th St; ♿ The sleek, polished Whitney exterior is as cool as its massive collection of predominantly American 20th-century art, featuring established artists like Rothko and Hopper, but also newcomers like Kiki Smith. The Whitney's a must for lovers of modern American works.

Soloman R Guggenheim Museum

 SHOP

🏠 LUCA LUCA
☎ 212-753-2444; www.lucaluca.com;
690 Madison Ave; ⏰ 11am-6:30pm
Mon-Wed & Sat, 11am-8pm Thu; 🚇 N,
R, W to Fifth Ave-59th St, 4, 5, 6 to
59th St
Italian designer Orlandi Luca
achieves what so few can: sultry,
sensual clothes that can be worn
by women of all ages. Famous for
glittery, flowing evening gowns
that cling in all the right places,
Luca Luca also has a stellar line of
separates for day.

🏠 NELLIE M BOUTIQUE
☎ 212-996-4410; 1309 Lexington Ave;
⏰ 10am-8pm Mon-Fri, 11am-8pm Sat,
to 7pm Sun; 🚇 4, 5, 6 to 86th
Located off Madison Ave, this
inviting boutique carries upscale-
but-hip clothing from smaller
designer labels (such as Rebecca
Taylor) that are found at most
Upper East Side (UES) giants.
There're also plenty of accessories
and evening wear, as well as more
sporty finds.

🏠 RALPH LAUREN
☎ 212-606-2100; 867 Madison Ave;
⏰ 10am-6pm Mon-Wed & Fri, to 7pm

NEIGHBORHOODS

UPPER EAST SIDE

Thu, noon-5pm Sun; 🚇 6 to 68th St-Hunter College
Housed in a beautiful 1890s mansion (one of Manhattan's few remaining residences of that era), Ralph's flagship store is worth the long stroll up Madison Ave, even if you've already stocked up on Polo gear elsewhere. There's a big selection here, with an emphasis on more formal wear, particularly for men.

🍽 EAT

🍽 ANDRE'S PATISSERIE
European/Hungarian Bakery $-$$
☎ 212-327-1105; 1631 Second Ave;
🕙 10am-9pm; 🚇 4,5, 6 to 86th St; V ♿
An Upper East Side secret, Andre's is a fabulous Hungarian eatery and bakery, with some of the best desserts in town, and homemade stews, goulashes, crepes and more. It's a narrow room with pretty blond wood and friendly waitresses who all come from the Old Country.

🍽 BEYOGLU
Turkish/Middle Eastern $$
☎ 212-650-0850; 1431 Third Ave;
🕙 lunch & dinner; 🚇 4, 5, 6 to 86th St; ♿ V
Blue tiles and pretty plates make dining at Beyoglu a festive affair,

especially if it's summer and you can join the beautiful people sitting at the sidewalk tables. There's a delectable meze, plenty of vegetarian options and lots of fresh seafood. Check out the Turkish wines, too.

🍽 CAFE SABARSKY
Austrian $$
☎ 212-288-0665; www.wallse.com; 1048 Fifth Ave; 🕙 breakfast, lunch & dinner; 🚇 4, 5, 6 to 86th St; V ♿
It can get a little tight in this popular Neue Galerie café on the weekends, but the food, and opulent Old-World ambience make it worth the fight for a table. Authentic Austrian food – trout-filled crepes, goulash, sausage and strudel – are served on heavy platters and silver cups brought from Vienna.

🍽 CANDLE CAFÉ
Vegetarian $$
☎ 212-472-0970; 1307 Third Ave; 🕙 lunch & dinner daily; 🚇 6 to 77th St; ♿ ♿
It's not just the delicious, healthy fare that pulls in the crowds – the energy is surprisingly romantic and decadent, making it a great date location. The food is plentiful and straightforward, with greens, roots, grains and some layered casserole dishes. The vegan cakes are surprisingly moist and sweet,

and the wine list long and enticing. It's food and atmosphere for all fives senses.

🍴 DANIEL French $$$$
☎ 212-288-0033; www.danielnyc.com; 60 E 65th St; 🕑 dinner Mon-Sat; ⊚ 6 to 86th St; ♿

So few things live up to their hype once – it's rare to see a place that, over time, continues to surpass its own excellent reputation. Daniel Boulod's eponymous eatery is spacious and gracious, the food delicate and hearty at the same time. But it's the friendliness of the staff that adds the final, special touch. If you can't get a reservation, consider **Cafe Boulod** (20 E 76th St) just around the corner, or DB Bistro Moderne for a different, but still stellar Boulod meal.

🍴 DAVID BURKE & DONATELLA
New American $$$$
☎ 212-813-2121; www.dbrestaurant .com; 133 E 61 St; 🕑 lunch & dinner daily, brunch Sat-Sun; ⊚ F to Lexington Ave-63rd St, N, R, W to Lexington Ave-59th St

It might look like a member of the Versace family decorated this lush red space, but the Donatella in question has no ties to any fashion empire – she and partner David Burke are strictly about food, like salmon with warm potato knish,

pretzel-crusted crabcake, yellowfin tuna on saltrock, and 'crispy and angry' lobster cocktail.

🍴 JO JO French $$$$
☎ 212-223-5656; www.jean-georges .com; 160 E 64th St; 🕑 lunch & dinner; ⊚ 4, 5, 6 to 59th St, N, R, W to Lexington Ave-59th St

No matter how far down the fusion highway Jean-Georges Vongerichten chooses to stray, his first, and best hotspot retains its iconic status. The townhouse decor is dark and sultry and the dishes equally so: venison cubes tossed with pomegranate seeds, roast chicken with green olives. The not-to-be-missed signature dish is a dessert – decadent Valrhona cake that oozes chocolate.

🍴 MAYA Mexican $$
☎ 212-585-1818; www.modernmexican .com; 1191 First Ave; 🕑 dinner; ⊚ 4, 5, 6 to 59th St; ♿ 🚻

Newly renovated Maya now looks something akin to an 18th-century Mexican hacienda, and the decor perfectly complements the powerful, mole-infused dishes. Chef Richard Sandoval's menu has, among other things, corn masa with *oaxaca* cheese and *chile poblano rajas*, seviche halibut, marinated filet mignon, and chunky, rich guacamole as a side.

DRINK

☉ BAR EAST
☎ 212-876-0203; 1733 First Ave btwn 89th & 90th Sts; ⊕ 6 to 86th St

Kind of off the beaten path (it's quite a hike from the subway, after all), this friendly neighborhood bar is tricked out with a pool table, good pop-rock DJs, darts and a nice mirror-backed bar. If you want to see locals drinking and yammering without pretense, head east and grab a stool.

☉ BEMELMANS BAR
☎ 212-744-1600; www.thecarlyle.com; Carlyle Hotel, 35 E 76th St; after 9:30pm $20, after 9:30pm Sat $25; ☽ noon-2am Mon-Sat, noon-12:30am Sun; ⊕ 6 to 77th St

The only surviving commissioned mural from Ludwig Bemelmans still on display to the public infuses this namesake café with the artist's legendary wit. Bemelmans' plush red interior is a perfect place to canoodle, making it a favorite for in-love couples and those wishing to conduct an affair of the heart with discretion. Suave and sophisticated piano jazz is the musical mainstay.

☉ SUBWAY INN
☎ 212-223-8929; 143 E 60th St btwn Lexington & Third Aves; ⊕ 4, 5, 6 to 59th St

This is a classic old-geezer watering hole, with cheap drinks and loads of authenticity, right down to the barmen's white shirts and their thin black ties. It should truly be landmarked, as the entire scene – from the vintage neon sign outside, to the well-worn red booths and old geezers huddled inside – is truly reminiscent of by-gone days. The dive, which offers, amongst other things, plenty of cheapo shots, is an amusing place to recover from a shopping spree at posh Bloomingdale's (p162), just around the corner.

PLAY

☆ 92ND ST Y
☎ 212-415-5500; www.92y.org; 1395 Lexington Ave at 92nd St; ☽ times vary depending on events; ⊕ 6 to 96th St

The Y is a bastion of literary greatness (as well as a venue that caters for music and dance), with its Unterburg Poetry Center hosting frequent readings, plus a Biographers and Brunch lecture series on Sundays, featuring top-shelf authors. Recent appearances have included Paul Auster, Margaret Atwood, Joan Didion and Michael Chabon. Almost all the big-name readings sell out, so if there's a particular author you want to hear, reserve well in advance.

⭐ **CAFÉ CARLYLE**
☎ 212-744-1600; www.thecarlyle.com;
35 E 76th St at Madison Ave; 🕑 6:30-
10pm Mon-Wed, 6:30pm-midnight
Thu-Sat, closed Sun; 🚇 6 to 77th St
Monday nights it's Woody Allen
on the clarinet, playing with his
jazz ensemble; sometimes Ute
Lemper's headlining, and if she's
unavailable, it could be Eartha
Kitt, although that depends on
whether or not she's doing a
Broadway show. In short, it's an
A-list crowd all the way.

UPPER WEST SIDE

What can you experience on the Upper West Side? The best bagels in town, magnificent brownstones and tons of books – in stores, on sidewalks and lining the tweedy bars around the American Museum of Natural History (another big draw).

Not as upper crust as the East Side, the UWS has long been the bastion of the city's intellectual circles. The Dakota, where John Lennon lived, is one of its most famous buildings, but many of the old-fashioned beaux arts facades merit a closer look.

Strong on the arts, it houses Lincoln Center, where you can see the Metropolitan Opera House, Jazz at Lincoln Center, the world-famous Juilliard School of Music and, in summer, outdoor performances and free dance nights (mostly salsa, tango and swing, with lessons thrown in).

Nearby Columbia University translates into a college-town feeling on its upper reaches – the bars are plentiful and cheap. It's a great slice of laid-back New York, where families and grown-ups comingle with bright young minds in a friendly, bohemian atmosphere.

UPPER WEST SIDE

NEW YORK

W 99th St
W 98th St
W 97th St
96th St
W 96th St
W 95th St
W 94th St
W 93rd St
W 92nd St
W 91st St
W 90th St
W 89th St
W 88th St
W 87th St
W 86th St
86th St
W 85th St
W 84th St
W 83rd St
W 82nd St
W 81st St
W 80th St
W 79th St
79th St
W 78th St
W 77th St
W 76th St
W 75th St
W 74th St
W 73rd St
W 72nd St
72nd St
W 71st St
W 70th St
W 69th St
W 68th St
W 67th St
66th St-Lincoln Center
W 66th St
W 65th St
W 64th St
W 63rd St
W 62nd St
W 61st St
W 60th St
59th St-Columbus Circle
W 59th St
W 58th St
W 57th St
57th St
W 56th St
W 55th St
55th St
W 52nd St
7th Ave
W 51st St
W 50th St
50th St

Broadway
Amsterdam Ave
Columbus Ave
Central Park West
West Dr
Central Park West
W End Ave (Eleventh Avenue)
Riverside Dr
Twelfth Ave (West Side Hwy)
Freedom Pl
Tenth Ave
Ninth Ave
Eighth Ave
Seventh Ave
Sixth Ave (Avenue of the Americas)
Center Dr

Hudson River

Jacqueline Kennedy Onassis Reservoir

Central Park

Belvedere Lake
86th St Transverse Rd
79th St Transverse Rd
72nd St Transverse Rd
65th St Transverse Rd

Conservatory Pond
The Lake
The Pond
Central Park South

UPPER WEST SIDE

Dewitt Clinton Park
MIDTOWN
TIMES SQUARE

81st St-Museum of Natural History

0   600 m
0   0.3 miles

A   B   C   D

⊙ SEE

◉ AMERICAN MUSEUM OF NATURAL HISTORY

☎ 212-769-5000; www.amnh.org; Central Park West at 79th St; suggested donation adult/child/senior & student $14/8/10.50, last hr free; ⏱ 10am-5:45pm, Rose Center till 8:45pm Fri; ◉ B, C to 81st St-Museum of Natural History, 1 to 79th St

There's something for everyone in this museum; it's truly amazing.

Kids go crazy for the touchy-feely artifacts they can actually handle, parents love the interactive exhibits, three huge halls, and the Rose Center for Earth and Space, home to space-show theaters and a planetarium (not to mention free jazz, drinks and tapas Friday nights), and even experts can't help but be dazzled by the more than 30 million bits and bobs filling the massive building. You can spend the day here and still not see it all.

◉ CHILDREN'S MUSEUM OF MANHATTAN

☎ 212-721-1234; www.cmom.org; 212 W 83rd St btwn Amsterdam Ave & Broadway; admission $9, child under 1 yr free; ⏱ 10am-5pm Wed-Sun; ◉ 86th St, B, C to 81st St-Museum of Natural History

This museum is a favorite for area mommies. It features discovery centers for toddlers, a postmodern media center where technologically savvy kids can work in a TV studio, and the cutting-edge Inventor Center, where all the latest, cool tech stuff like digital imaging and scanners are made available. Expect the kids' stuff to be filtered through a sophisticated city lens, though, as recent exhibitions showed the art of Andy Warhol and shaped interactive art projects around the works of William Wegman,

American Museum of Natural History

Elizabeth Murray and Fred Wilson. During summer months, little ones can splash around with outdoor waterwheels and boats for lessons on buoyancy and currents. The museum also runs craft workshops on the weekends and sponsors special exhibitions.

LINCOLN CENTER
☎ 212-875-5900; www.newyorkphil harmonic.org; Lincoln Center Plaza, Broadway at W 64th St; ⓜ 1 to 66th St; ♿ ♻

Sprawling Lincoln Center is a miniature city in its own right: Avery Fisher Hall, home to the New York Philharmonic, currently undergoing a redesign, sits next to Alice Tully Hall, locus of the Chamber Music Society. The New York State Theater plays host to the New York City Ballet (www .nycballet.com), and the New York City Opera (www.nycopera.com). Walter Reade Theater hosts the New York Film Festival and shows quality films daily – there are the Newhouse and Beaumont theaters, Juilliard School and, last but not least, the Metropolitan Opera House, with its sweeping, grand red-carpeted staircase.

NEW-YORK HISTORICAL SOCIETY
☎ 212-873-3400; www.nyhistory.org; 2 W 77th St at Central Park West;

⏰ 10am-6pm Tue-Sun; ⓜ 1 to 79th St, B, C to 81st St-Museum of Natural History

As the antiquated, hyphenated name implies, the New-York Historical Society is the city's oldest museum, founded in 1804 to preserve the city's historical and cultural artifacts. It was also New York's only public art museum until the Metropolitan Museum of Art was founded in the late 19th century. Though it's often overlooked by visitors tramping to the nearby American Museum of Natural History, it shouldn't be, as its collection is as quirky and fascinating as NYC itself. Only here can you see 17th-century cowbells, baby rattles and the mounted wooden leg of Gouverneur Morris. The Henry Luce III Center for the Study of American Culture, which opened in 2000, is a 21,000-sq-ft showcase of more than 40,000 objects from the museum's permanent collection, and features fine portraits, Tiffany lamps and model ships. The place hosts unique special exhibits, too, with recent examples including *Slavery in New York* and *Nature and the American Vision: the Hudson River School at the New-York Historical Society*.

RIVERSIDE PARK
www.riversideparkfund.org; Riverside Dr from 68th to 155th Sts; ⏰ 6am-1am; ⓜ 1, 2, 3 to any stop btwn 66th & 157th St; ♿

Another classic beauty designed by Olmsted and Vaux, this waterside spot seems forever overshadowed by the more famous Central Park. But Riverside, running north on the Upper West Side, banked by the Hudson River, is lusciously leafy and tranquil. Plenty of bike paths and playgrounds make it a family favorite.

SHOP

☐ CHILDREN'S GENERAL STORE

☎ 212-580-2723; 2473 Broadway; ⏰ 10am-6pm Mon-Fri, 11am-6pm Sat & Sun; ⓜ 1, 2, 3 to 96th St

Packed with stuffed animals, wind-up toys, costumes and puzzles priced for every budget. As a cute touch, it's laid out like a real general store, with dolls and toys stocked as practically as dry goods. Kids will love it. There is another store in Grand Central Terminal – it's a perfect place to grab something before jumping on a train.

☐ HARRY'S SHOES

☎ 212-874-2035; www.harrys-shoes .com; 2299 Broadway; ⏰ 10am-6:45pm Tue, Fri & Sat, 10am-7:45pm Mon, Wed & Thu, 11am-6pm Sun; ⓜ 1 to 86th St

While not specifically for children, with an extensive collection of fine European brands sized for the wee ones, it'd be a shame to overlook

Harry's. Plus, it makes a great first-time experience for a tot; the sales staff still use the old-style classic metal rulers to take clients' foot sizes.

☐ LIBERTY HOUSE

☎ 212-799-7640; 2466 Broadway near 92nd St; ⏰ 10am-6:45pm Mon-Wed, 10am-7:45pm Thu-Fri, noon-5:45pm Sun; ⓜ 1, 2, 3 to 96th St

A 1960s grassroots cooperative designed to promote the work of American artisans and farmers, Liberty House retains is eco-friendly mission even in today's global economy. Women and children can pick up organic, natural-fiber clothes (no sweatshop labor here, thank you very much!) and its imported goods are bought directly from artists and artisan collectives who use only recycled or nonendangered woods and materials.

☐ PENNY WHISTLE TOYS

☎ 212-873-9090; 448 Columbus Ave btwn 81st & 82nd Sts; ⏰ 9am-6pm Mon-Fri, 10am-6pm Sat, 11am-5pm Sun; ⓜ B, C to 81st St

A small, indie, old-fashioned toy store, this bright shop is full of quality fun stuff, including display-worthy kites, Brio train sets, Czech marionettes, puzzles, costumes and collectible dolls.

🏠 PLAZA, TOO

☎ 212-362-6871; 2231 Broadway at 79th St; 🚇 1 to 79th St

If Harry's Shoes is a bit too practical, find your high-fashion footwear at this brand-new outpost of the suburban favorite – it's the first and only NYC location. It's got fancy footwork from the likes of Marc Jacobs, Chlóe, Adrienne, Cynthia Rowley, Sigerson Morrison and many more, and the prices are frequently reduced by nearly half at fabulous sales events.

🏠 ZABAR'S

☎ 212-787-2000; www.zabars.com; 2245 Broadway; 🕙 8:30am-7:30pm Mon-Fri, 8am-8pm Sat, 9am-6pm Sun; 🚇 1 to 79th St

An unofficial Upper West Side landmark, Zabar's still has that special 'only-in-New York' vibe that makes you feel you're in an original Woody Allen movie. People bustle and bump around the gourmet foods discussing their lives, politics and the freshness of the gefilte fish as if they were the only ones in the room.

🍴 EAT

🍴 'CESCA Italian $$-$$$

☎ 212-787-6300; 164 W 75th St; 🕙 dinner; 🚇 1, 2, 3 to 72nd St

Be prepared to eat hearty and eat well at 'Cesca, where the earthy decor and rustic tables are a precursor to the bulky platters of meat and pasta that await you. The slabs of tuna, grilled perfectly and dipped in tomato sauce, and chunks of tender lamb are totally worth wading through, but you better be hungry. Lighter fare like paninis is available at the bar. It's a great place for cocktails, too.

🍴 CITRUS
Sushi/Mexican/Latin
American $$

☎ 212-595-0500; www.citrusnyc.com; 320 Amsterdam Ave; 🕙 dinner Mon-Fri, lunch & dinner Sat & Sun; 🚇 1, 2, 3 to 72nd St; 👤 V

Adding a little sultry heat to sushi with chipotle spice and habanero peppers, Citrus likes to take culinary traditions and mix 'em up. The results, brash and brassy on the tongue, go well with the bright and splashy colors at Citrus, part bar, part eatery and very, very busy.

🍴 JOSIE'S RESTAURANT
Health Food $$

☎ 212-769-1212; 300 Amsterdam Ave; 🕙 dinner Mon-Fri, lunch & dinner Sat & Sun; 🚇 1, 2, 3 to 72nd St; 👤 V 👤

Organic fare (with its provenance listed on the menu) that satisfies vegans, vegetarians and meat eaters alike has kept Josie's around for more than a decade. Its clean,

NEIGHBORHOODS

UPPER WEST SIDE

simple ambience is reflected in the food – steak, salads, gorgeous veggie dishes, but nothing too processed or tortured.

🍴 OUEST
American/French $$$

☎ 212-580-8700; www.ouestny.com; 2315 Broadway; ⏰ dinner Mon-Fri, lunch & dinner Sat & Sun; ◉ 1 to 86th St; ♿

The addition of a smooth jazz combo has enhanced the sophisticated energy at Tom Valenti's red-boothed wonder, which still rates high with New Yorkers thanks to delicately stacked combo dishes like house-smoked sturgeon with frisée and poached egg, oyster pan roast with yukon gold potatoes and grilled

---

TOWERS OF FOOD POWER

Seven high-end restaurants are spread through Time Warner Center (p172). Among the offerings: **Rare** (mains $30 & up), a sprawling steakhouse from Jean-Georges Vongerichten; American creative at **Per Se** (☎ 212-823-9335; tasting menu $210); French-Asian fusion at **Café Grey** (☎ 212-823-6338; mains $50-75), and **Masa** (☎ 212-823-9800; tasting menu $325), a Japanese lair that requires reservations, oh…about a lifetime in advance.

---

free-range chicken. The bar food is just as nice, and less damaging to the pocketbook.

🍴 REGIONAL *Italian* $$

☎ 212-666-1915; www.eatregional .com; 2607 Broadway; ⏰ dinner daily, lunch & dinner Sat; ◉ 1, 2, 3 to 96th St; ♿ Ⓥ ⚦

Cuisine from 20 Italian regions can be sampled in a series of small plates, or you can hone in on a particular favorite – pizza from Naples, for example – and get your starters, wine and dessert from that region. The name gives the gimmick away, but Regional is on to a good thing. The pastas – filled with cheese and veggies and/or spicy meats – steal the show.

🍴 ROPPONGI
Japanese/Sushi $$

☎ 212-362-8182; 434 Amsterdam Ave; ⏰ lunch & dinner; ◉ 1 at 79th St, B, C to 81st St-Museum of Natural History; ♿ Ⓥ ⚦

Melt-in-your-mouth, five-flavor sashimi, perfectly round rice and delicately cooked noodles, salmon with green-olive moromi miso, and sushi rolls accompanied by mango salsa and orange compote are regular fixtures at this Upper West Side standout that has the friendliest waiters ever.

DRINK
AMSTERDAM BILLIARDS & BAR
☎ 212-496-8180; 334 Amsterdam Ave btwn 75th & 76th Sts; ◉ 1, 2, 3 to 72nd St

A flight above Amsterdam Ave, this expansive boîte featuring exposed brick and a friendly vibe is way more than a bar – though the drinks are well mixed and the stools cozy. The main event is the collection of about a dozen well-maintained pool tables.

DEAD POET
☎ 212-595-5670; 450 Amsterdam Ave; ◷ 9am-4am Mon-Sat, noon-4am Sun; ◉ 1 to 79th St, B, C to 81st St-Museum of Natural History

Good beers on tap (Smithwicks, Blue Moon, Brooklyn Lager), tons of Irish whiskey, and a narrow, bookish bar where literary types (and even better, serious readers) come to leaf through old pages and compare interpretations of Proust.

EVELYN LOUNGE
☎ 212-724-2363; 380 Columbus Ave; ◷ 6pm-4am Mon-Fri, 5pm-4am Sat & Sun; ◉ 1 to 79th St, B, C to 81st St-Museum of Natural History

Slinky Evelyn has long, lush banquettes, flickering sconces and lots of theatrical, billowy drapes to round out the sharp edges of its cold, stone walls. This sexy boîte isn't heralded for its bar food, but is popular because of its 1st-floor lounge, which is quiet and romantic during the week and thronged on the weekend.

MARITIME CAFÉ AT PIER 1
☎ 917-612-4330; 70th St at the Hudson River; ◉ 1, 2, 3 to 72nd St

Come the warm season, this ingenious use of the Riverside Park esplanade – an outdoor café with grilled grub, fruity cocktails and lounge chairs set up on the grass for those who reserve in advance – is totally hopping. It's no wonder, as there are few better city spots for a front-row view of the sunset, let alone those with such service. Summertime brings frequent live music, as well as movies, shown al fresco at the end of the connecting pier.

SHALEL
☎ 212-799-9030; 65 W 70th St btwn Central Park West & Columbus Ave; ◉ B, C, 1, 2, 3 to 72nd St

Craving some downtown style? Then enter the Greek Metsovo restaurant and head down the candlelit stairway to the cavernous, underground thriller of a Moroccan lounge. You'll find low couches, flickering votives, tossed pillows and even an in-house waterfall. A good selection of spicy wines adds to the mystique, and private little dining rooms can add to the romanticism.

 PLAY

⭐ CARNEGIE HALL
☎ 212-903-9750; www.carnegiehall .org; 881 Seventh Ave at 57th St; adult/child under 12 yr/senior & student $9/free/$3; ⏱ tours are offered at 11:30am, 2pm & 3pm Mon-Fri, tickets can be purchased at the box office from 11am-3pm; ⊖ A, B, C, D, 1 to Columbus Circle, N, Q, R, W to 57th St-Seventh Ave, E to Seventh Ave; ♿

Step through the arched doors and fluttering flags into the lobby, and you've entered the world of Toscanini, Tchaikovsky, Ravi Shankar and Frank Sinatra. The Carnegie has hosted some of the world's greatest musicians and continues to fill its cream-colored, multitiered main hall with crowd-pleasing performers.

⭐ CLEOPATRA'S NEEDLE
☎ 212-769-6969; www.cleopatras needleny.com; 2485 Broadway btwn W 92nd & 93rd Sts; ⊖ 1, 2, 3 to 96th St

Late-night and open-mike jams are a hallmark at Cleopatra's Needle, where the music goes until 4am. Some of the best band views are from the bar, where you can have a pint on tap and nosh on surprisingly good Mediterranean-influenced fare. There's never a cover, but mind the $10 drink and/or food minimum, as well as the fact that some performers resent being seen as background music to your dinner conversation.

⭐ THE DAKOTA
1 W 72nd St at Central Park West; ⊖ B, C to 72nd St; ♿

A turreted, gabled building described in 1884 as so far uptown it was in 'the Dakotas,' this sand-colored gem quickly became the epitome of cool, housing Boris Karloff, Rudolph Nureyev, Lauren Bacall, and most famously, John Lennon, who was fatally shot at its gated entrance.

⭐ IRIDIUM
☎ 212-582-2121; www.iridiumjazzclub.com; 1650 Broadway; cover $25-40; 🕙 6:30pm-closing; ⊕ 1, C, E to 50th St

The cover is high, but you get what you pay for at the Iridium. Great food, perfect sight lines and glossy, sophisticated jazz that will carry you away on a swell of music. Space is tight so reserve early, especially for the Les Paul trio on Monday nights and the Mingus Big Band on Thursdays.

⭐ JAZZ AT LINCOLN CENTER
☎ 212-258-9595; www.jazzatlincoln center.org; Time Warner Center, Broadway at 60th St; ⊕ A, B, C, D, 1 to 59th St-Columbus Circle

Of the three venues, the other two being the fancy Rose Theater and Allen Room, it's Dizzy's Club Coca-Cola that you're most likely to wind up in, as it's got nightly shows. And how lucky for you, since, with the exception of its

awful name, the nightclub is flawless, with stunning views overlooking Central Park and excellent line-ups of both local and touring artists.

⭐ LEONARD NIMOY THALIA
☎ 212-236-5849; www.symphonyspace .org; 2537 Broadway; tickets $7-10; 🕙 daily; ⊕ 1, 2, 3 to 96th St; ♿ ♿

Want to see a double feature of *Rear Window* and *On the Waterfront*? How about *The Big Heat* and *Mean Streets*? The Leonard Nimoy Thalia Theater at Symphony Space can be counted on to provide the most eclectic and entertaining showings in town. A film buff's fantasy come true.

⭐ SYMPHONY SPACE
☎ 212-864-1414; www.symphonyspace .com; 2537 Broadway; ⊕ 1, 2, 3 to 96th St; ♿ ♿

Founded and supported by community contributions, Symphony Space is renowned for its three-day series dedicated to one musician. The first one was given over to Bach, but they've also included Joni Mitchell, Stephen Sondheim, Burt Bacharach and others. It's got an affinity for world music – Gypsy Kings, Salif Keita, Cesaria Evora, and many more.

HARLEM

A whole new era is being ushered into Harlem – you can hear it, literally, in the constant buzz of construction crews busy gutting old brownstones and prepping foundations to hold soaring skyscrapers.

It's a region in flux; as new wealth and residents come in, local entrepreneurs open clubs, restaurants, performance spaces and retail outlets. It's good for the area's many working-class and business-owning residents, but it's hard on the working poor, and the homeless.

Settepani's, the iconic Lenox Lounge jazz club, the Malcolm Shabazz Market and other well-known parts of Harlem are along Lenox Ave, the main drag. The west side, by Columbia University, has Riverside Church, St John the Divine, and Smoke, a funky jazz club. Historic Harlem is above 125th St, where the Apollo, Studio Museum and the Schomburg Center are located. The east side has El Museo del Barrio, a grassroots museum featuring Puerto Rican, Dominican and Caribbean artists.

HARLEM

◉ SEE
Abyssinian Baptist Church	1	B3
Apollo Theater	2	B4
Cathedral of St John the Divine	3	A5
El Museo del Barrio	4	C6
General US Grant National Memorial	5	A4
Hispanic Society of America	6	A1
Museum of the City of New York	7	C6
Riverside Church	8	A4
Schomburg Center for Research in Black Culture	9	B3
Studio Museum in Harlem	10	B4

🛍 SHOP
125th St Shopping	11	B4
B Oyama Homme	12	B3
Bobby's Happy House	13	B4
Jumel Terrace Books	14	A1
Malcolm Shabazz Market	15	C5
Pieces of Harlem	16	B3
Scarf Lady	17	B3
Wearable Harlem Art	18	C5

🍽 EAT
Africa Kine	19	B5
Amy Ruth's Restaurant	20	B5
Ginger	21	C5
Le Baobab	22	B5
M&G Diner	23	B4

Native	24	B5
Rao's Restaurant	25	D5
River Room of Harlem	26	A2
Settepani's	27	B4

🍸 DRINK
Den	28	C3
MoBay Uptown	29	C4
Revival	30	B4

⭐ PLAY
Lenox Lounge	31	B4
Moca	32	B5
Perk's	33	B4
Smoke	34	A6
St Nick's Pub	35	A2

SEE

ABYSSINIAN BAPTIST CHURCH

☎ 212-862-7474; www.abyssinian.org; 132 Odell Pl (W 138th St) btwn Adam Clayton Powell Jr & Malcolm X Blvds; ⏱ services 9am & 11am Sun; ⓣ 2, 3 to 135th St

Founded by an Ethiopian businessman, the Abyssinian Baptist Church began as a downtown institution but moved north to Harlem in 1923, mirroring the migration of the city's black population. Its charismatic pastor, Calvin O Butts III, is an important community activist whose support is sought by politicians of all parties. The church has a superb choir and the building is a beauty. If you plan on visiting with a group of 10 or more, the congregation requests that you call in advance to see if space is available.

APOLLO THEATER

☎ 212-531-5337; 5253 W 125th St at Frederick Douglass Blvd; tours Mon/Sat & Sun $12/14; ⏱ tours 11am, 1pm & 3pm Mon, Tue & Fri, 11am, 1pm Sat & Sun; ⓣ A, B, C, D to 125th St

This has been Harlem's leading space for political rallies and concerts since 1914. Virtually every major black artist of note in the 1930s and '40s performed here,

including Duke Ellington and Charlie Parker. After a desultory spell as a movie theater and several years of darkness, the Apollo was bought in 1983 and revived as a live venue. After the completion of a two-year renovation (phase one in a long-range plan), the Apollo is more beautiful than ever, with a restored facade, marquee, glass-and-steel storefront and brand-new box office. Its famous weekly Amateur Night, 'where stars are born and legends are made,' still takes place on Wednesdays, with a wild and ruthless crowd that's as fun to watch as the performers. On other nights, the Apollo hosts performances by established artists like Stevie Wonder and the O'Jays.

CATHEDRAL OF ST JOHN THE DIVINE

☎ 212-316-7540; www.stjohndivine .org; 1047 Amsterdam Ave at 112th St; ⏱ 7am-6pm Mon-Sat, 7am-7pm Sun; ⓣ 1 to 110th St; ♿

A beloved spiritual and artistic center in Manhattan, the cathedral's massive nave is a mix of Romanesque and Gothic Revival styles blended harmoniously together. Started in 1892, the cathedral's still not done – the finishing touches on the towers should be in place by 2050, if workers stay on schedule.

EL MUSEO DEL BARRIO
☎ 212-831-7272; www.elmuseo.org;
1230 Fifth Ave at 104th St; suggested
donation adults/seniors & students
$6/$4, child under 12 yr free, seniors free
on Thu; ☷ 11am-5pm Wed-Sun; ☉ 2, 3
to 110th-Lenox Ave; ♿
Growing out of the Nuyorican
and Civil Rights Movement in East
Harlem, El Museo remains the only
major museum in the city dedicated to Puerto Rican and Latin
work, with a permanent collection of pre-Colombian and Taino
artifacts, and revolving modern-
art exhibits.

GENERAL US GRANT
NATIONAL MEMORIAL
☎ 212-666-1640; www.nps.gov/gegr;
Riverside Dr at W 122nd St; ☷ 9am-5pm;
☉ 1 to 125th St
Popularly known as Grant's Tomb,
this landmark holds the remains
of Civil War hero and president
Ulysses S Grant and those of his
wife, Julia. Completed in 1897 (12
years after his death) the granite
structure cost $600,000 and is the
largest mausoleum in the country.
Though it plagiarizes Mausoleus'
tomb at Halicarnassus, this version
doesn't qualify as one of the Seven
Wonders of the World. The building languished as a graffiti-scarred
mess for years until Grant's relatives
shamed the National Park Service
into cleaning it up by threatening
to move his body elsewhere.

HISPANIC SOCIETY OF
AMERICA
☎ 212-926-2234; www.hispanicsociety
.org; Audubon Tce on Broadway btwn
155th & 156th Sts, Washington Heights;
admission by suggested donation;
☷ 10am-4:30pm Tue-Sat, 1-4pm Sun;
☉ 1 to Broadway-157th St; ♿
Preparing for a move downtown,
the Hispanic Society hopes to draw
more attention to its outstanding
collection of Goya, Velázquez,
Sorolla and El Greco masterpieces.
Until it finds a new home, you can
survey the Spanish masters in
relative solitude way uptown.

MUSEUM OF THE CITY OF
NEW YORK
☎ 212-534-1672; www.mcny.org;
1220 Fifth Ave at 103rd St; admission by
suggested donation; ☷ 10am-5pm Tue-
Sun; ☉ 2, 3 to 110th St-Lenox Ave; ♿
This collection spans the past,
present and future of the five
boroughs in lithographs, photographs, cartoons, clothes and
more. Exhibits cover all facets of
city life, from hard-core skaters in
Brooklyn, to famous city interior
designers.

RIVERSIDE CHURCH
☎ 212-870-6700; www.theriverside
churchny.org; 490 Riverside Dr at 120th
St; ☷ 7am-10pm via Claremont Ave
entrance, visitors center 10am-7pm Wed;
☉ 1 to 116th St; ♿

Famous for combining its spiritual beliefs with progressive politics, Riverside Church has had Martin Luther King Jr, Fidel Castro and Nelson Mandela holding forth from its pulpit.

SCHOMBURG CENTER FOR RESEARCH IN BLACK CULTURE
☎ 212-491-2200; www.nypl.org/research/sc/sc.html; 515 Malcolm X Blvd; ☾ noon-8pm Tue & Wed, noon-6pm Thu & Fri, 10am-6pm Sat; ◉ 2, 3 to 135th St

The nation's largest collection of documents, rare books, recordings and photographs relating to the African American experience resides at this center near W 135th. St Arthur Schomburg, born in Puerto Rico, started gathering works on black history during the early 20th century while becoming active in the movements for civil rights and Puerto Rican independence. His impressive collection was purchased by the Carnegie Foundation and eventually expanded and stored in this branch of the New York Public Library. Lectures and concerts are regularly held in the theater here.

STUDIO MUSEUM IN HARLEM
☎ 212-864-4500; www.studiomuseum.org; 144 W 125th St at Adam Clayton Powell Blvd; admission by suggested donation; ☾ noon-6pm Wed-Fri & Sun, 10am-6pm Sat; ◉ 3 to 125th St, 4, 5, 6 to 125th St-Lexington Ave; ♿

An eclectic mix of work by African American and Caribbean artists hangs on the walls of the Studio Museum. Exhibits range from abstract expressionism to political cartoons, and they go a long way towards debunking the myth that there have been no great African American artists to emerge in the first half of the 20th century.

SHOP

BOBBY'S HAPPY HOUSE
☎ 212-663-5240; 2335 Frederick Douglass Blvd; ☾ 11am-8pm; ◉ A, B, C, D to 125th St-Nicholas Ave

Part of Harlem history, Bobby's specializes in deep gospel sounds. The owner, Bobby Robinson, worked with Elmore James and produced Gladys Knight & the Pips, whom he also named. The store has R&B, blues and just a few funk albums to go along with the gospel.

B OYAMA HOMME
☎ 212-234-5128; www.boyamahomme.com; 2330 Adam Clayton Powell Blvd at 136th St; ☾ 2-8pm Mon, 11am-8pm Tue-Fri, 10:30am-6pm Sat, closed Sun; ◉ C to 135th St

Bernard Oyama is the 'Haberdasher of Harlem,' and one look at his wing-tipped shoes, two-tone suits and sleek fedoras and you'll get an urge to shoot your cuffs, too. His boutique sells tailor-cut suits, an assortment of shirts, and items like ties, pocket squares, gloves, cuff links, and suspenders.

☐ JUMEL TERRACE BOOKS
☎ 646-472-5938; www.jumelterrace books.com; 426 W 160th St; 🕑 by appointment only; ◉ 1 to 163rd St-Amsterdam Ave
Housed in a historic private home, this shop specializes in tomes on Africana, Harlem history and African American literature. You've got to set up an appointment, but if you're fascinated by rare books, and rare opportunities to shop at a beautiful home, it's worth it.

☐ MALCOLM SHABAZZ MARKET
☎ 212-987-8131; 52 W 116th St; 🕑 10am-5pm; ◉ 2, 3 to 116th St
Enjoy some alfresco shopping at this popular marketplace, where you'll find items including African crafts, essential oils, incense, tra-ditional clothing, CDs and bootleg videos. The fish market next door is also a popular snack stop for Harlemites who like the catch of the day deep-fried with a side of french fries.

☐ PIECES OF HARLEM
☎ 212-234-1725; 228 W 135th St; 🕑 noon-6pm Sun & Mon, 11am-7pm

Tue-Thu, to 8pm Fri & Sat; ◉ 2, 3 to 135th St
Owned by the husband-and-wife duo who opened the first Pieces in Brooklyn, this new outpost has the same eclectic, handpicked col-lection of clothing and accessories from local and national designers. Find funky, sexy halter dresses, flouncy blouses and Pucci-like tunics, plus a range of hip acces-sories and unique outerwear.

☐ SCARF LADY
☎ 212-862-7369; 408 Lenox Ave; 🕑 11:30am-7pm Tue-Sat; ◉ 2, 3 to 125th St
Mystery revealed: Paulette Gay is the Scarf Lady. Her small boutique is crammed with hundreds of her colorful, handmade scarves, hats and other accessories.

☐ WEARABLE HARLEM ART
☎ 212-987-2500; 174 Lenox Ave btwn 118th & 119th Sts; 🕑 11:30am-7pm Mon-Fri, 11am-7pm Sat, noon-6pm Sun; ◉ 2, 3 to 116th St
Decked out with beautiful vintage tables and sporting a mellow vibe, this boutique is filled with designer-made clothing and memorabilia that celebrates the 'hood. Check out the tees and tote bags silkscreened with the profile of a woman with a 'fro, plus earth-tone messenger bags, caps, mugs and aprons that say 'Harlem.'

🍴 EAT

🍴 AFRICA KINE RESTAURANT
Senegalese/Moroccan $-$$
☎ 212-666-9400; www.africakine.com;
256 W 116th St; 🕐 lunch & dinner; 🚇 B,
C to 116th St; 🚹

One of the first African restaurants
to open up along the stretch of
W 116th St now known as Little
Senegal, Kine's got the best *Thu
Yap* and *Thiebu Djeun* in New York.
Succulent lamb and fish dishes
backed with big bowls of brown
rice, garlicky veggies and sometimes couscous bring in droves
of Senegalese every lunch hour.
Located on the 2nd floor, Kine
doesn't look like much from the
outside, but don't let that deter
you – it's a real treat for Africa
aficionados.

🍴 AMY RUTH'S RESTAURANT
*Homestyle Southern Cuisine/
Southern Soul* $-$$
☎ 212-280-8779; www.amyruthsrestau
rant.com; 113 W 116th St; 🕐 breakfast,
lunch & dinner Sun-Thu, 24hr Fri & Sat;
🚇 2, 3 to 116th St; 🚹 🚹

Weekend throngs are frequent,
such is the fame of Amy Ruth's
waffles – you can choose from
chocolate, strawberry, blueberry
or one with fried chicken – but
during weekdays it's usually calm
enough to enjoy your candied

yams, deep-fried fish with okra,
collard greens and red-velvet cake
in relative peace.

🍴 GINGER *Healthy Chinese* $$
☎ 212-423-1111; www.gingerexpress
.com; 1400 Fifth Ave; 🕐 dinner; 🚇 2, 3,
6 to 116th St; 🚹 Ⓥ 🚹

A welcome addition to a neighborhood where eating Chinese
usually means putting your life on
the line, Ginger is committed to
healthy fare that still satisfies your
cravings. The pretty brick exterior
gives way to a deep purple interior
with an open kitchen so you can
watch your baby-back ribs, shrimp
fried rice or chicken and broccoli
come together.

🍴 LE BAOBAB *Senagalese* $
☎ 212-864-4700; 120 W 116th St;
🕐 lunch & dinner; 🚇 2, 3 to 116th
St; Ⓥ

Step right into this homey spot
and find some room among the
cab drivers, bus drivers, local
construction workers and shop-
keepers who have crowded in as
well. Le Baobab is acknowledged
as one of the best (if not the best)
African restaurants in Harlem.

🍴 M & G DINER *Soul Food* $
☎ 212-864-7326; 383 W 125th St;
🕐 8am-midnight; 🚇 2, 3 to 125th
St; 🚹

Many claim to cook soul food, but few really do. For those who know the difference, there's M & G Diner, where chefs fry chicken like its an Olympic event and braise their meats more tenderly than most people cradle a child.

🍴 NATIVE
Moroccan/Caribbean $-$$

☎ 212-665-2525; 161 Lenox Ave; 🕑 dinner; 🚇 2, 3 to 116th St; 🚻 🚼

Native prefers grilling to deep-frying, so dishes like cumin-flecked fried chicken, plantain fritters, red curry coconut shrimp and pan-seared catfish are served flaky and light. Its outside tables are nice, but the candle-lit interior much more romantic.

🍴 RAO'S RESTAURANT
Italian $$$

☎ 12-722-6709; www.raos.com; 455 E 114th St; 🕑 dinner Mon-Fri, reservations required; 🚇 6 to 116th St; 🚻

So you want to go to Rao's. Who doesn't? Getting a reservation is like trying to find a shamrock – you just gotta be lucky. Serving clams, baked ziti and classic lasagna without pause since 1896, Rao's is an institution, a standard-bearer, a disappearing slice of New York. If you can't get a table, stop for a drink at the bar; it's worth the trip.

🍴 RIVER ROOM OF HARLEM
American/Southern $$-$$$

☎ 212-491-1500; www.riverroomof harlem.com; Riverside Dr at 145th St; 🕑 lunch Thu-Sat, dinner Tue-Sat, jazz brunch Sun; 🚇 1 to 145th St; 🚻

Get a load of that view – the George Washington Bridge to the north, and a sweeping panorama of the Hudson River to the south. Add to that some delectable dishes – paprika-grilled skirt steak, jumbo shrimp and gravy, corn mean and okra over market fish – let-down-your-hair dancing (salsa in the bar), groovy music (fusion, acid and all types of jazz), and general bonhomie, and you have a real winner.

Native

NEIGHBORHOODS

HARLEM

⏹ SETTEPANI'S
American/Italian $-$$

☎ 917-492-4806; www.settepani.com; 196 Lenox Ave; ⏱ lunch & dinner; ⊖ 2, 3 to 116th St; ⓖ ⓥ ⓧ

Pretty Settepani's is a glorious sight on a warm day – its rust-colored awning flutters in breezes that flow up and down broad Lenox Ave, and people of many different backgrounds enjoy fresh salads, sandwiches, quiches and desserts. It's one of several bright coffee hangouts springing up in Harlem. The service is sometimes a little slow, but people are rarely in a rush to leave anyway.

⏹ DRINK

⏹ DEN
☎ 212-234-3045; www.thedenharlem .com; 2150 Fifth Ave near 132nd St; ⏱ 6pm-2am Mon-Fri, 8pm-4am Sat,11am-5am Sun; ⊖ 2, 3 at 135th St.

This is a very sexy place, visited by some very sexy people who like to laugh, drink and eat, as well as share the stage on open-mike night (Wednesday). Part art gallery (local painters are shown on the walls), part gin joint (sip your Uncle Tom Collins with your tongue in cheek) and part soul restaurant (with pulled park and sushi on the menu), the Den is also gorgeous to look at. It's located on the 1st floor of a restored brownstone,

and you'll feel right at home. Live music on weekends, also a monthly Black Film Friday and a Kung Foo'd Saturday.

⏹ MOBAY UPTOWN
☎ 212-876-9300; www.mobayrestau rant.com/harlem/home.htm; 17 W 125th St; ⏱ 11am-11pm Mon-Wed, 11am-12:30am Thu-Sat, 11am-10pm Sun; ⊖ A, C, E, 2, 3 to 125th St

An extension of MoBay's in Brooklyn, this Caribbean eatery (with Jamaican, Haitian and vegetarian dishes) likes to add a little jazz to its cooking. It has jazz nights every Tuesday to Sunday from 8pm until midnight in the lounge (where you can order nibbles) and gospel brunches every Sunday from 11am to 5pm, and then a live band comes in for the evening.

⏹ REVIVAL
☎ 212-222-8338; www.harlemrevival .com; 2367 Frederick Douglass Blvd at 127th St; ⏱ lunch Tue-Fri, dinner daily, brunch Sat & Sun, daily happy hour 5-7pm; ⊖ A, C, E to 125th St

Swing by for happy hour, when drinks are two for one, and try the Frangelico-flavored Harlem Hazelnut specialty cocktail, or the chocolate martini that's named for Frederick Douglass – they're delicious! Revival is a sleek, upscale restaurant and a pleasant place to have a drink at any time of night.

PLAY

⭐ LENOX LOUNGE

☎ 212-427-0253; www.lenoxlounge
.com; 288 Malcolm X Blvd btwn 124th
& 125th Sts; 🕐 noon-4am; 🚇 2, 3 to
125th St

The classic art deco Lounge, which frequently hosts big names, is an old favorite of local jazz cats, though it's a beautiful and historic house for anyone who wants a nice place to imbibe. Don't miss the luxe Zebra Room in the back.

⭐ MOCA

☎ 212-665-8081; 2210 Frederick
Douglass Blvd at 119th St; 🕐 5pm-2am
Mon-Thu, 5pm-4am Fri & Sat, 5pm-mid-
night Sun; 🚇 2, 3 to 116th St, 1 to 116th
St-Columbia University

Save your best moves for Moca because you're going to need them! The thumping sound system (no live music) really has the dancefloor heaving on weekend nights, mostly to reggae, salsa and hip-hop. Don't let the security frisk at the door bother you – it's just standard procedure. Two-drink minimum on weekends, but there's a nightly happy hour, too.

⭐ PERK'S

☎ 212-666-8500; 553 Manhattan Ave at
123rd St; 🕐 4pm-4am Mon-Sat; 🚇 2, 3
to 125th St

On the weekends Perk's is packed with hip swinging dancers who take over the floor and move to the fusion sounds produced by the DJ. On weeknights this sedate-looking club pulls in the best local jazz artists to play live sets. You can't go wrong either way.

⭐ SMOKE

☎ 212-864-6662; 2751 Broadway near
106th St; 🕐 5pm-4am; 🚇 1 at 103rd St

Smoke has defied the odds of its no-man's-land location (not deep in Harlem but north of the Upper East Side) and flourished as an intimate and welcoming club. Its long dark drapes and fluffy sofas give it a homey feel, and the low covers appeal to the local student population.

⭐ ST NICK'S PUB

☎ 212-283-9728; www.stnicksjazzpub
.com; 773 St Nicholas Ave at 149th St;
🕐 7pm till late; 🚇 A, B, C, D to 145th St

Started in 1940 by Duke Ellington's piano player, St Nick's launched the careers of Billie Holiday, Sonny Rollins and many other American greats. In keeping with its tradition of encouraging collaboration, Monday and Wednesday nights are open-mike, under the careful direction of the house manager. You can hear amazing jam sessions in a no-fuss atmosphere, sitting at one of the city's most comfortable bars.

>BROOKLYN

New York City's most densely populated borough is a sprawling amalgamation of brownstones, skyscrapers, cobblestone streets and narrow highways, with an eclectic mix of hipster yuppies, working-class Latino and Caribbean families, and a surging influx of Eastern European immigrants. It's mesmerizing, overwhelming, and ripe for exploration. For old-school Brooklyn, start with the skyline across the East River from Lower Manhattan. After moving on to the gorgeous warren of reclaimed factories and historic brownstones, try Carroll Gardens, Red Hook or Cobble Hill for a fabulous restaurant. Park Slope is a laid-back, gay-friendly neighborhood mirroring Manhattan's upscale lifestyle, or, for a singular experience, head to Coney Island and check out the freak shows and 1926 roller coaster.

BROOKLYN

🜂 SEE

111 Front Street Galleries	1	G4
Brooklyn Historical Society	2	F4
Coney Island Boardwalk	3	A6
DUMBO Arts Center	4	G4
New York Transit Museum	5	F5
Pierogi 2000	6	G2
Prospect Park	7	E3
Roebling Hall	8	G2
Schroeder Romero	9	G2

🏠 SHOP

3R Living	10	E6
Academy Records and CDs	11	G2
Amarcord	12	G2
Brooklyn Artisans Gallery	13	F5
Clothier Brooklyn	14	F6
Dear Fieldbinder	15	F5
Ghostown	16	G2

Jacques Torres Chocolate	17	G4
Loopy Mango	18	G4
Prague Kolektiv	19	G4
Sahadi's	20	F5
Spring Gallery Store	21	G4

🍴 EAT

360	22	D4
Al di La	23	E6
Applewood	24	D3
Blue Ribbon Sushi Brooklyn	25	E6
Bubby's Brooklyn	26	G4
Chestnut	27	E5
Dumont	28	G2
Frankie's 457 Sputino	29	E5
Good Fork	30	D4
Grimaldi's	31	G4
Grocery	32	E5
Nathan's Famous Hot Dogs	33	A5
Pedro's Restaurant	34	G4
Peter Luger	35	F2
Pies-n-Thighs	36	G2

| River Cafe | 37 | G4 |
| Totonno's | 38 | A5 |

🍸 DRINK

68 Jay St	39	G4
Abilene	40	E5
Alligator Lounge	41	G3
Bar 4	42	D3
Bar Reis	43	E6
Cattyshack	44	E6
Ginger's	45	E6
Low-Bar	46	G4
O'Connors	47	F6
Spuyten Duyvil	48	G2
Superfine	49	G4
Waterfront Ale House	50	F4

⭐ PLAY

Bar Below	51	F5
Barbes	52	D6
Brick Theater	53	G3
Galapagos Art Space	54	G2
St Ann's Warehouse	55	G4

Please see over for map

SEE

111 FRONT STREET GALLERIES
www.frontstreetgalleries.com; 111 Front St near Washington St; ❹ A, C to High St
You'll recognize this building immediately thanks to the arresting orange banner at the front door. More than 11 independent artists and art organizations are housed inside, each one maintaining its own distinct office or atelier. Visitors are more than welcome to browse through and check out the work going on in each one, but opening hours vary.

BROOKLYN HISTORICAL SOCIETY
☎ 718-222-4111; www.brooklynhistory .org; 128 Pierrepont St; ⏱ 10am-5pm Wed-Sun; ❹ M, R to Court St, 2, 3, 4, 5 to Borough Hall
Built in 1881 and renovated in 2002, this four-story Queen Anne–style landmark building (a gem in its own right) houses a library (with some 33,000 grainy digitized photos from decades past), auditorium and museum devoted to the borough. The society also leads several Brooklyn walking tours (some free), and an occasional bus tour of the riverside Navy Yard.

CONEY ISLAND BOARDWALK
www.coneyisland.com; 1000 Surf Ave; ❹ D, N, Q or F train to Stillwell Ave
The kitschy and somewhat dissolute charm of Coney Island is not long for this world – a major developer has scooped up many of its most famous sights, including the Astroland Amusement Park. Plans include a major overhaul, adding gleaming rides and high-rise condos. But the stunning Atlantic beach views that can be seen while strolling the boardwalk are unchanged, as is the surrounding Russian community.

DUMBO ARTS CENTER
☎ 718-694-0831; www.dumboartscent er.org; 30 Washington St; ⏱ noon-6pm Thu-Mon; ❹ A, C to High St
One of Washington St's best galleries, this collective also puts together the D.U.M.B.O. Arts Festival each year. It offers a great overview of the neighborhood – who is working on what and showing where – and maintains a rotating exhibit of various artists.

NEW YORK TRANSIT MUSEUM
☎ 718-694-1600; www.mta.info/mta /museum; Boerum Pl at Schermerhorn St; admission $5, some tours $15; ⏱ 10am-4pm Tue-Fri, noon-5pm Sat & Sun; ❹ 2, 3, 4, 5 to Borough Hall, M, R to Court St

Occupying an old subway station built in 1936 (and out of service since 1946), this museum takes on 100-plus years of getting around the Big Apple. Kids love the models of old subway cars, bus drivers' seats, and the chronological display of turnstiles from the late 19th century. Best is the downstairs area, on the platform, where everyone can climb aboard 13 original subway and elevated-train cars, dating from the 1904 wicker-seat, army green–and-crimson Brooklyn Union Elevated Car.

◉ PIEROGI 2000
☎ 718-599-2144; 177 N 9th St btwn Bedford & Driggs Aves; ◷ noon-6pm Thu-Mon; ◉ L to Bedford Ave
An early arrival to Williamsburg, Pierogi 2000 has made a name for itself by handling a rotating roster of 800 artists in its front room, as well as letting people don white gloves to flip through drawings and other artist renderings. The back room is a community center/meeting space for cultural gatherings.

◉ PROSPECT PARK
www.prospectpark.org; Grand Army Plaza; ◷ 5am-1am; ◉ 2, 3 to Grand Army Plaza, F to 15th St-Prospect Park; ♿
Not quite as famous as the iconic Central Park, this lush green oasis is considered an equal master-piece from designers Olmsted and Vaux. Its 585 acres contain the gorgeous Brooklyn Botanical Gardens, numerous lakes, bike paths, meadows and running routes. The soaring arched entrance at Grand Army Plaza, not far from the Brooklyn Museum and next to the Brooklyn Public Library, is one of the borough's most celebrated sights.

◉ ROEBLING HALL
☎ 718-599-5352; www.roeblinghall .com; 390 Wythe Ave at S 4th St; ◷ noon-6pm Mon-Fri, or by appointment; ◉ J, M, Z to Marcy Ave, L to Bedford Ave
It's been around for seven years and done a lot to advance Brooklyn's art world in that time through installation, photography, painting, video and film. Roebling makes a point of bringing foreign artists here (and vice versa); at the time of writing, it was hosting 19 artists from 10 countries.

◉ SCHROEDER ROMERO
☎ 718-486-8992; 173A N 3rd St at Bedford Ave; ◷ noon-6pm Mon-Fri, or by appointment; ◉ L to Bedford Ave
Focusing on emerging and mid-career artists whose works address socio-political themes, gallery director Lisa Schroeder has curated some of the most

> [!NOTE]
> **STATEN ISLAND FERRY**
> This is the life – you've got a nice breeze, plenty of room, a good long look at Lower Manhattan, the Statue of Liberty and Ellis Island, and it costs nothing. The **Staten Island Ferry** (☎ 718-815-BOAT; www.nyc.gov/html/dot/html/masstran/ferries/statfery.html; Whitehall Terminal at Whitehall & South Sts; admission free; 24hr; &) has got to be the best deal in town.

talked-about shows in recent years, including one chronicling an artist's transition from male to female and *Proof of Mary*, featuring gravestone art.

SHOP

🔲 3R LIVING
☎ 718-832-0951; 276L Fifth Ave, near Garfield Pl; 11am-7pm Sun-Wed, 11am-8pm Thu-Sat; M, R to Union St
At last, a design-conscious eco store that still manages to emphasize the three Rs – Reduce, Reuse and Recycle. This shop is full of nifty home ideas and solutions, and all use 'green' products imported under fair-trade agreements. The in-store recycling center has separate bins for old batteries, crayons, laser-printer cartridges, CDs and cell phones.

🔲 ACADEMY RECORDS AND CDS
☎ 718-218-8200; 96 N 6th St near Wythe Ave; noon-8pm Sun-Thu, noon-10pm Fri & Sat; L to Bedford Ave
Stacks and stacks of vinyl, CDs, even some old DVDs, fill every bit of available space at this hipster hangout, where the music-obsessed come to pay homage and search for classic recordings amid the sprawl.

🔲 AMARCORD
☎ 718-963-4001; 223 Bedford Ave near N 5th St; noon-8pm; L to Bedford Ave
A vintage store that's stocked with vintage European dresses, bags and shoes that the owner hunts down on the continent, Amarcord is a favorite for thrift-store mavens, and on weekends gets visits from Manhattanites too.

🔲 BROOKLYN ARTISANS GALLERY
☎ 718-330-0343; 221A Court St; 11am-7pm Wed-Sat, 11am-6pm Sun; F, G to Bergen St
Run as a collective, this store only carries knick-knacks and things made by local craftspeople. Anything goes – scarves, frames, jewelry, handbags, paintings, and stained-glass bookends shaped like cats and dogs.

NEIGHBORHOODS

BROOKLYN

☐ CLOTHIER BROOKLYN

☎ 718-623-2444; 44 Fifth Ave near Dean St; ⏰ 11am-8pm Tue-Sat, noon-6pm Sun; ⊕ B, Q, 2, 3, 4, 5 to Atlantic Ave

Jeans and jackets in all shapes and sizes in denim, denim and more denim.

☐ DEAR FIELDBINDER

☎ 718-852-3620; www.dearfieldbinder .com; 198 Smith St near Baltic St; ⏰ 11am-7pm; ⊕ F, G to Bergen St

Located on big-name Smith St, this white-walled store more than holds its own with some big-name designers – A Cheng, for one – while making sure to showcase some raw talent too (Wendy Hil, Para Gabia, Tom K Nguyen). The clothes are eclectic, but classically feminine.

☐ GHOSTOWN

☎ 718-387-0990; 335 Grand St near Havemeyer St; ⏰ noon-8pm; ⊕ J, M, Z to Marcy Ave, G, L to Metropolitan Ave-Lorimer St

A used and gently worn clothing store that also doubles as a club on certain nights of the week, Ghostown carries men's and women's streetwear from local designers and brands. The parties come and go; check in with the owners while you're in town.

☐ JACQUES TORRES CHOCOLATE

☎ 718-875-9772; www.mrchocolate .com; 66 Water St, Dumbo; ⏰ 9am-7pm Mon-Sat; ⊕ A, C to High St

Treats from Jacques Torres Chocolate

Oyunchimeg Blease,
Bodega owner, Brooklyn

Best thing about your neighborhood? Rents are still affordable! **How has New York changed in the past five years?** I think it's more diverse. In my neighborhood, around Flatbush Ave, there used to be mostly African Americans. Now there's a lot of Asians from all over. **What will your neighborhood look like in five years?** Even more mixed, with a lot of Africans and Asians, but not too many Europeans. **What's a tourist trap worth the trip?** When my friends and family come from Mongolia, I always tell them to go to the Statue of Liberty. **Favorite season?** Summer, because then I can go to Jones Beach and swim. **What's your favorite thing about New York City?** The skyscrapers. When I first came here I'd never seen one before. I am still always looking up and wondering how they built those buildings.

Serious chocolatier JT runs this small European-style store with three-table café, filled with the most velvety and innovative chocolates ever crafted. Take a few to the nearby Empire Fulton Ferry State Park for a snack and a view between the Brooklyn and Manhattan Bridges. The shop also does a brisk internet business, and makes its delicacies available at Chocolate Bar (p126) in the Meatpacking District.

☐ LOOPY MANGO
☎ 718-222-0595; www.loopymango .com; 68 Jay St (& 117 Front St); ☽ noon-8pm Tue-Sat, noon-7pm Sun; ◎ A, C to High St

The brainchild of crochet designer Waejong Kim and artist Anna Pul-vermakher, Loopy Mango features Waejong's one-of-a-kind crochet clothes and accessories, and Anna's series of woodcuts and crochet jewelry and accessories. The two women, both artists, opened a second Dumbo store on Front St; they carry other designers like Cynthia Rowley and Vera Wang.

☐ PRAGUE KOLEKTIV
☎ 718-260-8013; 143B Front St near Jay St; ☽ noon-7pm Tue-Fri, 11am-7pm Sat & Sun, closed Mon; ◎ A, C to High St

Red-lacquered chairs and chrome-trimmed tables are just two of the retro Czech styles you'll find at this furniture store specializing in 1920s and '30s Eastern European designs.

☐ SAHADI'S
☎ 718-624-4550; 187 Atlantic Ave near Clinton St; ☽ 9am-7pm Mon-Sat; ◎ 2, 3, 4, 5 to Borough Hall

Kalamata olives, fresh hummus, sweet figs and dates, and briny pickles – all sorts of Middle Eastern treats are sold at this specialty store, run by a Middle Eastern family.

☐ SPRING GALLERY STORE
☎ 718-222-1054; 126A Front St cnr Jay St; ☽ 1-7pm Thu-Sun, closed Mon-Wed; ◎ A, C to High St

A decidedly anti-establishment mentality reigns at Spring Gallery Store, where design objects like Richard Saja's Historically Inaccurate pillows are displayed in the windows. The latest in European home furnishings is sold here.

🍴 EAT
🍴 360 *French Bistro* $$
☎ 718-246-0360; www.360brooklyn .com; 360 Van Brunt St near Sullivan St, Red Hook; ☽ 5:30-11:30pm Wed-Sat, 5:30-10pm Sun; ◎ A, C, F to Jay St-Borough Hall; Ⓥ

360's three-course prix fixe ($25 at press time) is a steal, and the owner will talk your ear off about which organic or biodynamic wine you should order with the veal-tongue confit with pickled radishes and cornichon, or the steamed PEI mussels in Thai curry, or even the red-wine-braised short ribs with oil-cured black olives, smoked bacon and orange zest, sautéed kale and penne pasta.

🍴 AL DI LA TRATTORIA
Italian $$

☎ 718-783-4565; www.aldilatrattoria .com; 248 Fifth Ave at Carroll St; ⏲ dinner Wed-Mon; Ⓜ F to 15th St-Prospect Park, M, R to Union St; Ⓥ

Make reservations waaaay in advance as this place is perpetually packed – for good reason though: the food. There are plenty of pastas and antipasti, but also braised rabbit with black olives and polenta, calf liver, and pan-roasted cod.

🍴 APPLEWOOD *American* $$
☎ 718-768-2044; www.applewoodny .com; 501 11th St btwn Seventh & Eighth Aves; ⏲ dinner Tue-Sat, lunch Sun; Ⓜ F to Seventh Ave; ♿ Ⓥ ♨

Applewood fills nightly with chatty locals who like the working fireplace and back bar with its cocktails and a long wine list. The upstate venison – sliced and grilled – comes with leeks and shallots ($26). There's always a lone veggie option – like the

spinach and basil risotto with mascarpone cheese – and several fish dishes.

🍴 BLUE RIBBON SUSHI BROOKLYN *Sushi* $$
☎ 718-840-0408; 278 Fifth Ave btwn 1st St & Garfield Pl; ⏲ dinner; Ⓜ M, R to Union St; Ⓥ

Next to Blue Ribbon's meat- and oyster-filled restaurant, the sushi counterpart features sleek wooden benches and a long list of sashimi, sushi and maki rolls. If you can't choose, the sushi sashimi combo is $27.50.

🍴 BUBBY'S BROOKLYN
American Traditional $$
☎ 718-222-0666; 1 Main St at Water St; ⏲ lunch & dinner Thu-Tue; Ⓜ A, C to High St; ♿ Ⓥ ♨

Bubby's is a family-friendly haven when you're foot-sore and hungry. Its juicy burgers, mac 'n' cheese and heaping plates of BBQ chicken are impossible to resist.

🍴 CHESTNUT
American Nouveau $$
☎ 718-243-0049; 271 Smith St near Degraw St; ⏲ 5:30-11pm Tue-Sat, 11am-3pm & 5:30-10pm Sun; Ⓜ F, G to Carroll St; Ⓥ

Chef Daniel Eardley seeks out the best upstate and local organic farm goods for his delectable meals. Good bets are the Sunday brunch,

NEIGHBORHOODS

BROOKLYN

nightly tasting menus (wine pairings optional), or the prix-fixe chef's specials with charred octopus, stuffed pork chop or halibut with wild mushrooms.

🍴 DUMONT
American Traditional $

☎ 718-486-7717; www.dumontrestaurant.com; 432 Union Ave; 🕐 lunch & dinner; 🚇 G, L to Metropolitan Ave-Lorimer St; 🚻 Ⓥ

Eating beet salads, big burgers, crab cakes, 'Dumac 'n' cheese,' and more serious mains like skate and roasted olives, grilled half-chicken, and steak *bordelaise* in the garden bar or treehouse is great summer fun.

🍴 FRANKIE'S 457 SPUTINO
Italian $$

☎ 718-403-0033; www.frankiessputino.com; 🕐 lunch & dinner; 🚇 F, G to Carroll St; 🚻 Ⓥ

There's no end to the inventive sides Frankie's dishes up – roasted cauliflower, artichokes, beets, sweet potatoes, brussels sprouts and mushrooms – to go along with your choice of salty cured meats, or deep-dish sandwiches with tasty meatballs or crunchy veggies.

🍴 GOOD FORK
Korean/American $$

☎ 718-643-6636; www.goodfork.com; 391 Van Brunt St near Coffey St;

🕐 5:30pm-10:30pm Tue-Sun; 🚇 F, G to Smith-9th Sts; 🚻 Ⓥ

You get two types of cuisine in a convivial atmosphere here. If 'Korean style' steak, kimchi rice and fried egg don't appeal, try dumplings, the gumbo, or the ravioli, or even the slow-braised Korean pork. It's all good.

🍴 GRIMALDI'S *Pizza* $

☎ 718-858-4300; www.grimaldisbrooklyn.com; 19 Old Fulton St; 🕐 lunch & dinner; 🚇 A, C to High St; 🚻 Ⓥ 👶

Grimaldi's

Legendary pizza with perfect crust and spicy sauces, topped with bubbling cheeses of all types. If the 'no reservations' policy creates long lines, everybody stops complaining once the pizza's dished up.

GROCERY
New American $$$
☎ 718-596-3335; 288 Smith St; dinner Mon-Sat, lunch Sat; F, G to Carroll St;
Even with the additional space, it's still hard to get a table at what's become Smith St's hottest eatery. Semolina-crusted fluke, pan-roasted monkfish, octopus, teenage greens, home-smoked trout and spaetzle on the side are perennial favorites.

NATHAN'S FAMOUS HOT DOGS *Hot Dogs* $
☎ 718-946-2202; 1310 Surf Ave; breakfast, lunch & dinner till late; D, F to Coney Island-Stillwell Ave
If you eat 'em, this is the place for an all-beef dog with sauerkraut and mustard. A frightening time to visit is July 4, when Nathan's holds a hot dog-eating contest (the record stands at Takeru Kobayashi's 50 and a half).

PEDRO'S RESTAURANT
Latin American $
☎ 718-797-2851; 73 Jay St at Front St; lunch & dinner daily; A, C to High St;

Pedro's battered facade doesn't instill confidence, but aesthetics aside, it's one heckuva place. It's been serving up tasty tacos and burritos with ice-cold beer for years and has a loyal following. Sitting outside on its strange-shaped stools certainly adds to the fun.

PETER LUGER
Steakhouse $$
☎ 718-387-7400; www.peterluger.com; 178 Broadway; lunch & dinner; J, M, Z to Marcy Ave;
There are a couple of rules to follow here: bring cash, first of all, and make a reservation. Be prepared to wait, and check your shyness at the door – these are long, communal tables. Expect rapid but slightly mechanical service, but just when you start to wonder why you came, your steak – juicy, perfect and tender – stifles all your doubts.

PIES-N-THIGHS
Southern/Soul $
☎ 347-282-6005; 351 Kent Ave near S 5th St; 11am-9pm Tue-Sun; J, M, Z to Marcy Ave;
It's a bit rough-looking from the outside, but once you get through the Williamsburg Rock Star Bar to where the cooking gets done, you'll have forgotten the 15-foot barbed-wire fence outside. This is southern cooking done right –

NEIGHBORHOODS

BROOKLYN

pulled pork, mac 'n' cheese, home-made bread and double-crusted pies oozing organic berries.

🍴 RIVER CAFE *American* $$$$
☎ 718-522-5200; www.rivercafe.com; 1 Water St; 🕐 lunch & dinner daily, brunch Sat & Sun; 🚇 A,C to High St; V 🚼

It takes a beating from purists who sniff the words 'tourist trap,' but they've probably never actually been to this floating wonder with beautiful views from under Manhattan Bridge. The seared mahi-mahi with almond crust and scallop seviche are just two of many innovative dishes the kitchen produces, and River Cafe's brunches are legendary for their bloody marys and perfect eggs.

🍴 TOTONNO'S *Pizza* $
☎ 718-372-8606; 1524 Neptune Ave near 16th St; 🕐 noon-8pm Wed-Sun; 🚇 D, F, N, Q to Coney Island-Stillwell Ave; 🚼

Open daily as long as there's fresh dough – when it goes, the shop closes for the day. It's part of the only-do-it-when-it's-fresh ethos that's run this place for decades. The crust tastes better and the sauce sweeter, making the experience worth a Coney Island trip.

🍸 DRINK
🍸 68 JAY ST
☎ 718-260-8207; 68 Jay St; 🚇 A, C to High St

Paint-spattered but still elegant, with rounded arches and a big columned doorway, 68 Jay St is a rarity among bars – it turns the music down to a comfortable level for discussion among patrons. Consequently, you hear a lot of art-world buzz as the regulars – all members of said world – dish the dirt over drinks.

🍸 ABILENE
☎ 718-522-6900; 442 Court St at 3rd Pl; 🕐 6pm-4am; 🚇 F, G to Carroll St

Chess and domino lovers will feel right at home at this low-key beer and bourbon joint, where the back tables are set aside for gamers. The bar has a good assortment of beers on tap, and the usual assortment of well drinks, but it's the gentle aura that pulls in the regulars.

🍸 ALLIGATOR LOUNGE
☎ 718-599-4440; 600 Metropolitan Ave, Williamsburg; 🚇 L to Lorimer St

In Williamsburg's northern reaches, the Alligator draws a mixed crowd of hipsters and working-class locals, who sit on U-shaped leather settees or in Japanese tea-house nooks in the back. The real draw is the free, freshly made brick-oven pizza. And, hey, a pitcher of Yuengling is $14. Karaoke on Thursdays, live jazz on Sundays.

BAR 4
☎ 718-832-9800; 444 Seventh Ave at 15th St; 🕑 6pm-4am; 🚇 F to Seventh Ave, M, R to Prospect Ave

Grungy and a little worn down, Bar 4 is nonetheless relaxing, and it serves up some mean Martinis – flavored with juice, or straight up. DJ styles change daily, and Tuesday nights are open mic starting at 9pm.

BAR REIS
☎ 718-832-5716; 375 Fifth Ave; 🕑 5:30pm-2am Sun-Wed, 5:30pm-4am Thu-Sat; 🚇 F, M, R to Fourth Ave-9th St

You've got choices here – climb the spiral staircase to the upper floor and survey the scene from above, or head out back to the wisteria-filled garden, strung with romantic lights, or hang at the street-level bar. The drinks are delicious, the crowd is friendly and the vibe sophisticated and relaxed.

CATTYSHACK
☎ 718-230-5740; 249 Fourth Ave near President St; 🕑 2pm-4am Mon-Fri, noon-4am Sat & Sun; 🚇 M, R to Union St

Two floors of pulsing beats, raw industrial views and a queer-friendly atmosphere that's mainly for the ladies but also welcoming to gays, trannies and heterosexuals. Weekend nights turn into a dance party; weeknights tend to be slower and more communal.

GINGER'S
☎ 718-778-0924; 363 Fifth Ave; 🚇 F, M, R to Fourth Ave-9th St

Let-love-rule lesbian bar with ruby-red walls that sees a lot of gays and straights at its long bar up front and big garden in the back. More laid-back than Manhattan's lesbian bars? Sure, this is Brookburg, baby.

LOW-BAR
☎ 718-222-1LOW; 81 Washington St; 🕑 7pm-2am Fri & Sat; 🚇 A, C to High St

Low-Bar, an offshoot of the popular Rice (p90) eatery in Manhattan, serves the same delicious mixtures of black, green and long-grain rice, but it also has a secret gathering spot in its basement that's a popular nightclub on weekends. It starts out slow but generally heats up after midnight, when the dancing breaks out and people start to live a little.

O'CONNORS
☎ 718-783-9721; 39 Fifth Ave, btwn Bergen & Dean Sts; 🕑 noon-4am; 🚇 2, 3 to Bergen St

All dive-bar infrastructurally, with fluorescent lights, old wall paneling, and Yankees games flickering on the TV, O'Connor's cheap drinks (gin-and-tonics are $2.50!), its glorious 1931 roots and quiet vibe bring in the hipster youth, too.

NEIGHBORHOODS

BROOKLYN

SPUYTEN DUYVIL
☎ 718-963-4140;
spuytenduyvil@verizon.net; 359 Metropolitan Ave; ⏱ 5pm-1/2am Sun-Thu, 5pm-3/4am Fri & Sat; ⊕ L to Bedford Ave

Painted-red tin ceilings, vintage maps and ashtray displays look over wooden floors, with armchairs set by library racks of old paperbacks no-one would want to lift. In good weather, the au-naturale back courtyard is open. There's cheeses, pickles and cured meats for snacking.

SUPERFINE
☎ 718-243-9005; 126 Front St; ⊕ A, C to High St; Ⓥ

Superfine isn't only a good place to eat and play pool – it's a cool bar, too. Late nights on weekends keep it open well past 2am.

WATERFRONT ALE HOUSE
☎ 718-522-3794; 155 Atlantic Ave near Clinton St; ⏱ 11:30am-2am Mon-Thu, 11:30am-4am Fri & Sat; ⊕ M, R to Court St, 2, 3, 4, 5 to Borough Hall, F, G to Bergen St; Ⓥ

Solid pub grub, like burgers, fries, smoky meats in big paninis and hearty salads, combined with a neighborhood vibe, a wide beer selection and live blues and jazz makes this place a winner night after night.

★ PLAY
BAR BELOW
☎ 718-694-2277; 209 Smith St; ⏱ 7:30pm-4am Thu-Sat; ⊕ F, G to Bergen St, A, C, G to Hoyt-Schermerhorn Sts

Tucked underneath the Faan restaurant, which does decent Asian food, Bar Below has a strict 'no sportswear' rule and a loungey, cluby feel even though, in theory, dancing isn't allowed. Once the DJ hits a certain stride though, all bets are off and things start moving.

BARBES
☎ 718-965-9177; www.barbesbrooklyn.com; 376 9th St at Sixth Ave; ⊕ F to Seventh Ave

This bar and performance space, owned by two French musicians and longtime Brooklyn residents, is named after the North African enclave of Paris. It hosts music, readings and film screenings in the back room, and plays eclectic music, ranging from Lebanese diva Asmahan to Mexican *bandas,* Venezuelan *joropos* and Romanian brass bands.

BRICK THEATER
☎ 718-907-6189; www.bricktheater.com; 575 Metropolitan Ave btwn Union Ave & Lorimer St; ⏱ times vary depending on show; ⊕ G, L to Metropolitan Ave-Lorimer St

Formerly an auto-body shop, a yoga studio and various storage spaces, this brick-walled garage has been completely refurbished into a state-of-the-art dance and theater complex, with a large sprung floor, professional lighting and sound package. Now it does critically acclaimed productions like *Jenna is Nuts*, *Habitat*, *In a Strange Room* (based on Faulkner's *As I Lay Dying*) and stagings of Chekhov's *Three Sisters* and O'Neill's *Beyond the Horizon*. Its productions range from $10 to $20 and profits go back into the project.

☆ GALAPAGOS ART SPACE
☎ 718-384-4586; www.galapagosart space.com; 70 N 6th St; 🕑 6pm-2am Sun-Thu, 6pm-4am Fri-Sat; 🚇 L to Bedford Ave
They call it an 'art space,' but it's more of an atmospheric hangout

with a diverse line-up of experimental music, disco and campy ukulele bands singing of gay paradise. The entry is a giant dark reflecting pool (the size of some East Village bars), with an elevated stage and long bar (serving $6 cocktails) in back. Some events are free, others are $6 to $8.

☆ ST ANN'S WAREHOUSE
☎ 718-254-8779; 38 Water St btwn Main & Dock Sts; 🕑 1-7pm Tue-Sat; 🚇 A, C to High St
This avant-garde performance company took over an old spice mill and turned it into an exciting venue for the arts. Now the cavernous space regularly hosts innovative theater, and features some big names like Philip Seymour Hoffman and Meryl Streep.

>SNAPSHOTS

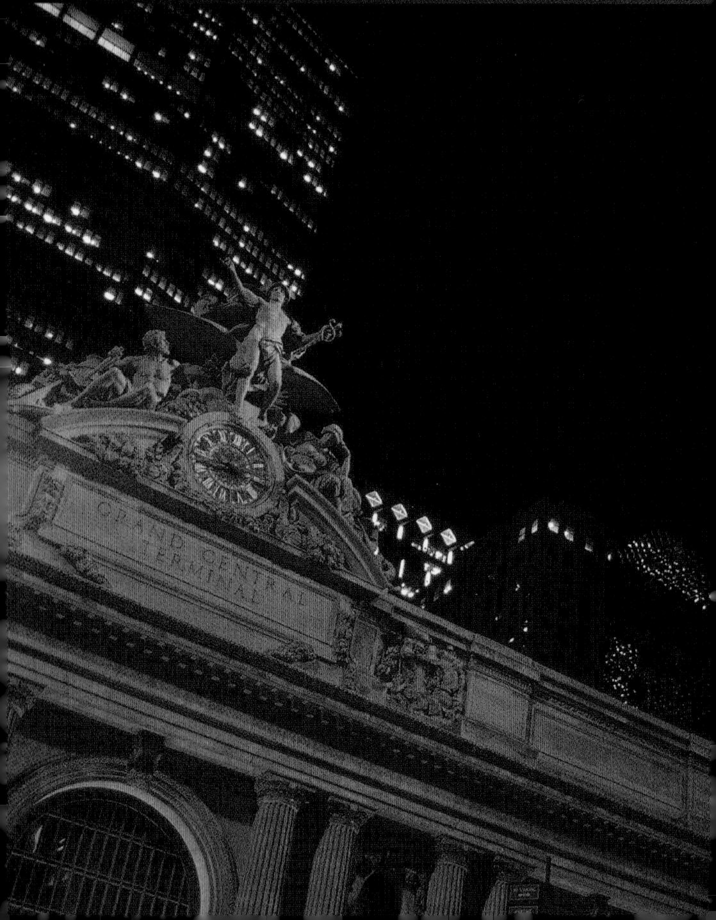

How do you best experience New York like the locals do? Simple – join them in their favorite pastimes. Whether it's gallery hopping or roller-skating at the Roxy, you won't be alone. There are so many options in the city, the challenge is finding time and energy for them all.

Grand Central Terminal and the Chrysler Building

ACCOMMODATIONS

With a little luck and careful planning, it's possible to find a great place in NYC that won't break your budget. Possible, but not likely.

The good news is that you'll get some bang for your buck in terms of service and decor (truly spacious rooms are a rarity in just about every price range). Hotels in Manhattan tend to come with sleek bars, beautiful restaurants, even nightclubs, day spas and gyms. If you're looking for a relaxing visit with museum hopping and cultural activity, look for accommodations on the Upper East and West Sides. Business travelers or those bent on seeing Broadway shows should focus on Midtown West first, and then Midtown East around Grand Central Station. Trendy boutique and theme hotels are popping up all over – Times Sq, Bryant Park, Union Sq and now on the Lower East Side. You can find bargains in older hotels in Chelsea, and among the B&Bs of Greenwich Village and the East Village.

Good resources to use include Lonely Planet's haystack (haystack .lonelyplanet.com), Just New York Hotels (www.justnewyorkhotels.com), New York Deals on Hotels (www.newyork.dealsonhotels.com), New York City Hotels Today (www.newyorkcityhotelstoday.com) and NYC Hotels (www.nyc-hotels.net). Hotels sometimes offer special internet-only deals on their own websites too. Priceline (www.priceline.com), Hotwire (www .hotwire.com), Orbitz (www.orbitz.com), Hotels.com (www.hotels.com), Hoteldiscounts.com (www.hoteldiscounts.com) and Travelzoo (www .travelzoo.com) all claim prices that are up to 70 % less than the standard rates.

haystack.lonelyplanet.com

Need a place to stay? Find and book it at lonelyplanet.com. More than 90 properties are featured for New York City – each personally visited, thoroughly reviewed and happily recommended by a Lonely Planet author. From hostels to high-end hotels, we've hunted out the places that will bring you unique and special experiences. Read independent reviews by authors and other travel aficionados like you, and get practical information including amenities, maps and photos. Then reserve your room simply and securely via Haystack – our online booking service. It's all at www.lonelyplanet.com/accommodation.

BEST BOUTIQUES
> Hudson (www.hudsonhotel.com)
> W Hotel Times Sq (www.whotels
  .com)
> 70 Park Ave (www.70parkave.com)
> Bryant Park Hotel (www.bryant
  parkhotel.com)
> Casablanca Hotel (www.casablanca
  hotel.com)

BEST 'OLD NEW YORK' HOTELS
> Chelsea (www.hotelchelsea.com)
> Dylan (www.dylanhotel.com)
> Hotel Deauville (www.hoteldeauville
  .com)
> The Mark (www.themarkhotel.com)
> Hotel Beacon (www.beaconhotel
  .com)

Above Taxis outside W Hotel Times Sq

SNAPSHOTS

ARCHITECTURE

Hong Kong may have more skyscrapers, but New York's are the tallest – this city invented the vertical high-rise. With the World Trade Center Towers in Lower Manhattan gone, the most striking examples of modern construction can be found in the midtown area. It's home to many of the iconic structures that symbolize the city, such as the Empire State Building, a 102-story art deco creation finished in 193,1 and the Chrysler Building, a popular landmark finished in 1930. Inside Rockefeller Center you'll find the GE Building, another art deco construction that's lauded for the frieze over the main entrance depicting Wisdom.

The Time Warner Center, a mixed-use building at Columbus Circle, was the first major skyscraper built in the city after September 11. Its striking, black-glass exterior and sloping facade are considered an architectural feat and it's one of the city's most exclusive addresses – the penthouse condo went for $45 million. The newly finished Conde Nast Building (officially at 4 Times Sq) is a modern skyscraper built on 'green principles,' a first for Manhattan. It's got high-performing insulation and shading to keep the air-conditioning and heating systems turned off on most days.

For many residents, however, the city's most beloved buildings are the short, squat rows of Federalist-style houses left intact from colonial (or at least pre-WWI) times. New York's surviving original buildings were all built of rock; the great fire of 1831 wiped out anything built of flammable material. Colonnade Row (p95) along Astor Pl is a great example of pre-1900s architecture.

FIVE FAMOUS BUILDINGS
> Chrysler Building (p158)
> Empire State Building (p158)
> Flatiron Building (p148)
> Rockefeller Center (p160)
> Dakota (p206)

ART GALLERIES

The official count for art galleries in New York City is around 500 – include every offbeat storefront and studio-cum-display-center and the figure would probably double. Art is in the air here, and it can pop up in some of the strangest places. Soho, once a stronghold of creativity, still houses a few fantastic galleries, but most of the up-and-coming work is developed and shown in Dumbo, where prices are more affordable. Chelsea – from about 21st to 26th Sts on 10th and 11th Aves – is one long strip of salons, shops, art dealers and galleries. Midtown Manhattan has become an art world offshoot – what can't fit into Chelsea has moved there.

New York Magazine's free online reviews (www.nymetro.com), Time Out New York's comprehensive listings (www.timeoutny.com) and the Gallery Guide in major galleries are indispensable in sorting through your options. The New York Times' weekend edition and the venerable Village Voice (www.villagevoice.com) are your backup sources, and www.westchelseaarts.com provides an exhaustive database of all current galleries. The city's Department of Cultural Affairs (www .nyc.gov/html/dcla) maintains an event calendar for the five boroughs and allows you to search for galleries and attractions by art type and borough. If you're pressed for time, head out on a comprehensive tour through Chelsea and Soho by calling **New York Gallery tours** (☎ 212-946-1548; www.nygallerytours.com).

MUST-SEE GALLERIES
> Chelsea Art Museum (p133)
> gallery group (p21)
> Cheim & Read (p133)
> Matthew Marks (p137)
> Gagosian (p136)
> Soho Galleries (p91)
> Louis Meisel Gallery (p92)
> galleryonetwentyeight (p67)
> Participant Inc (p70)
> Drawing Center (p81)

SNAPSHOTS

BARS

New York, a city that loves to imbibe and socialize, has a whole vocabulary devoted to the business of drinking. Every classic drink has at least one twist – try a dirty martini, an apple-tini, a sake-tini, a lychee Martini or a ginger martini – there's always a race to create the next big winner.

Wine-lovers have always felt at home in New York, where sommelier is not a foreign word, and now beer-aficionados are blissfully enveloped in a microbrewery boom.

Cigarette smoking is out (outdoors, that is) since Mayor Bloomberg made it illegal to puff in public establishments. Cigars, however, are in, as long as you're inside a cigar bar.

Gastro-pubs (pubs with good food) are popular in Brooklyn, Lower Manhattan and the Upper West Side; former speakeasies and 'hidden' bars proliferate on the Lower East Side. The East Village is full of eclectic choices, swinging from posh to punk in two doors, and the West Village has some quaint gay, lesbian, cabaret and literary establishments. Most of the energetic stuff happens in the Meatpacking District and Chelsea, where the extreme west side is kind of a 'club row.'

Many bars, particularly those downtown, have late afternoon happy hours, when drinks are half their regular price, and some clubs repeat the fun after midnight, all the better to draw in the club-hopping crowd.

BEST NEIGHBORHOOD BARS
> Bridge Café (p50)
> Pete's Tavern (pictured above; p153)
> Chumley's (p118)
> Ear Inn (p90)
> West Side Tavern (p144)

BEST WINE & BEER BARS
> Morrell Wine Bar & Café (p176)
> Ginger Man (p166)
> Xicala (p91)
> Single Room Occupancy (p176)
> D.B.A. (p104)

CLUBBING & NIGHTLIFE

Legendary nightclub Studio 54 has long since shut down, but its free-wheeling spirit still moves around Manhattan, bouncing from club to club. As one closes its doors, another one opens. This constant shuffling of clubs is the byproduct of increased vigilance from local authorities who for the past decade have been cracking down on the notorious drug dealing and pervasive underage drinking that occur in many locations.

There's still plenty of nightlife to be had, mostly along the extreme west side of nonresidential Chelsea, where club owners have taken refuge from frequent police raids.

To get on top of the options that are out there, grab the Sunday and Friday editions of the *New York Times*, and the weekly editions of *New York Magazine, Time Out New York* and *The New Yorker*. *The Village Voice* has good information on dance clubs and a weekly column (Fly Life) that runs down where the best DJs are playing. Also try **Clubfone** (☎ 212-777-2582; www.clubfone.com).

FIVE BIG CLUBS
> Cain (p144)
> Movida (pictured above; p131)
> Lotus (p145)
> Happy Valley (p154)
> Level V (p131)

FIVE DANCE PARTIES
> Cielo (p130)
> Pyramid (p107)
> Happy Ending (p63)
> Subtonic Lounge (p76)
> Sapphire Lounge (p76)

SNAPSHOTS

COMEDY & CABARET

It might shock you to know that dancing and cabaret clubs don't mix in this town. Thanks to a Prohibition-era crackdown on all things fun, clubs must apply for a special license if they want to have more than three people dancing at the same time. Don't ask why these laws are still around – it's a mystery. Mayor Michael Bloomberg has made it clear he's got bigger fish to fry, but the city still fights every legal challenge brought to the 'Cabaret Laws.'

Luckily that hasn't hurt the cabaret business, which is as strong as ever. World-class performers like Eartha Kitt, Ute Lemper, Elaine Stritch and others keep the blues away, old chum, with regular gigs around town. The city's two campiest and most endearing clubs are in the West Village, naturally, and if you're lucky, Alan Cumming, who played in the Broadway show *Cabaret*, will drop by for a cameo.

Comedy is alive and well in Gotham, feeding its talent straight into live TV shows taped at Comedy Central in Times Sq. The newest and glossiest comedy clubs exist around the neon lights of Broadway, while the somewhat dingy stalwarts that spawned Jon Lovitz, Eddie Murphy, Chevy Chase, Jerry Seinfeld and others are still alive and kicking in the West Village and Upper East Side.

BEST CABARET & COMEDY
> Café Carlyle (p197)
> Comedy Cellar (p119)
> Mo Pitkins (p103)
> The Oak Room (p178)

FASHION & COUTURE

You've got the old guard, the new guard, the very, very avant-garde, and a lot of everything in between. There's so much on display that it's best to have a zen-like approach to clothes shopping in New York: beauty abounds, but find the right fit.

If money is no object, head right to the 'Gold Coast' along Madison Ave. It's a forty-block stretch of extremely high-end shopping, featuring couturiers like Luca Luca, Herrera, Bulgari and others. You'll be able to find the absolute best in menswear, womenswear, kids' clothing, accessories, watches, sunglasses – even the coffee and cake tastes extra special here.

Equally expensive stores line Fifth Ave near Columbus Circle. You can walk from Tiffany's into the houses of Balenciaga and Prada in just a few strides. There's also Ferragamo, Van Cleef & Arpels, Burberry and several of Manhattan's most famous department stores.

If you like your clothes on the cutting edge, your kind of shops will be found in the Meatpacking District, around the Nolita quadrant above Little Italy, and in the East Village. Don't forget to sign up for a list of the day's sample sales at www.dailycandy.com and nymag.com/shopping before you go.

MUST-STOP SHOPS
> Carlos Miele (p123)
> Alexander McQueen (p123)
> Catherine Malandrino (p126)
> Buckler (p123)
> Mayle (p86)

FIVE BEST SHOPPING DISTRICTS
> Madison Ave from 59th to 96th St (p193)
> Fifth Ave (p23)
> Mulberry & Mott Sts (pictured above) below Houston (p57)
> Orchard St and Grand St (p70)
> Grand Central Terminal (p158)

FOOD

There are more than 18,000 restaurants spread out across the five boroughs, and it's a safe bet that at any given time, at least half of them are serving up dishes that will knock your socks off. Choosing where to eat can be an agonizing process, but don't let it spoil your fun – when it doubt, consult the locals at www.chowhound.com. It's full of saucy and opinionated reviews from the pickiest customers around – New Yorkers.

Restaurants can go from hot to passé overnight, but the very best ones keep pulling in regulars long after the opening buzz is over, so it never hurts to make a reservation. New Yorkers are addicted to Open Table (www.opentable.com), which lets you read reviews, follow the 'buzz,' and book and instantly confirm reservations at hundreds of eateries. Of course, there are high-end and middle-to-low-end places where reservations are booked months in advance, or not taken at all. For the former, go early on a weeknight and hope for the best, or consider sitting in the lounge and eating from the bar menu – it's just as good as the formal menu and often half the price. For the latter, be prepared to wait.

Pick up a copy of *Time Out New York*, which reviews 100 restaurants in every issue, or a Zagat guide at any newsstand. *The Village Voice* also has a database of cheap eats on its website (www.villagevoice.com). With so much to choose from, you definitely won't go hungry.

BEST CHANCE AT ROMANCE
> Bridge Café (p50)
> Rise (p54)
> The Grocery (p229)
> Bao III (p101)
> Peasant (p89)

BEST LOUNGES FOR GOURMET FOOD
> Daniel (p195)
> Tenement (p75)
> Eleven Madison Park (p152)
> Spice Market (p129)
> Thalassa (p51)

BEST BRUNCHES
> Public (p89)
> Town (p175)
> Prune (p103)
> Schillers Liquor Bar (p74)
> Alias (p73)

BEST BETS IN BROOKLYN
> The Grocery (p229)
> 360 (p226)
> Applewood (p227)
> Superfine (p232)
> Al di la (p227)

Top left Diner food in the Meatpacking District **Above** Dinner at Schiller's Liquor Bar.

GAY & LESBIAN NEW YORK

Gay Pride – it's a month-long celebration in June of the city's longstand-ing and diverse queer communities, and an apt description of New York's gay and lesbian lifestyle, unabashedly out and empowered in a city noted for its overachievers. For more details on Gay Pride, check out www.heritageofpride.org.

New York doesn't differentiate much between hetero-and homo-sexual—at least, not when it comes to dancing, drinking and eating. Chelsea, Greenwich Village, Jackson Heights and Park Slope are famously gay-friendly communities, but there's hardly any establishment in town where gays and lesbians wouldn't feel welcome. The one rule to remem-ber is that the age of consent in New York for sex (of any kind) is 17.

The magazines *HX* and *Next* are available at restaurants and bars, or pick up *LGNY* and *NY Blade* from street-corner boxes and the lifestyle magazine *Metrosource* at shops and the Lesbian & Gay Community Services Center. *Time Out New York* features a good events section. Useful counseling, referral and information centers include the **Gay & Lesbian Hotline** (☎ 212-989-0999; glnh@glnh.org) and the **Lesbian & Gay Community Services Center** (☎ 212-620-7310; www.gaycenter.org; 208 W 13th St at Seventh Ave).

BEST GAY PRIDE EVENTS	LGBT BARS
> Gay Pride March	> Henrietta Hudson (p112)
> Dyke March	> Splash (p143)
> Mermaid Day Parade	> Gym (p143)
> Dance on the Pier	> Starlight Lounge (p107)
> Rapture on the River	

LITERARY NEW YORK

The ever-present backdrop in thousands of published and unpublished novels, articles, essays, memoirs and nonfiction books, New York City has become a literary character in its own right.

Edna St Vincent Millay, ee cummings, James Baldwin and many other celebrated writers have lived in the West Village, probably still the most literary neighborhood in Manhattan. In the East Village, the roiling Socialist speeches of fiery Emma Goldman and pro-birth-control advocate Margaret Sanger, handed out on seditious pamphlets, still hang in the rebellious air.

The Oak Room in the Algonquin Hotel is hallowed ground (Dorothy Parker drank there, along with many celebrated New Yorker writers), and Harlem resounds with the energy of Ralph Ellison, Zora Neale Thurston, Langston Hughes and others.

Bookish Brooklyn has Henry Miller, Paul Auster, Walt Whitman, Colson Whitehead, Nicole Krauss, Jonathan Lethem, Kathyrn Harris, Darin Strauss and Jhumpa Lahiri, to name but a few.

The Village Voice (villagevoice.com) has reading listings, and *New York Magazine* has a daily run down of literary events on its website (www.nymag.com).

The 92nd St Y stages the most interesting and laid-back author events you can find north of 14th St. Bluestockings, a shabby-chic run down bookstore, is your best bet if you want to actually talk face-to-face with an author. For the inside scoop, visit www.clubfreetime.com, for all the latest details.

WHERE THE AUTHORS DRANK
> White Horse Tavern (Dylan Thomas)
> The Oak Room (Dorothy Parker)
> Chumley's (Norman Mailer)
> Nuyorican Café (Pedro Pietri)
> Pete's Tavern (O.Henry)

LITERARY BARS
> KGB Bar (p105)
> Half-King (p143)
> Mo Pitkins (p103)
> Ear Inn (p90)
> Happy Ending (p63)

SNAPSHOTS

LIVE MUSIC

Catching a live band in New York is easy – just head towards the sound of music. In the summer and spring, New Yorkers take the party outside. Bluesy jazz on the lawn in Battery Park, salsa and swing at South St Seaport and Lincoln Center, all kinds of bands at Central Park Summerstage, and somewhat unplanned but free (and very popular) breakout performances at McCarren Park Pool in Williamsburg (www.freewilliamsburg.com).

To stay on top of what's happening year round, check out www .whatsupnyc.com, which posts tips about spontaneous performances in the city that aren't promoted anywhere but passed around by word of mouth (like the surprise early-morning show once put on by His Purpleness, Prince, in Brooklyn's Prospect Park).

There are still plenty of old jazz haunts in the West Village and Harlem, and some laid-back dive bars paying homage to punk and grunge on the Lower East Side and in Hell's Kitchen. Lincoln Center has set the standard for high-quality performances for decades now and continues to showcase artists from all genres. Symphony Space on the Upper West Side is known for live world music from under-appreciated performers.

BEST ROCK & INDIE LIVE MUSIC
> Bowery Ballroom (p78)
> Arlene Grocery (p77)
> Joe's Pub
> The Living Room (p78)

BEST JAZZ, BLUES & WORLD LIVE MUSIC
> 55 Bar (p119)
> Smoke (p217)
> St Nick's Pub (p217)
> Village Vanguard (p120)
> Lenox Lounge (p217)

MARKETS

What could be better than a good bargain? That's why the weekend market was invented. New Yorkers love to amble around the city's parks and squares, eyeing other people's cast-offs and hand-me-downs.

There's also a whole network of green markets set up around the city, making it easier than ever to find fresh produce. The main bazaar, which often feature crafts as well during the holiday seasons, gets set up in Union Square, but there are now outposts in parts of Upper and Lower Manhattan as well.

If outdoor markets are too rustic for you, there are plenty of big chains and revered mom-and-pop type bodegas to be found. Check out the many Whole Foods stores around the city for the best in organic eats, the latest craze to hit health-obsessed New Yorkers. Trader Joe's, another high-end gourmet organic shop, just opened two doors down from Whole Foods in Union Square. If you're looking for old-school New York, it's Zabar's on the Upper East Side, Balducci's on the west side, or the quaint market inside Grand Central Terminal.

POPULAR MARKETS
> Grand Central Terminal Markets
> Trader Joe's
> Balducci's

> Elizabeth & Vine
> Zabar's (pictured above)
> Chelsea Market

MUSEUMS

There's at least one in Manhattan for every type of visitor, and if you want to see even a handful of them, budget your time wisely. If you're going to do a marathon art day, make it a Friday, when many museums hold extended hours and offer drinks and sometimes jazz along with free admission in the evening. Just about every museum has at least one 'suggested donation' day when you pay what you wish.

Aside from the big-name attractions, where you can easily spend a day covering just one floor, there are many world-class medium- and small-sized museums that are worth a look, too. Some of them are even on 'Museum Mile,' the expanse of Fifth Ave that runs parallel to Central Park on the Upper East Side and features more than 100 cultural offerings all in a row.

Lower Manhattan has many of the city's best historic museums, and the outer boroughs have hidden gems focusing on up-and-coming artists, or exhibits tracing the history of art in developing immigrant communities.

BEST-KNOWN MUSEUMS
> Metropolitan Museum (p190)
> Museum of Modern Art (p159)
> Guggenheim (p192)
> Whitney Museum (p192)

BEST 'UNDISCOVERED' MUSEUMS
> Museo del Barrio (p211)
> Neue Galerie (p191)
> Lower East Side Tenement Museum (p67)
> National Museum of the American Indian (p47)
> Studio Museum in Harlem (p212)

NYC FOR LOVERS

Ahhh, *l'amour* – it's not just for Paris. New York has plenty of ways for you to get a romantic thrill. Be it rowing in Central Park, canoodling on the roof of the Empire State Building, dining at the Top of the Rock or strolling the Museum Mile, you'll find that this hard-nosed business town really has quite a soft side.

There's no need to be shy about your affection, either. New Yorkers are quite accustomed to seeing couples – same-sex or otherwise – walking arm-in-arm, holding hands, trading smooches, and even snuggling closely while enjoying a night concert in Central Park. The only time you might run into trouble is if you unintentionally block the sidewalk by moving in tandem.

Famously romantic NYC experiences include a ride around Central Park in a horse-and-buggy, a kiss in the middle of blaring Times Sq, dressing to the nines for a concert at Lincoln Center, hand-holding across the table at a dark and secluded Greenwich Village jazz club, and sharing a drink at legendary Top of the Tower, an intimate bar atop the Beekman Tower Hotel in midtown Manhattan.

BEST ROMANTIC SIGHTS & ATTRACTIONS
> The Cloisters at Fort Tyron
> Rockefeller Center (p160)
> Lincoln Center (pictured above; p201)
> Staten Island Ferry at sunset (p54)
> Brooklyn Botanical Gardens (p222)

BEST ROMANTIC RESTAURANTS
> Tavern on the Green (p186)
> Central Park Boathouse (p184)
> River Café (p230)
> Blue Hill (p116)
> Blaue Gans (p49)

NYC WITH KIDS

Tots can enjoy the Big Apple just as much as adults can – in fact, maybe more, because they won't be hauling *you* in and out of ill-configured subway and bus doors. Plus, there are plenty of attractions and entertainments designed just for them. The too-skinny-turnstiles at subway exits and entrances do make life with a stroller a challenge; catch the attention of the station clerk to get buzzed through the larger gates to the side. Don't panic if someone grabs your stroller from behind as you approach the stairs – it's proper New York etiquette to help overburdened solo parents. There are a few museums that don't allow strollers on certain days but will give you baby carriers to make up for it.

Many restaurants, hotels and attractions are quite happy to cater to families; look for the 👶 icon listed with general reviews for kid-friendly options.

To make the cultural capital your personal playground, pick up a *Time Out New York Kids*, published four times a year and available at newsstands. It has tons of fabulous information and listings. GoCity Kids is a useful online reference (www.gocitykids.com) as is New York Kids (www.newyorkkids.net).

FUN PLACES FOR KIDS

> Bronx Zoo (p26)
> American Museum of Natural History (Discovery Room) (p200)
> Children's Museum of Manhattan (pictured above; p200)
> Central Park (p180)

FAMILY-FRIENDLY EATERIES

> One Fish Two Fish
> Bubby's Pie Co (p50)
> Schillers (p74)
> Jaya Food (p62)
> Eleven Madison Park (p152)

OUTDOOR ACTIVITIES

New York is a mecca for outdoor enthusiasts, with more than 28,000 acres of greenery (excluding national and state parks and the Statue of Liberty). All told, there are more than 1,700 public parks, playgrounds, swimming pools and recreational facilities around the five boroughs, covering territory from woods to wetlands to skating rinks. And let's not forget the beach – 14 miles of sandy coast to enjoy, too.

To use any of the city's 614 baseball fields, 550 tennis courts, numerous basketball courts, golf and track courses, as well as its indoor and outdoor swimming pools, go to www.nycgovparks.org for locations and details.

For outdoor fun that doesn't involve a workout, there's the Monday night film series in Bryant Park, Shakespeare in the Park, Central Park Summerstage concerts, Hudson River Park concerts, River to River Festivals and Lincoln Center Dance Nights (OK, that one will work up a sweat). Plus, a whole series of unplanned, spontaneous concerts that pop up in the city's public parks and along the waterfronts whenever a group of musicians get together.

FUN OUTDOOR ACTIVITIES
> Playing basketball at West 4th St and Sixth Ave (p113)
> Dancing at Lincoln Center under the stars (p201)
> Biking Hudson River Park (p109)
> In-line skating in Central Park (p180)
> Kayaking around the Statue of Liberty (p48)

BEST PARKS
> Central Park in Manhattan (p180)
> Prospect Park in Brooklyn (pictured above; p222)
> Flushing Meadows/Corona Park in Queens
> Jamaica Bay Gateway National Recreation Area
> Pelham Bay Park in the Bronx

v

SNAPSHOTS

SHOPPING

Doesn't matter what you want – New York's got it. The streets are packed with high-end department stores, sleek designer ateliers, offbeat boutiques, kitschy memorabilia and miles upon miles of shoes, music and books.

Fifth Ave and the Upper East Side feature old-school glamour at sky-high prices. Unique couture, break-out designs, the coolest in handmade jewelry and other accessories are downtown, in Soho, Tribeca and Nolita. The Villages – Greenwich and East – offer a unique mix of everything and cover all price ranges, while the Meatpacking District has the latest in chic, modern looks from whiz-kids like Alexander McQueen.

Chinatown and Times Sq are famous for T-shirts. Shops are generally open from 10am to 8pm daily, with stores owned by Orthodox Jews closing Fridays and reopening Sunday mornings.

There are sample sales year round – www.dailycandy.com has a sample sale page devoted to nothing else. Other good sources to check include www.lazarshopping.com, www.nysale.com and *New York Magazine*'s rundown at http://nymag.com/shopping.

BEST DEPARTMENT STORES
> Barney's (p139)
> Century 21 (p48)
> Macy's (p172)
> Pearl River Mart (p60)
> Saks Fifth Ave

BEST FOR SHOES & ACCESSORIES
> Sigerson Morrison (p87)
> Me & Ro
> Bond 07 (p85)
> Bond 09 (p85)
> Otto Tootsi Plohound (p87)

SPAS

Rejuvenation can be squeezed into a busy New York schedule at any time of day – and that means all night, too, thanks to Juvenex, a 24-hour salon in Little Korea that caters to dancers and performers from Broadway shows.

A visit to the spa means different things to different people, of course. In New York, it can be a simple and straightforward after-work-out massage, a mani-pedi (manicure and pedicure), a waxing (bikini, Brazilian or otherwise), any number of different facials and topical skin treatments, or a combination of minimally-invasive procedures to erase fine lines, peel away surface layers of old skin, zap broken capillaries, and so on and so on. New York's got oxygen masks, fruit masks, organic masks, deep-sea particle masks – the list is endless. And it's not just for women: several spas cater exclusively to men, and even unisex places offer male facials and 'handshake upkeep' treatments (instead of the more girly 'manicure').

Many hotels have an on-site spas, although you may have to book in advance for an appointment. Don't undergo chemical peels lightly – they're non-invasive, true, but in the wrong hands, damned uncomfortable with unsightly after-effects.

SPORTS

Baseball's known as the 'New York Game' for a reason – the city's two professional teams are the extraordinarily successful Yankees (American League), who have won the World Series more times than any other franchise, and the perpetual runner-up, the Mets (National League). The season runs from April to October.

You can catch a game at Yankee Stadium in the Bronx, Shea Stadium in Queens, or at the farm team locations in Coney Island (Brooklyn Cyclones) and Staten Island (the Staten Island Yankees).

The New York Knicks basketball team plays through the winter and early spring at Madison Sq Garden. The women's professional team, New York Liberty, plays there too. The New Jersey Nets basketball team may soon be moving to Brooklyn, and a new stadium is under development there to house them.

NY Giants football tickets sell out years in advance, but tickets to New York Jets football games are easier to come by. The season runs from September to January; both teams play at the Meadowlands Sports Complex in New Jersey.

The New York Rangers play ice hockey at Madison Sq Garden from October to April.

The US Open is the year's final Grand Slam tennis event (spanning the Labor Day weekend) and is held at Flushing Meadows. Reserved tickets are only required for Arthur Ashe Stadium, which is sold out months ahead. Day-session ground passes are sold on the morning of each day's play – if you're in line before 9am you might snag one.

Belmont Park is the area's biggest horseracing track. The season runs from May to July.

Most sporting events can be booked through **Ticketmaster** (☎ 212-307-7171).

THEATER

The Big Apple is especially juicy when it comes to the art of performance. There's literally always something on, be it experimental theater on the Lower East Side, world-class ballet in Lincoln Center, a blow-out Broadway extravaganza in Times Sq, or a low-key, nonprofit production of Chekhov, Stoppard or Miller in downtown revival theaters.

To keep track of it all, start with the Sunday and Friday editions of the *New York Times*, as well as the weekly editions of *New York Magazine*, *Time Out New York* and *The New Yorker*. *The Village Voice* has good information on alternative and off-off Broadway productions. The **Department of Cultural Affairs** (☎ 212-643-7770) has a hotline that lists events and concerts at cultural institutions, while **NYC On Stage** (☎ 212-768-1818), a 24-hour information line, publicizes music, theater and dance events. Other good sources include **All That Chat** (www.talkinbroadway.com/all thatchat/), **NYC Theater** (www.nyc.com/theater) and the **Broadway Line** (☎ 888-276-2392).

CELEBRATED THEATERS
> Soho Playhouse
> Joseph Papp Public Theater (p106)
> Ambassador Theater (p177)
> New Amsterdam Theater (p178)
> Repertorio Español, a bilingual theater (tilde over the ñ in Español, por favor)

POPULAR AND LONG-RUNNING SHOWS
> Avenue Q (www.avenueq.com)
> Chicago (www.chicagothemusical.com)
> The Lion King (pictured above; www .thelionking.org/musical)
> Mamma Mia! (www.mamma-mia.com)
> The Phantom of the Opera (www.the phantomoftheopera.com)

V

SNAPSHOTS

VISTAS & VIEWPOINTS

Keep your camera handy, because life in New York goes by in a flash. Luckily there are a thousand ways to see the city and as many places to see it from. Now that Rockefeller Center has reopened its panoramic observation deck, Top of the Rock, you've got two chances to endure vertigo while peering down on the city from impossible heights. (The other option being the Empire State Building, of course.)

The views from the top seem to be the most sought after, but Manhattan can be entrancing from many different angles. Take a trek to the NY Transit Museum to see how it looks from the bottom up. Their tours take you through now-defunct parts of the city's subway system.

More scenic options can be found in Central Park, especially at its gorgeous central fountain located at Bethesda Terrace, near the Ramble. (The adjacent Bow Bridge is a popular place to pop the question, by the way.) A stroll along Hudson River Park gives you a shoreline view of the city, and for the quintessential image of Manhattan that's graced many a postcard, take the Staten Island Ferry just before sunset. The views headed to Staten Island are great and you really hit the jackpot on the return trip if you catch the glowing sun descending behind Manhattan's skyscrapers.

WHERE TO FIND GREAT VIEWS
> Stroll over the Brooklyn Bridge to Dumbo (p219)
> Catch a ride on the Staten Island Ferry (p54)
> Take the water taxi to Long Island City
> Tour the town from a double-decker bus
> Visit the Empire State Building (p158)

Street outside Grand Central Terminal

BACKGROUND

HISTORY

Long before Giovanni da Verrazano sailed by Staten Island in 1524, or Henry Hudson came looking for land to claim for the Dutch East India Company in 1609, great numbers of Algonquin-speaking people had made the Manhattan area their home.

The Lenape natives fished New York Bay for oysters and striped bass, and laid down well worn trading routes across the hilly island (Manhattan means 'island of hills' in one native dialect); those same routes later became Broadway, Amsterdam Ave and other major city thoroughfares. Legend says that Dutch trader Peter Minuit bought the island from the Lenape for trinkets worth about $24, but historians say it's unlikely the Lenape agreed to anything of the sort since it was a culture that didn't adhere to the idea of private property. In any case, the Dutch assumed control of the island and by 1630 the colony numbered 270, with a number of Belgians (Walloons), French Huguenots and English mixed in.

Peter Stuyvesant arrived to impose order on the unruly colony of New Amsterdam in 1647, but his intolerant religious views led to unrest. Few resisted the bloodless coup by the British in 1664, and the colony was renamed as New York. It became a British stronghold and remained steadfastly loyal to George III through much of the Revolutionary War in the 1770s. George Washington's ragtag army of farm boys was almost wiped out by Britain's General Cornwallis and his troops in what is currently Brooklyn Heights – only a daring, all-night march north saved them.

Post-Revolutionary times were good for most New Yorkers, even though the founding fathers disliked the bustling seaport city. The capital moved further south but the masses didn't go with it. By 1830, the population had expanded to 250,000, mostly composed of immigrants working in dangerous factories and living in tenements on the Lower East Side. At the same time, corrupt politicians bilked millions from public works projects and industrial barons amassed tax-free fortunes. A lack of space forced building sprawl upward rather than outward; skyscrapers peppered the horizon and the city continued to expand its network of subways and elevated trains. In 1898 the independent districts of Staten Island, Queens, the Bronx and Brooklyn merged with Manhattan and they became the five 'boroughs' of New York City. With the waves of immigrant arrivals, the population reached three million in 1900.

Speakeasies, flappers, gangsters, the 19th Amendment (which gave women the right to vote) and a Harlem Renaissance brought incredible

> **AFRICAN BURIAL GROUND**
> Africans have been in New York City since the 17th-century Dutch era. Brought over as slaves, they built many of the colonial attractions of Lower Manhattan. Their contributions were largely forgotten as slavery disappeared from the north, but the African Burial Ground – the final resting place of some 400 slaves taken mostly from Ghana that was discovered accidentally in 1991 – is a poignant reminder of their suffering. The site is at Duane and Elk Sts, adjacent to 290 Broadway, and a permanent exhibition is on display at the Schomburg Center in Harlem (p212).

vitality to New York in the years preceding and following WWI. Margaret Sanger preached about birth control in Washington Sq Park, Wall St made golden boys out of hayseeds, and F Scott Fitzgerald chronicled it all in *The Great Gatsby*. When the bottom fell out of the stock market on Black Tuesday (October 29, 1929), the glittering, apparently limitless future of New York was smashed overnight. Hard times followed and, even though Manhattan was the nation's premier city after WWII, economically things continued to stagnate. Only a massive federal loan program rescued the city from bankruptcy in the 1970s.

LIFE AS A NEW YORK RESIDENT

New York City is the original 'melting pot,' the term used by the nation's leaders to encourage mixing between old settlers and new arrivals at the turn of the 20th century. Popular theory held that incoming immigrants would assimilate to the dominant culture (primarily Anglo-Saxon at the time) and create a unified population free of ethnic and class divisions. Instead, the opposite happened: Italians coming into New York City didn't settle in the Irish enclave of Greenwich Village, or the Eastern European Jewish communities of the Lower East Side. They established their own beachhead, known as Little Italy, and proudly spoke their language and practiced their traditions. Dominicans of the 1950s and 1960s settled in what became Spanish Harlem, and Puerto Ricans still own most of the Bronx. Along the way other nationalities arrived and rubbed shoulders and traded quips, and if the perfect homogeneity the city planners envisioned never materialized, well, nobody misses it because a vibrant, hybrid culture has taken its place. No matter what their ethnic roots, your average New Yorker today knows a smattering of Spanish or another foreign language (or is perfectly bilingual), has a good sense of the Chinese

> **TANGO PORTEÑO**
> If you love this steamy Argentinean dance, stop by Pier 16 at South St Seaport any Sunday evening from May through the end of October and join the throngs moving in sultry fashion around the docks. This free weekly event (www.tangoporteno.org) is open to anyone – beginners and experts alike. All that's needed is an appreciation for moonlight, music and romance.

lunar calendar (how else to know when the Chinese New Year is coming with its fabulous dragon parade?) and can order a bagel with a *schmear* (dab of cream cheese) without batting an eyelid.

Which is not to say that all New Yorkers live together in perfect harmony – in a city of more than 8 million people, there are bound to be a few problems. Politicians are expected to resolve most of these conflicts and if they don't, they can kiss that second term goodbye. When it comes to the city's overall well-being though, New Yorkers have no problem banding together in amazing displays of solidarity.

Pedestrian street traffic is expected to move in double-time and you'll hear rapid-fire exchanges everywhere ('How you doin', 'Hey, what's happening,' 'You got the time, buddy?'), so don't hold back if someone sends a well meaning inquiry your way. Politeness – please, thank you, etc – is also important, and displays of class status like slighting the taxi driver or doorman do not go over well in democratic Manhattan. There are a few things that raise local ire: do not exit the subway stairs and stop to pull out your map, thereby blocking the exit. Move to the corner before figuring out your location. Don't go into an eatery during the busy lunch hour rush and keep everyone waiting while you decide. You're just asking for the counterperson to zing you with a typical New York barb. Hang back until you are ready to order. A jacket and tie are expected at upscale restaurants, but otherwise feel free to wear what you wish.

GOVERNMENT & POLITICS

Billionaire businessman Michael Bloomberg's steady economic hand and fair but unimpassioned leadership pulled New York City out of its financial doldrums post–September 11, and got him re-elected in 2006. The city is undeniably wealthier than ever before, but also less affordable. Discontent with the Republican leadership that dominated Albany for 12 years led to a major change in 2006 – Democrat Eliot Spitzer became governor, backed by a Democratic Attorney General and State Comptroller. Senator Hillary Clinton, re-elected by a landslide in 2006, is widely believed to be making a run for the presidency in 2008.

New York City has five borough presidents, a city-wide comptroller, a public advocate and a 51-member city council to balance mayoral power. The economy has bounced back with a vengeance after a few rocky years, and the city's entrenched liberalness has started to reassert itself – most visibly in the grassroots push to improve housing options for the low-income and working-class families who have been priced out of Manhattan and practically all of the surrounding boroughs. America's ongoing debate on immigration reform has also fired up pockets of resistance in New York City, home to some of the largest émigré communities in the country. Local politicians pressured to take a stand have come out in favor of amnesty programs that would grant legal status to long-time undocumented residents. With an overwhelmingly Democratic City Council (only three members are not registered Democrats), and no strong contenders in sight to replace outgoing Republican city and state leaders, New York City looks to be leaning a little further to the left after decades of moderate Republicanism.

ENVIRONMENT

Most New Yorkers are die-hard recycling enthusiasts (although you'll be hard-pressed to find any recycling receptacles on the streets) and have a reverence for the green spaces poking through the concrete jungle. But in this development-crazed city, the push to build has given rise to some fairly outlandish schemes – including a new aquatic park of water slides to be built on Randalls Island in the East River. The rush to throw up buildings also threatens the pristine and delicate ecosystem in the Croton Watershed, a wetland system that naturally cleans much of the rainwater that flows into the city and into New Yorkers' taps. Environmentalists have held off the worst of the development, but it's a battle that will only get harder in coming years. The dangers of too much building can be already seen in the Gateway National Park in Jamaica Bay, Queens. The once massive wetland system has been reduced to just a few miles of shoreline, and Army Corp of Engineer scientists predict the marshland – dying of unknown reasons – will be gone entirely in 25 years. The city has recently taken steps to limit building on the marshy edges, but many fear it's too little too late.

FURTHER READING
NYC IN LITERATURE

Low Life (1991; Luc Sante). New York's underbelly is laid bare in this hefty work by a former East Village resident. All the city's seedy activities from 1840 through 1920 are chronicled with unsparing attention to detail.

Motherless Brooklyn (1999; Jonathan Lethem). Lionel Essrog, Lethem's beloved Brooklyn gumshoe, takes you on a wild insider's ride through a bleak but undeniably alluring borough while attempting to solve a local crime.

Rudy!: An Investigative Biography of Rudolph Giuliani (2003; Wayne Barrett). *Village Voice* reporter Wayne Barrett dishes the dirt on former mayor Rudy Giuliani, revealing the inner workings of city government and the power brokers that shape it.

Random Family: Love, Drugs, Trouble, and Coming of Age in the Bronx (2004; Adrian Nicole LeBlanc). An award-winning nonfiction work that follows the ups and downs of an inner-city Bronx family for 10 years.

Go Tell it on the Mountain (1953; James Baldwin). Short and intense, Baldwin's debut novel focuses on 24 hours in the life of a young Harlem teen undergoing what he believes to be a spiritual awakening. It was hailed as the first work of fiction to use black idiom in a natural setting, and also showcases the effects of northern migration upon rural blacks.

The Institutionist (2000; Colson Whitehead). Okay, so it's never overtly stated that the city in this fabulous first novel is New York — but what other city could it be? Brooklyn resident Whitehead knows how to draw you into his strange metropolis, where elevators are a symbol of lofty financial expansion, as well as soulful growth.

Cosmopolis (2003; Don DeLillo). A very Joycean romp through the streets of Manhattan. Well, make that one street in particular, as 28-year-old billionaire Eric Packer, the protagonist, tries to make it across Midtown for a haircut on a very eventful day.

Bergdorf Blondes (2004; Plum Sykes). If you liked *Sex and the City*, this novel picks up where Carrie Bradshaw left off. Penned by Vogue editor and 'it' girl Plum Sykes, it delivers a wallop of Manhattan's lush life in a few short but entertaining chapters.

Up from Orchard Street (2006; Eleanor Widmer). Three generations of a Jewish family struggle to break out of the Lower East Side tenements that they've called home since leaving the Old Country far behind. It's a loving look at 20th-century family life, as well as a sharply drawn rendition of immigrant conditions in the city.

FILMS & TV
NYC IN FILM

The Squid and the Whale (2005). Director Noah Baumbach returns to his roots in this tale of family love and separation set amid the quiet life of literary Brooklyn. The father's hapless search for the perfect parking spot never fails to strike a chord with city dwellers everywhere.

Manhattan (1979). It's hard to decide which Woody Allen movie best showcases his beloved island – *Annie Hall* is always a strong contender. But in the end this masterpiece, shot in unsparing black and white, wins everybody over with its humorous depiction of living and loving in what can be a very lonely city.

Ghost Busters (1984). If the wacked out and loony humor of Dan Aykroyd and Bill Murray doesn't captivate you, the fantastic shots of Manhattan – minus the huge stores, malls, chain restaurants and condo developments of today – certainly will.

Jungle Fever (1991). Spike Lee's dissection of bi-racial love leaves many of its emotional plots undeveloped, but his bracing frankness about race, sexuality and discrimination – in the upscale homes of African American professionals in Harlem and the Italian suburb of Bensonhurst, Brooklyn – give the movie tremendous energy as it plays out in neighborhoods around the city.

Torch Song Trilogy (1988). First presented as three separate stage acts done a month apart at experimental theater space La MaMa in the 1980s, Harvey Fierstein's masterful work on gay life is even more entrancing on the big screen. If the depiction of homophobic violence seems anachronistic, remember that in 2006 a drag queen was severely beaten not far from the West Village store where the film's pivotal moment was shot some 20 years ago.

Gangs of New York (2002). Directed by Martin Scorsese and starring Daniel Day Lewis, among others, this tale of immigrant suffering doesn't quite come together as well as it could have, but the visual detail brings Manhattan's notorious Five Points area – now in Chinatown – to vivid life. The film does a good job of showcasing the competing economic interests of 19th century immigrants that often erupted along ethnic lines as gang warfare.

Dave Chappelle's Block Party (2005). Comedian Dave Chappelle's loosely constructed documentary of a block party jumps around a bit geographically and plot-wise (there's no definable documentary narrative) but in the end, it's full of fabulous music and amazing natural performances, and after viewing footage of the actual block party that was held in Brooklyn, it's hard not to say, 'I wish I had been there'.

DIRECTORY
TRANSPORTATION
ARRIVAL & DEPARTURE
AIR

Multiple direct flights from just about every major city in North and South America and western Europe arrive in New York daily, as do many stopover flights from Asia. The majority (but not all) of domestic air travel gets routed to LaGuardia Airport, while John F Kennedy Airport handles mostly international traffic. New York City's airports sit just east of Manhattan but traffic often turns the short commute into a two-hour drive.

JFK International Airport
John F Kennedy International Airport (JFK; www.kennedyairport.com), in southeastern Queens, is about 15 miles from Midtown, or 45 to 75 minutes by car – longer in peak hours.

Travel to/from JFK

	AirTrain/Subway	Taxi	Bus	Car Service
Pick-up point	Look for AirTrain signs at terminals that take you to the Rockaway subway station; from there take the A train into Manhattan.	Outside any terminal. Look for the lines, as there are specific pick-up points under 'Taxi' signs.	Outside any terminal. Buses run every 15-20 min to midnight.	At any JFK terminal.
Drop-off point	Anywhere on the A train line.	Anywhere you want.	Penn Station, Port Authority Bus Terminal and Grand Central Terminal.	Anywhere in Manhattan.
Cost	AirTrain/Subway $5/$2	$45 to Manhattan and most of Brooklyn	$12-15 one way	$50-75
Duration	1 hr	1-2 hrs	Allow 60-75 min	1 hr
Contact	www.airtrainjfk.com, www.mta.info		For express bus service, 718-875-8200; www.nyairportservice.com	Operators include **Big Apple** (☎ 718-232-1015), **Carmel** (☎ 212-666-666), **Citywide** (☎ 718-405-5822), **Dial** (☎ 718-743-2877) and **Tel Aviv** (☎ 212-777-7777)

Left Luggage

Terminal 1 (☎ 718-751-4020; ⏱ 24hr) baggage facilities are on the first floor, and cost anywhere from $4 to $16, as do **Terminal 4** (☎ 718-751-2947; ⏱ 7am-11pm) baggage facilities. Prices depend on the size of your bags.

Information

General inquiries ☎ 718-244-4444
Parking information ☎ 718-244-4444
Hotel booking service ☎ 212-267-5500
Lost and Found ☎ 718-244-4225/6
Medical services ☎ 718-656-5344
Wi-fi Terminals 1, 8 and 9, with more coverage planned.

Located in the arrival areas of terminals;1, 3, 4, 6, 7, 8 and 9, **Traveler's Aid** (☎ 718-656-4870; ⏱ 10am-6pm daily except national holidays), a nonprofit organization, helps stranded travelers, providing access to free phone service, food and other assistance. If you have to spend the night in the airport,

the second floor of Terminal 4 is the designated place to crash.

LaGuardia Airport

LaGuardia (www.laguardiaairport .com) is in northern Queens, 8 miles from Midtown, or 20 to 45 minutes by car (contact information for car services is the same as for JFK; see p266 for details).

Information

General inquiries ☎ 718-533-3400
Parking information ☎ 718-533-3400
Hotel booking service ☎ 212-267-5500
Wi-fi Central Terminal; US Airways Terminal
Lost and Found ☎ 718-639-1839

TRAIN

Amtrak trains come right into midtown Manhattan – you can pick them up in Boston, Philadelphia and Washington DC and at some smaller stops along the way.

Travel to/from LaGuardia

	New York Airport Service	Taxis	Train/Subway
Pick-up point	To LaGuardia, buses leave every 20 min between 6am and midnight from Penn Station, Port Authority Bus Terminal and Grand Central Terminal.	Outside any terminal. From the airport, take the M60 to W 106th St and Broadway. The M60 also connects with trains and the subway into Manhattan.	A taxi can take you to the N and W trains in Astoria Queens, the 2 4, 5, 6, A, B, C, D subways along 125th St and the 1 subway at 116th, 110th Sts and Broadway.
Cost	$15	$15-30	$2
Duration	1 hr	20-40 min	Allow 1 hr
Contact	718-875-8200; www .nyairportservice.com		www.mta.info

TRAVELING THE NORTHEAST CORRIDOR INTO NYC

Out-of-state buses arrive at and depart from **Port Authority Bus Terminal** (☎ 212-564-8484; 625 Eighth Ave) with carriers going to just about anywhere in the US and parts of Canada. For bare-bones jaunts to Boston, DC and parts of Philly, check out the 'Chinatown to Chinatown' line. Run by **Fung-Wah Company** (☎ 212-925-8889; www.fungwahbus .com). Direct buses leave out of New York's Chinatown; the fare is $15—$20 one way. Other innovative and low-budget carriers serving the northeast from Manhattan include the follllowing:

Apex (☎ 212-343-3280; www.apexbus.com)
Lucky Star (☎ 1-888-881-0887; www.luckystarbus.com)
Vamoose Bus (☎ 877-393-2828; www.vamoosebus.com)

Long-distance Amtrak and Long Island Rail Road trains arrive at **Pennsylvania (Penn) Station** (☎ 212-582-6875, 800-872-7245; 33rd St btwn Seventh & Eighth Aves). Commuter trains (MetroNorth) use **Grand Central Terminal** (☎ 212-532-4900; Park Ave at 42nd St). **New Jersey PATH** (Port Authority Trans-Hudson; ☎ 800-234-7284) trains stop at several stations in Manhattan but don't venture above 33rd St.

TRAVEL DOCUMENTS
PASSPORT

To enter the US, visitors are now required to have a passport that's valid for at least six months after their intended stay in the USA ends.

VISA

The US State Department has set up a Visa Waiver Program that allows Canadian citizens and citizens from most European countries to enter the country without a tourist visa. Certain restrictions do apply depending on your country of origin; for the most up-to-date regulations, check with the American embassy nearest you before departing. As members of the Visa Waiver Program, residents of the UK, Ireland, Norway, Spain, France, Austria, Germany, and also Australia and New Zealand do not usually need visas for temporary visits. However, some European passports issued prior to October 2005 don't carry the machine-readable identity chips that US customs now requires. Tourists from any country with an old-fashioned passport must get a visa to enter the country. Visitors from non-European countries must apply for a visa at the nearest American embassy, and allow at least six weeks for the paperwork to go through. Many of the application forms and further information can be found at the US State Depart-

ment website (http://travel.state
.gov/visa).

RETURN/ONWARD TICKET
To enter the United States, you
will need a return ticket that's
nonrefundable in the USA.

SECURITY
Security is very visible and tight at
the two airports. Allow extra time
for check-in and always have your
identification on hand. Don't try
to carry on metal nail files, Swiss
Army knives, pocketknives, razors,
corkscrews, or any other sharp
implements. Of course, any kind
of firearm or other weapon, explo-
sives, flammable liquids or solids,
or any other hazardous materials
are prohibited. Some camping and
scuba equipment – butane tanks,

air tanks, inflatable rafts – must
also be checked with your bags.

GETTING AROUND
Subway is generally the fastest,
cheapest way to get around Manhattan because busy city streets
get clogged by 'gridlock,' with cars
sitting bumper to bumper waiting
for lights to change. City buses can
be useful, especially for cross-
town travel, provided that traffic is
moving – pick up a public transit
map from subway ticket booths.
Taxis are the most convenient
mode of transportation after 1am.

TRAVEL PASSES
A **MetroCard** (☎ 718-330-1234) is the
easiest way to pay for travel on
New York's public transit system,
and are required to travel by

Travel Around New York City

	Theater District	The Met	American Museum of Natural History	Harlem	Dumbo	Coney Island	Williamsburg
Lower Manhattan	Subway 10 min	Subway 15 min	Subway 15 min	Subway 25 min	Subway 10 min	Subway 45 min	Subway 30 min
Upper East Side	Cab 10 min	Cab/walk 5/10 min	Cab 10 min	Subway 15 min	Subway 30 min	Subway 1 hr	Subway 30 min
Upper West Side	Cab/walk 5/10 min	Cab 10 min	Walk 5-10 min	Subway 10 min	Subway 20-25 min	Subway 1 hr	Subway 40 min
Theater District	n/a	Walk/ subway 15/ 10-15 min	Walk/subway 15/10 min	Subway 15 min	Subway 20-30 min	Subway 45 min- 1hr	Subway 40 min
Southern Brooklyn	Subway 40 min	Subway 30 min	Subway 40 min	Subway 45 min	Subway 20 min	Subway 30 min	Subway 35 min

> **CLIMATE CHANGE & TRAVEL**
>
> Travel – especially air travel – is a significant contributor to global climate change. At Lonely
> Planet, we believe that all who travel have a responsibility to limit their personal impact. As
> a result, we have teamed with Rough Guides and other concerned industry partners to sup-
> port Climate Care, which allows people to offset the greenhouse gases they are responsible
> for with contributions to energy-saving projects and other climate-friendly initiatives in the
> developing world. Lonely Planet offsets all staff and author travel.
>
> For more information, turn to the responsible travel pages on www.lonelyplanet
> .com. For details on offsetting your carbon emissions and a carbon calculator, go to www
> .climatecare.org.

subway. Pick one up at any news-stand or subway entrance. The one-day Fun Pass ($7) is a major money-saver, giving you unlimited access to subways and buses from the first swipe until 3am the next morning. The seven-day ($24) or 30-day ($76) unlimited cards are great deals, but you must let 18 minutes elapse between each swipe, making it harder for two people to share one card. Pay-per-ride options are also available – either a vending machine or a subway clerk can put any dollar amount you want on your Metro-Card, with bonus rides when you buy several at a time. Be aware that the single-ride cards sold from machines in subway stations expire after two hours. At print time, the single ride fare was $2, though that's subject to change.

SUBWAY

The subway system (☎ 718-330-1234) runs 24 hours a day. In this

book, our subway listings note the nearest stop's name. If you transfer from the subway to the bus or from the bus to the subway within 18 minutes of paying a fare, there's no double charge – free transfers are permitted. To get the latest bus and subway routes, and up-to-the-minute service changes, visit www.mta.info and follow the links to NYC Transit. Other useful websites are www.hopstop .com; www.trips123.com and www.publicroutes.com. These for-profit sites offer free informa-tion on traveling around New York and surrounding cities via public transport.

BUS

City buses (☎ 718-330-1234) operate 24 hours per day and generally run north–south along avenues, and crosstown along the major east–west thoroughfares.

You need exact change of $2 (no dollar bills allowed) or a Metro-Card to board a bus as the driver will not make change.

Bus routes that begin and end in Manhattan start with M (eg M5); Queens bus routes start with Q, Brooklyn with B, and the Bronx with BX. Some 'limited stop' buses pull over only every 10 blocks. 'Express' buses ($6.50) are primarily for outer-borough commuters, not for people taking short trips.

TRAIN

New Jersey PATH trains (☎ 800-234-7284) run down Sixth Ave to Jersey City, Hoboken and Newark, with stops at 33rd, 23rd, 14th, 9th and Christopher Sts in Manhattan. A second line goes from the World Trade Center to Jersey City and Newark. These reliable trains run every 15 to 45 minutes, 24 hours a day. The fare is currently $1.50.

BOAT

New York Waterway ferries (☎ 800-533-3779; www.nywaterway.com) make runs up the Hudson River Valley and from Midtown to Yankee Stadium in the Bronx. A popular commuter route goes from the New Jersey Transit train station in Hoboken to the World Financial Center in Lower Manhattan; boats leave every five

to 10 minutes at peak times, and the 10 minute ride costs $4 each way.

Port Authority Ferries (www.panynj.gov) run between Battery Park and New Jersey, stopping mainly at Hoboken and Colgate (Exchange Place), across from Lower Manhattan. They also run ferries from Manhattan's East River to Fulton Ferry Landing and Brooklyn Army Terminal in Brooklyn, and Hunter's Point in Long Island City, Queens.

New York Water Taxi (☎ 212-742-1969; www.nywatertaxi.com; one-stop $5) is a new service that's really taken off in New York. These yellow taxi boats stop at various piers along Manhattan's West Side and are a wonderful way to travel to Midtown, lower Manhattan, and parts of Brooklyn and Queens. The Water Taxi Beach is a favorite pit stop.

TAXI

Taxis are available when the rooftop number is glowing (as opposed to the 'off duty' side lights). Fares are metered and start at $2.50; tip is 10% to 15% (minimum 50¢) and there's a 50¢ surcharge from 8pm to 6am. For long trips uptown or downtown, ask the driver to take the FDR Highway (East Side) or West Side Highway (West Side).

LIMOUSINE

Limousines and car services can be an inexpensive way to travel, especially for groups. **Affordable Limousine Service** (☎ 888-338-4567) and **Carmel** (☎ 212-666-6666) charge about $45 per hour for up to four people; a night on the town (ie three hours) for eight costs $150.

CAR & MOTORCYCLE

Parking is a nightmare, traffic horrendous, and gas tremendously expensive – if you don't have to rent a car, save yourself the hassle. Motorcycles are better for squeezing into tight spaces, but with cabs and subways so readily available, why bother?

RENTAL

The main rental agencies in New York City include **Avis** (☎ 800-331-1212), **Budget** (☎ 800-527-0700), **Dollar** (☎ 800-800-4000), **Hertz** (☎ 800-654-3131) and **Thrifty** (☎ 800-367-2277).

PRACTICALITIES
BUSINESS HOURS

Shops are generally open Monday to Saturday 10am to 6pm and Sunday noon to 6pm, with some extended hours Thursday nights; many shops close Monday. Some businesses change their operating hours with the seasons, usually

resulting in shorter hours in the summer. Banks and institutional businesses keep a 9am to 5pm Monday to Friday schedule, but many also keep 9am to 3pm hours on Saturday.

Museums and art galleries are usually open Tuesday to Sunday 10am to 5pm. On public holidays, banks, schools and government offices (including post offices) close, and transportation services operate on a Sunday schedule.

DISCOUNTS

Students, children (under 12) and seniors get discounts at most attractions and on most forms of transportation. Many attractions also offer reduced-price tickets for families. Students must present their student IDs for discounts. Seniors over 62 can also expect cut rates on hotel charges, drugstore (pharmacy) prescriptions and cinema prices. Buy a CityPass (www.citypass.com) to avoid long ticket lines at six major attractions and for a 50% discount on admission.

EMBASSIES & CONSULATES

The UN's presence in New York means that nearly every country in the world maintains diplomatic offices here. Most are listed in the white pages of the phone book under 'Consulates General of (country).' Some embassies include the following:

Australia (☎ 212-351-6500; 150 E 42nd St btwn Lexington & Third Aves)

Canada (☎ 212-596-1783; 1251 Sixth Ave btwn 49th & 50th Sts)

Ireland (☎ 212-319-2555; 345 Park Ave btwn 51st & 52nd Sts)

New Zealand (☎ 212-832-4038; 780 Third Ave btwn 48th & 49th Sts)

South Africa (☎ 212-213-4880; 333 E 38th St btwn First & Second Aves)

UK (☎ 212-745-0202; 845 Third Ave btwn 51st & 52nd Sts)

EMERGENCIES

You can always get help by dialing 911 from any phone, including mobiles. There are also emergency call boxes on many city corners; some look like bright orange bulbs, others are old-fashioned iron boxes bolted to the crosswalk signals. In either case, push the button, and the cavalry will come running.

Police, fire, ambulance (☎ 911)

Police information operator (☎ 212-374-5000)

PRECAUTIONS

Tap water is safe to drink, but most New Yorkers prefer bottled. Regular summer outbreaks of West Nile Virus, transmitted through mosquitoes, prompt widespread pesticide spraying in the outer boroughs, but few humans catch the disease. Wear long sleeves and insect repellent if you're worried.

Condoms are readily available in drugstores, corner bodegas and nightclub vending machines – use them.

MEDICAL SERVICES

New York Hotel Urgent Medical Services (☎ 212-737-1212) offers medical services to visitors; doctors make 24-hour house (and hotel) calls, but expect to pay top dollar (prices start at $200). Medical care gets very expensive very fast in the US if you don't have insurance. All hospitals do have 24-hour emergency departments though that must treat the uninsured. The following is a list of reputable hospitals.

Bellevue Hospital (☎ 212-562-4141; NYU Medical Center, First Ave at E 27th St)

Lenox Hill Hospital (☎ 212-434-2000; 100 E 77th St btwn Park & Lexington Aves)

New York Hospital (☎ 212-746-5050; 525 E 68th St btwn York Ave & Franklin D Roosevelt Dr)

For tricky tooth situations that can't wait, try **AAA Dental Care** (☎ 212-744-3928; 30th East 60th St., Suite 1504; www.emergencydentalnyc.com).

There are a number of 24-hour pharmacies in New York City:

Duane Reade (☎ 212-541-9708; W 57th St at Broadway)

Duane Reade (☎ 212-674-5357; Sixth Ave at Waverly Pl)

Genovese (☎ 212-772-0104; 1299 Second Ave at 68th St)

DIRECTORY

IMPERIAL SYSTEM

Americans hate the metric system and continue to resist it. Distances are in feet, yards and miles. Dry weights are measured by the ounce, pound and ton; liquid measures differ from dry measures. Gasoline is dispensed by the US gallon (about 20% less than the imperial gallon) and US pints and quarts are also 20% less than imperial ones.

INTERNET

Public libraries offer free web access; internet cafés are common.

INTERNET SERVICE PROVIDERS

Major national ISPs include AOL (dial-in: ☎ 212-871-1021) and AT&T (dial-in: ☎ 212-824-2405). Earthlink (www.earthlink.net) is another popular ISP while Metconnect (☎ 212-359-2000, 646-496-0000; www.metconnect.com) offers a free service.

INTERNET CAFÉS

Times Sq Cybercafé (☎ 212-333-4109; www.cyber-café.com; 250 W 49th St btwn Broadway & Eighth Ave; per 1/2 hr $6.40; ⏰ 8am-11pm Mon-Fri, 11am-11pm Sat-Sun)

Web2Zone (☎ 212-614-7300; www.web2zone.com; 54 Cooper Square; per 15 min $3, per hr $12, unlimited day $60; ⏰ 9am-11pm Mon-Fri, 10am-11pm Sat, noon-10pm Sun) They offer three services in one place – internet access, interactive video games in its entertainment center and a Small Business Center.

WI-FI

Bryant Park decided to go wireless in 2005, and now all of New York City has followed suit. WiFi Salon (http://wifisalon.com) has brought interconnectivity to most city parks.

Details on what you need to connect are on the WiFi Salon website; Bryant Park requires an 802.11b compatible wireless card or built-in 802.11b wireless capability. Instructions on how to configure your laptop or handheld device can be found at www.bryantpark.org/amenities/wireless.php.

TELEPHONE

Public phones are either coin- or card-operated; some accept credit cards. Use a major carrier such as AT&T (☎ 800-321-0288) for long distance calls.

The US uses the GSM mobile phone system – you'll need a GSM compatible phone if you want to make and receive calls.

PHONE CARDS

Newsstands and pharmacies sell prepaid phone cards but they can be huge rip-offs, charging per-minute prices a lot higher than those promised.

COUNTRY & CITY AREA CODES

The US country code is 1. Manhattan phone numbers are always preceded by a three-digit area code: ☎ 212, ☎ 646, and ☎ 917, although ☎ 646 and ☎ 917 also do double duty as mobile phone and pager area codes. Even when dialing in Manhattan you must use 1 plus the entire 10-digit number. For the outer boroughs, the area codes are ☎ 718 and ☎ 347.

USEFUL NUMBERS

City information (☎ 311)
Directory assistance (☎ 411)
International dialing code (☎ 011)
Operator (☎ 0)
Operator-assisted calls (☎ 01 + the number; an operator will come on the line once you have dialed)
Collect calls (☎ 0)
Time (☎ 212-976-1616)
Weather (☎ 212-976-1212)
Moviefone (☎ 212-777-FILM)
Clubfone (☎ 212-777-CLUB)

INTERNATIONAL CODES

Dial ☎ 00 followed by the code for the country you're calling:
Australia (☎ 61)
Canada (☎ 1)
Japan (☎ 81)
New Zealand (☎ 64)
South Africa (☎ 27)
UK (☎ 44)

TIPPING

Waiters work for less than minimum wage, so it's expected that satisfied customers will tip 15–20% of the total bill. Tips are not automatically included, but some restaurants add a 15% gratuity to the bills of parties of six or more. If you leave without tipping, it's not unheard of for a manager to ask you what was wrong. As a general rule you don't have to tip on tax (8.625% in New York). For an easy way to figure out the correct amount to tip, look at the tax you've been assessed and double it.

Other standard tipping amounts include:
Baggage carriers $3 for the first bag, $1 for each additional bag.
Bars At least $1 per drink (or more for faster service and stronger drinks).
Cloakroom attendants $1 per item.
Hotel service personnel $2 for each service performed.
Hairdressers 15%
Restaurants 15–20% (not expected in fast food, takeout or self-service restaurants).
Room cleaners Minimum $5 per day.
Taxis 10–15%
Tour guides $10 per family/group for a full-day tour.

TOURIST INFORMATION

NYC & Co (☎ 212-484-1222; www .nycvisit.com; 810 Seventh Ave at 53rd St; ⏱ 8:30am-6pm Mon-Fri & 9am-5pm Sat-Sun) operates a 24-hour toll-free

DIRECTORY

line with listings of special events and reservation details. Staff are helpful and knowledgeable and the information center is comprehensive.

You'll also find information counters and centers at airports, in Times Sq, at Grand Central Terminal and at Penn Station.

TRAVELERS WITH DISABILITIES

Federal laws require that all government offices have good elevator and ramp access for wheelchairs, and devices to aid the hearing impaired. Almost all major venues offer good bathroom facilities for those with wheelchairs, and all city buses are able to carry wheelchair passengers. Only some subway stations are accessible though (see MTA maps or call ☎ 718-596-8585 for more information).

Listings in this book that are wheelchair-friendly are indicated by the ♿ icon.

INFORMATION & ORGANIZATIONS

The book *Access for All* is a guide for the disabled to New York attractions. Contact **Hospital Audiences**

(☎ 212-575-7676; www.hospitalaudiences.org; 548 Broadway, New York, NY 10012) for a copy.

Helpful contacts include the following:

New York Society for the Deaf (☎ 212-777-3900)

People with Disabilities Office (☎ 212-788-2830, TTY 212-788-2838)

Public Transport Accessible Line (☎ 718-596-8585, TTY 800-734-7433)

Society for Accessible Travel and Hospitality (SATH; ☎ 212-447-7284; www.sath.org)

WOMEN TRAVELERS

It's a good idea to avoid public transportation after midnight, and watch your drink at all times in a bar – just as a precaution.

Tampons, pads and condoms are sold everywhere. The contraceptive pill and 'morning-after' pill are available by prescription only, although as this book went to press pharmacies were planning to carry 'Plan B' over the counter. New York City law stipulates that rape victims be offered the 'morning-after' pill while receiving treatment at hospitals, but it's not always automatically offered. If you're in a situation where you think you need it, insist upon getting it.

>INDEX

See also separate indexes for See (p282), Shop (p283), Eat (p285), Drink (p286) and Play (p287).

000 map pages

000 map pages

PLAY

Arts

Ballet & dance

Bars, clubs & pubs

Cabaret

Cinemas

000 map pages